International Perspectiv
Competence Developm

In today's complex and ever-changing world it has become obvious that even highly developed knowledge and skills are no longer sufficient to meet new challenges, situations and problems facing individuals, organizations and nations. This raises an enormous and potentially confusing issue for educators and trainers: how is it possible to generate and assess abilities to deal with challenges and problems unknown – or not even in existence – at the time when the learning takes place?

This book builds on the experiences and insights of its expert contributors, all of whom have worked with, studied and analysed competences and how they are developed. Their collected work presents:

- comprehensive explanation and analysis of the concept and nature of competence;
- specific contexts of competence development, e.g. in the public sector or small business;
- competence development as a national strategy for building an up-to-date education and training system.

With contributors from around the world, this book illustrates in an engaging and convincing manner the importance and innovative nature of the concept of competences, resulting in a varied, differentiated and empathetic guide to the topic. It will appeal to educators, both in academic and management circles, as well as students and administrators of education.

Knud Illeris is Professor of Lifelong Learning at the Danish University of Education. He is internationally acknowledged as an innovative contributor to learning theory and adult education. In 2005 he became Honorary Adjunct Professor of Teachers College, Columbia University, New York, and in 2006 he was inducted to The International Hall of Fame of Adult and Continuing Education. He is the author of numerous books, including *How We Learn*, which provides a comprehensive understanding of human learning and non-learning, and *Contemporary Theories of Learning*, which draws together the world's leading theorists of human learning.

International Perspectives on Competence Development

Developing skills and capabilities

Edited by Knud Illeris

Routledge
Taylor & Francis Group

LONDON AND NEW YORK

First published 2009
by Routledge
2 Park Square, Milton Park, Abingdon, Oxon, OX14 4RN

Simultaneously published in the USA and Canada
by Routledge
270 Madison Avenue, New York, NY 10016

Routledge is an imprint of the Taylor & Francis Group, an informa business

© 2009 editorial and selection, Knud Illeris; individual contributions, Karen E. Watkins, Maria Cseh, Moacir Gadotti, Per-Erik Ellström, Henrik Kock, Soonghee Han, David Beckett, Knud Illeris, Peter Jarvis, Katrin Hjort, Peter Sawchuk, Pam Irwin, Manuela Perrotta, Xianjin Dou, Ben Parker, Shirley Walters, Patcharawalai Wongboonsin and Kua Wongboonsin

Typeset in Garamond by
GreenGate Publishing Services, Tonbridge, Kent
Printed and bound in Great Britain by
TJ International Ltd, Padstow, Cornwall

British Library Cataloguing in Publication Data
A catalogue record for this book is available from the British Library

Library of Congress Cataloging-in-Publication Data
International perspectives on competence development : developing skills and capabilities / Edited by Knud Illeris.
p. cm.
Includes index.
1. Employees--Training of--Cross-cultural studies. 2. Core competencies--Cross-cultural studies. 3. Skilled labor--Cross-cultural studies. 4. Labor productivity--Effect of education on--Cross-cultural studies. 5. Continuing education--Cross-cultural studies. I. Illeris, Knud.
HF5549.5.T7I57 2009
658.3'124--dc22
2008052295

ISBN 10 0-415-49210-6 (hbk)
ISBN 10 0-415-49211-4 (pbk)

ISBN 13 978-0-415-49210-2 (hbk)
ISBN 13 978-0-415-49211-9 (pbk)

Contents

Figures and tables

Figures

Tables

Contributors

David Beckett is Associate Professor in the Melbourne Graduate School of Education, Australia (the new name for the Faculty of Education at The University of Melbourne), where he specializes in adults' workplace learning. He publishes widely in philosophy of education, policy analysis and vocational education. Since 2000, he has held various management roles in education, centred on international, off-shore activities and research higher degree students, and currently holds two associate deanships in these areas. He supervised about fifteen theses in 2008, and is preparing, with Professor Paul Hager at the University of Technology, Sydney, their next joint book.

Maria Cseh is Associate Professor of Human and Organizational Learning (HOL) at The George Washington University, Washington DC, USA, coordinator of the HOL Doctoral Program, and Lecturer at the University of Pécs, Hungary. Dr Cseh's cross-cultural and international research studies on workplace learning, organizational development and change, and leadership were published in peer-reviewed journals and book chapters and presented at international conferences. She is a member of the Advisory Board for four international journals and serves on the Board of Directors of the Academy of Human Resource Development, on the Advisory Councils of two non-profit organizations, and on the Executive Board of the inter-disciplinary Women Leadership Institute at The George Washington University.

Xianjin Dou is Director of Lifelong Education in the Chinese National Centre of Education Development Research. He has a Master Degree of Economics and is Doctor of Labour Economics. In the Chinese Ministry of Education he has been responsible for rural education, vocational education, curriculum development and technological education policies. His research has mainly been on national education policies. In 2006 he was a Visiting Professor at the Danish University of Education. He is also the coordinator of Career and Technical Education in the Education Network of the APEC Human Resource Development Working Group and of the Research Network on National Strategies of Lifelong Learning of the ASEM Education and Research Hub.

Per-Erik Ellström is Professor of Education at Linköping University, Sweden. He is also Director of the HELIX Centre of Excellence – a ten-year programme for research on mobility, learning, health and innovation (http://www.liu.se/helix). His research interests include studies of workplace learning and innovation processes in organizations, the interplay between formal and informal learning at work, interactive research, leadership and organization development. He is currently leading a government-funded research project on workplace learning and practice-based innovations. His publications in English include chapters in several books, and articles in journals such as *Human Resource Development Quarterly*, *International Journal of Action Research*, *Journal of European Industrial Training* and the *Journal of Workplace Learning*.

Moacir Gadotti is PhD in Education Sciences at the University of Geneva (1977), Professor at the University of São Paulo, Brazil, and director of the Paulo Freire Institute. Of his many books two have been published in English: *Reading Paulo Freire: His Life and Work* (1994); *Pedagogy of Praxis: A Dialectical Philosophy of Education*, with a preface by Paulo Freire (1996). In Portuguese and Spanish he has also published *The History of Pedagogical Ideas* (1996); *Paulo Freire: A Bibliography* (1999), and in Portuguese *Pedagogy of the Earth* (2001); *The Masters of Rousseau* (2004); *To Educate for Another Possible World* (2006); and *School and Teachers: Paulo Freire and the passion of teaching* (2007).

Soonghee Han is Professor of Lifelong Learning in the Department of Education at Seoul National University, South Korea. He earned his Master's degree from Seoul National University and his Doctorate from the State University of New York, Buffalo. His academic work has focused mainly on studies of the learning society and learning ecology, comparative and global studies lifelong learning, and critical theories in adult education. He is also deeply involved in studies of popular education and human rights education in the Korean context. Currently he is leading a government-funded research project, which mainly investigates the agenda of Competency-based Education Change (http://competency.snu.ac.kr).

Katrin Hjort is Professor of Educational Studies at the Institute of Philosophy, Pedagogy and the Study of Religions at The University of Southern Denmark and Guest Professor of Pedagogy at Kristianstad University, Sweden. Her main research area is contemporary transformations and modernization processes in the public sector in the Nordic Welfare States including the professional and democratic challenges these processes entail. Currently she is leading a research project on the reforms of the Danish upper secondary school (gymnasium). She is a member of the Danish Research Council of the Humanities and of the Danish Clearing House for Educational Studies.

Knud Illeris is Professor of Lifelong Learning at the Danish University of Education in Copenhagen. His academic work is focused on learning theory, youth and adult learning and education, learning in working life and the method of project studies. His publications in English include *The Three Dimensions of Learning* (2002); *Adult Education and Adult Learning* (2004); *Learning in Working Life* (2004); and *How We Learn: Learning and non-learning in school and beyond* (2007). He has also edited *Contemporary Theories of Learning* (2009). In 2005 he was appointed Honorary Adjunct Professor at Columbia University, New York, and in 2006 he was elected to the Adult Education International Hall of Fame.

Pam Irwin is Development Manager with the Greater Manchester Strategic Alliance, a membership consortium of higher education providers across Greater Manchester in the UK. She was initially involved in stimulating innovation in learning and teaching, and is currently responsible for evaluation and research. In addition, she has an extensive background in curriculum design, development and implementation in different disciplines, especially health related areas; as well as direct experience with informal, formal, blended and e-learning. Her research interests include practice based and work related learning, workforce development, and technology enhanced learning.

Peter Jarvis started his career in the Royal Air Force and later entered the Methodist ministry. After this he became a teacher trainer and then lecturer in adult education at the University of Surrey, UK, and after having gained his PhD he became Professor of Continuing Education – now part time. He has published over 200 papers and written or edited thirty-five books. He is also the founding editor of the *International Journal of Lifelong Education* and has received many awards for his work, including five honorary doctorates and membership of the Adult Education International Hall of Fame. His latest books are a trilogy on lifelong learning and the learning society (2006, 2007, 2008).

Henrik Kock is Senior Lecturer in Education at the department for Behavioral Sciences and Learning (IBL) at Linköping University, Sweden. He is also affiliated to HELIX Centre of Excellence in the field of working life research, where he is Director of HELIX Graduate School. His research involves issues on learning and competence development, workplace learning, leadership and organizational renewal. He has been engaged in several research projects on learning and competence development in organizations, and currently he is leading two projects within this area: 'Introduction of Lean Production in SMEs' and 'Coordinating Management – Leadership in a distributed and resource restricted organization' (www.liu.se/helix).

Ben Parker (1953–2008) was Director of Research at the South African Qualification Authority (SAQA). He spent over 30 years working in higher education in South Africa, beginning his career at the University of the Witwatersrand in 1976 as a lecturer in the department of philosophy. From 1984 to 2004, he was at the University of KwaZulu-Natal serving in various capacities including Professor and Head of the School of Education, and Professor of Ethics in the School of Philosophy and Ethics. He worked for the national government in various roles and produced numerous publications in the field of education. His main research interests included rural education, teacher education and education policy.

Manuela Perrotta graduated in Communication at the University of Siena and received a PhD in Sociology and Social Research at the University of Trento, Italy. She is a member of the Research Unit on Communication, Organizational Learning and Aesthetics (RUCOLA) at the University of Trento. Her interests include sociology of organizations and work, science and technology studies and sociology of the body. Her PhD research examined the relationships among technologies, practices and organizations in the field of Assisted Reproductive Technologies. Her current research focuses on the knowing and learning processes in the field of female entrepreneurship.

Peter Sawchuk is Associate Professor of Sociology and Equity Studies in Education at the University of Toronto, Canada. Prior to entering academia he worked as a high school teacher, a press-operator and union educator. He specializes in the area of work, learning, technological change and labour studies. His recent books include *Adult Learning and Technology in Working-Class Life* (2003); *Workplace Learning: A Critical Introduction* (2004); *Hidden Knowledge: Work and Learning in the Information Age* (2004); *Critical Perspectives on Activity* (2006); and *The Future of Learning and Work: Critical Perspectives* (2008).

Karen E. Watkins is Associate Dean and Professor of Human Resource and Organizational Development at The University of Georgia, USA. Previously, she directed the graduate programme in Adult and Human Resource Development Leadership at The University of Texas at Austin. She is the author or co-author of over seventy articles and chapters, and six books. Together with Victoria Marsick she developed the organizational survey, *Dimensions of the Learning Organization*, used throughout the world. She was voted Scholar of the Year by the Academy of Human Resource Development and inducted into the International Adult Education Hall of Fame.

Shirley Walters is Director of the Division for Lifelong Learning at the University of Western Cape, where she has been Professor of Adult and Continuing Education for 23 years. She has been active in building adult education and lifelong learning in South Africa and internationally through involvement in civil society organizations, policy development, research, teaching and writing. She has published widely including *Education for Democratic Participation* (1989), editor of *Globalisation, Adult Education and Training* (1997) and co-editor of *Gender in Popular Education: Methods for empowerment* (1996). She serves as the chairperson of the South African Qualifications Authority (SAQA).

Kua Wongboonsin is Professor of the College of Population Studies and Vice-President for Research Affairs at Chulalongkorn University, Bangkok, Thailand. He obtained his MA and PhD from the University of Pennsylvania. His fields of expertise include Demographic Analysis, Population and Development. He authored *Population and Development* (in Thai, 2002) and *Business Demography* (in Thai, 2002), *Population Projections for Thailand 2000–2025: Implications for Population Policy in the Future* (in Thai, 2003) and co-edited *The Demographic Dividend: Policy Options for Asia* (2005).

Patcharawalai Wongboonsin is a faculty member of the College of Population Studies, Chulalongkorn University, Bangkok, Thailand. She obtained her MA from the University of Pennsylvania and PhD from Kyushu University, Japan. Her fields of expertise include Population and Development, Human Development, Human Security and Migration. She is a member of the Executive Board of the Institute of Asian Studies, Chulalongkorn University, Asian Review Editor-in-Chief, Asia Trend Editor-in-Chief, East Asian Economic Cooperation Council member, Deputy Director of the European Studies Center in Thailand, and Representative of Thailand to the Network of East Asian Think Tank. She also served as Advisor to Thai Delegates, ASEAN Inter-Parliamentary Organization.

Introduction

Knud Illeris

During the last 15–20 years the concept of *competence* has gradually become a keyword in the area of education and training by taking over the traditional position of knowledge and skills as the central categories for expression of the intended outcomes of the efforts.

It is not least the intensive work of the Organisation for Economic Co-operation and Development (e.g. OECD 2005) that has contributed to the Member States' interest in the concept, and later many other states, especially in East Asia, have joined the trend.

Behind all this lies the fact that in our complex and ever changing late modern world and societies it has become obvious that even highly developed knowledge and skills are no longer sufficient to meet the new challenges, situations and problems that are constantly facing people, companies, organizations and nations. There must be something more, a personal or common commitment, a readiness to act and change, an overview and insight, an obliging and cooperative attitude, a totality of qualities necessary to follow new developments and changing demands.

This raises, however, an enormous and at the same time rather confusing issue for all kinds of educational and training activities: how is it possible to generate and assess abilities to deal with challenges and problems which are not known or do not even exist at the time when the learning takes place?

The endeavour of the OECD in this situation has been to try to help nations and governments to handle this demand in practice. And the organization has tried to do this by following the traditional scientific paradigm of splitting up the issue into its components and then trying to define these in ways that are as accurate and measurable as possible.

However, precisely in doing so it seems that the most fundamental nature and qualities of the object, the competences, have been lost, and what has emerged is a lot of elements, which in their totality seem to have missed the essence of what competences are about. This is, as I see it, because it has not been sufficiently acknowledged that what is special about competences, what is actually the very reason for introducing this concept instead of knowledge and skills, is that it does not only refer to abilities – which, at least to some extent, may be precisely defined and measured – but also to potentials, which are only unfolded in relation to the new and unknown challenges when they appear.

In the preparation of this book I have followed a different course. I have addressed specialists and experts round the world who, in very different ways and contexts, have worked with, studied and analysed competences and how they are developed. I have myself in no way tried to communicate to the contributors any fixed and ready conceptions of how the concept should be understood. But I have tried to find scholars who have engaged themselves in investigating the concept of competence and the practice of competence development from very different angles and in very different contexts.

What has come out of it, I believe, is a much more varied, differentiated and empathetic approach to the topic of competences and competence development – and it is not altogether surprising that many of the contributions criticize and distance themselves from the OECD approach and the way of thinking and working with competences that this approach represents.

There is a somewhat unusual story behind how all this came about. Back in the spring of 2007 I was contacted by my South Korean colleague Soonghee Han (who is also represented in this volume), who asked me if I would be guest editor of a special issue of the well reputed *Asia Pacific Education Review (APER)* on competence development. I felt honoured and challenged by this invitation and started to consider how to handle the task and who to contact for contributions. A great help in this process was my participation in June 2007 in the 3rd International Conference of the Centre for Research in Lifelong Learning (CRLL), University of Stirling, Scotland, on researching Lifelong Learning and Teaching. In this forum I met scholars from many countries with whom I could discuss the issue and possible contributors, and I also entered some agreements on contributions. So during the autumn of 2007 I succeeded in collecting six very interesting and qualified papers, which together with my own introduction comprised the special issue, which was published in February 2008 (*APER* 2008).

As I was not the only one who thought that in this issue I had collected some very qualified and important contributions to the on-going discussion on competence development, a new idea gradually came to my mind: Would this not be a good opportunity to try to collect some more contributions and then make a book out of it? So I contacted the *APER* and the authors from the special issue for permission to re-use the articles and received very positive replies from all. Then I contacted Routledge Education with a book proposal, and as they were also positive I asked the 'old' authors if they wished to make any changes in and/or additions to their contributions and I began to find new authors who could complete the collection.

In these efforts I followed two lines. The first was to get contributions that together would cover the topic from as many angles as possible. The second was to put together a collection including examples from all parts of the world. Great interest was shown in the project, and by June 2008 I had altogether promises of fourteen contributions from twelve countries covering all of the world's six continents.

I have chosen to arrange these contributions in four groups:

Part I includes three broad chapters that together cover the topic of competence development in a wide and comprehensive way. First, I have placed the contribution of American Karen E. Watkins and Maria Cseh on 'Competence development in the USA', which lines up and discusses the background and development of this approach in the country where it was first introduced. Second, Moacir Gadotti from Brazil, Director of the Paulo Freire Institute, takes up 'Adult education and competence development' in a critical perspective. And third, Swedish Per-Erik Ellström and Henrik Kock give an overview of 'Competence development in the workplace' and the many aspects involved in this.

Part II is about the concept and nature of competences. This is opened by the critical contribution of South Korean Soonghee Han on 'Competence: Commodification of human ability'. Next, in his chapter on 'Holistic competence: Putting judgements first', Australian David Beckett discusses judgement and decision making as the core area of competences. And in the two last chapters of this part, I myself take up the relationship 'Competence, learning and education' and British Peter Jarvis deals with 'Learning to be an expert: Competence development and expertise'.

Part III is about competence development in different contexts. First, Danish Katrin Hjort focuses on 'Competence development in the public sector'. After this, Canadian Peter Sawchuk goes on to 'Labour perspectives on the new politics of skill and competence formation'. Then British Pam Irwin looks at 'Competences and employer engagement'. And, finally, Italian Manuela Perrotta elaborates on the rather unusual but at the same time very interesting topic of 'Developing competence-in-practice: Female entrepreneurs in small business'.

In the closing Part IV, competence development is taken up as a national strategy for the generation of an up-to-date education and training system. This is done by three examples from very different developing countries dealing with the enormous challenge of raising the general educational level of big populations. Chinese Xianjin Dou gives an account of the gigantic project of 'Enhancing competences and skills in China'. Then South African Ben Parker and Shirley Walters describe the history of 'Competence-based training and National Qualifications Frameworks in South Africa' since 1994, when apartheid was abolished and a quite new educational system had to be built up. And, as the last chapter of the book, Patcharawalai and Kua Wongboonsin from Thailand deal with the development 'Towards enhanced competence of the Thai workforce'.

I am very satisfied and proud now to be able to present this collection of up-to-date and worldwide covering articles on the topic of competence development, and I hope that this book will illustrate in an engaging and convincing manner both the importance and the innovative nature of the concept of competences and simultaneously the many dangers that exist when such a concept is taken up and embraced as a kind of miraculous means to solve all problems in such a rapidly changing and very complex area as human learning, education and training.

Knud Illeris, Copenhagen

Part I

The issue of competence development

Chapter 1

Competence development in the USA

Limiting expectations or unleashing global capacities

Karen E. Watkins and Maria Cseh

Since the publication of Benjamin Bloom's *Taxonomy of Educational Objectives* in 1956, educators have been captured by the idea of defining the essential skills and knowledge of an educated individual. In the workplace, this has taken different forms over time – from a focus on competency profiling to performance analysis and design, to an emphasis on developing expertise and competency certification. As many corporations in Europe and Asia embrace qualifications frameworks as means to identify competence and certify skills, the USA continues to evolve new variations on these original concepts of competence, including a focus in the workplace on professional competence certification. In this chapter, we identify some workplace approaches and explore theories of competence, particularly those that are more holistic, organizational, or global capacities.

Why focus on competence development now? A global talent gap

As organizations face rapid changes that bring a need for ever-increasing skills and a shrinking supply of talented employees, they look to competency profiling to help them select and develop the strongest candidates. For example, at Danske Bank, competency profiles are developed for all employees (Competency Development 2008). The competency profile lists the specific professional and personal competencies that an employee needs to meet job requirements. The organization believes that these profiles will enable it to evaluate current skills and target competency development opportunities.

Human resource management specialists identify gaps in the leadership pipeline, particularly at the middle management level (Gurchiek 2007), rather than the retirement of key workers as the source of the most prevalent talent gap. There is increasing concern that, especially at leadership levels, there are fewer and fewer individuals who possess the complex array of skills needed to manage global businesses.

A recent national report, *Rising above the Gathering Storm* (by the Committee on Prospering in the Global Economy of the 21st Century (National Academy of Sciences 2005), stated that

> The enormous and growing supply of labor in the developing world is but one side of a global demographic transformation. The other side is the aging populations of developed nations. The working-age population is already shrinking in Italy and Japan, and it will begin to decline in the USA, the UK, and Canada by the 2020s. More than 70 million USA baby boomers will retire by 2020, but only 40 million new workers will enter the workforce. Europe is expected to face the greatest period of depopulation since the Black Death, shrinking to 7 pct. of world population by 2050 (from nearly 25 pct. just after World War II). East Asia (including China) is experiencing the most rapid aging in the world. At the same time, India's working-age population is projected to grow by 335 million people by 2030 — almost equivalent to the entire workforce of Europe and the United States of America today. These extreme global imbalances suggest that immigration will continue to increase. (p. 212)

The report suggests that employers will seek talent from a global pool.

The report also presents a letter from the leadership of the National Science Foundation to the President's Council of Advisors on Science and Technology that puts the case even more bluntly stating that,

> Civilization is on the brink of a new industrial order. The big winners in the increasingly fierce global scramble for supremacy will not be those who simply make commodities faster and cheaper than the competition. They will be those who develop talent, techniques and tools so advanced that there is no competition. (p. 1–3)

Thus, understanding the global labor market is crucial for the United States' strategic approaches to nurturing, attracting, and retaining its talent pool.

A bill was introduced to the USA Senate in May 2005, entitled Collaborative Opportunities to Mobilize and Promote Education, Technology, and Enterprise Act of 2005. Designed to address the skills gap in a knowledge economy, it provides for partnerships to provide science, technology, engineering, and math (STEM) education and incentives to spur research and development. The bill demonstrates concern that the USA is losing its competitive edge in a knowledge economy and the need to target funding to support new talent development in critical shortage areas. The America COMPETES bill passed in 2007 (American Society for Training and Development 2007).

Others argue that talent will come from hidden talent pools of people with existing talent not currently being utilized such as the underemployed, from people who delay retirement, outsourcing, off-shoring, and retraining programmes (Grantham & Ware 2005). A recent report by Deloitte Research (2007) describes a talent paradox as survival of the skilled – managers skilled in ensuring coordination among a globally dispersed workforce, managing a global workforce with varied demographic profiles, skill sets, expectations, who understand the impact of changing demographics and skill sets in different locations and can plan accordingly (p. 2). This report focuses on the availability of talent in Generation Y that has been elusive at present since corporations do not know how to attract these workers. The authors focus on the need to connect – to provide employees with tools and assistance to build networks to improve individual and organizational performance and to improve the quality of their interactions with others. Organizational environments that allow work–life flexibility are more effective with this generation.

Whether the talent gap is a lack of middle managers, key technical workers, globally astute leaders; whether the solution is to increase funding for pre-collegiate and retraining in STEM disciplines, finding and attracting underutilized and younger new entrants to key roles; the need for developing competence—especially new competences—is at the heart of the proposed solutions offered for the growing talent gap. The durability of this concept in the field of training and development may relate to these evolving profiles of competence in a changing workplace. On the other hand, the evolving scope of the concept may be the source of its sustained viability. In the section that follows, we show the evolution of our understanding of competency development in the workplace.

Differing definitions—increasing scope

From a focus on minute behaviors to patterns of behavior, to global mindsets, the history of competence development is one of an expanding scope. Reviewing definitions of competence over time, we see the evolution of foci and scope in our understanding of competence at the individual level.

Early definitions of competence focused on adequacy to function effectively in the world: "As used here, competence will refer to an organism's capacity to interact effectively with its environment" (White, 1959: 297). Working with David McClelland at Harvard to define behavioral competencies for individuals in key job roles, Klemp (1981) defined competence as

> any attribute of a person that underlies effective performance; a job competency is simply an attribute related to doing a job effectively. People carry with them a wide assortment of knowledge, abilities, interests, traits, and motives, but unless these attributes relate demonstrably to doing a job well, they are not job competencies. (p. 55)

A similar direction was found in the training and development field. McLagan (1982) conducted numerous studies of the competencies of trainers.

She wrote,

> many models developed for the training and development field do not distinguish between competencies and tasks. Although there is overlap, it is desirable to differentiate competencies (characteristics of people) from job tasks (tasks of jobs). We define jobs and roles in terms of tasks and responsibilities, but we describe (and develop) people in terms of competencies. (p. 20)

Elkin (1990) defined individual competencies similarly, but added a focus on transfer of these skills across job contexts,

> the Training Services Agency defines competency as "ability to perform the activities within an occupation", and so by implication includes job tasks. They continue: "competence is a wide concept which embodies the ability to transfer skills and knowledge to new situations within the occupational area. It encompasses organization, and planning of work, innovations and coping with non-routine activities. It includes those qualities of personal effectiveness that are required in the workplace to deal with co-workers, managers and customers." (p. 22).

In contrast, competence in Herling's (in Swanson & Holton 2001) view refers to minimal or nominally proficient performance. Earlier definitions of competence referred to competence as the knowledge, skills, and attitudes that, collectively, define an individual's capabilities. Bloom (1956) categorized educational objectives as cognitive, affective, and psychomotor in the hope that educators would design more holistic educational approaches, drawing on all of these domains. It's unfortunate that his ideas were used to develop exhaustive laundry lists of micro behaviors to guide instruction—and the idea of more synthetic or holistic approaches to education did not materialize.

Over time, broader conceptions of competence emerged.

> A competency is defined as a capability or ability. It is a set of related but different sets of behavior organized around an underlying construct, which we call the "intent." The behaviors are alternate manifestations of the intent, as appropriate in various situations or times. ... A theory of performance is the basis for the concept of competency. The theory used in this approach is a basic contingency theory. Maximum performance is believed to occur when the person's capability or talent is consistent with the needs of the job demands and the organizational environment.
> (Boyatzis 1982: 6)

In this view, competence includes not only behaviors but also intent and the idea of capacity—or the ability to deploy one's skills to meet job demands and environmental press.

Competencies are patterns of behavior in Rodriguez *et al.* (2002) who note that "OPM defines a competency as a measurable pattern of knowledge, skill, abilities, behaviors, and other characteristics that an individual needs to perform work roles or occupational functions successfully" (p. 310). Henderson *et al.* (1995) studied assessment center data and noted that competencies needed to be understood as behavioral repertoires or patterns of behaviors and competency profiling consists of identifying the broad patterns of behavior that are core to an individual in a particular job role.

These broad patterns of behavior are important to a concept of competence development. Consider a set of competencies for learning to drive. Some of those identified would probably focus on starting the car, steering, braking, speed limits, road conditions, etc. Yet, these micro skills are not enough. Learned separately, they do not add up to driving. If an individual is excellent at braking, but very poor at steering, he/she will not be a good driver. It is the ability to do all of these things well, in a smoothly integrated fashion, and at the appropriate time that constitutes driving ability. A focus on micro skills ignores the need for development of the whole—and of the judgment needed to know when to deploy skills.

Sandberg (2000), writing from an interpretive approach, defines competence as "competence is not seen as consisting of two separate entities; instead, worker and work form one entity through the lived experience of work. Competence is thus seen as constituted by the meaning the work takes on for the worker in his or her experience of it" (p. 11). Herling (in Swanson & Holton 2001) offers operational definitions of competence and expertise to illustrate why competence is no longer enough in an era of rapid, global change. The elements of expertise are knowledge, experience, and problem-solving. Drawing on research comparing the skills of novices vs. experts, advocates for the concept of expertise argue that experience is an accumulated repertoire of ways to apply knowledge and skills to solving complex organizational problems. Therefore, expertise is defined as "displayed behavior within a specialized domain and/or related domain in the form of consistently demonstrated actions of an individual that are both optimally efficient and effective in their results" (Swanson & Holton 2001: 241). To achieve this state, individuals have to have a set of competencies, experiences that hone those competencies, and judgment that enables them to choose wisely how to proceed in difficult situations.

Impact of the changing nature of work on competence development

Work is also changing in interesting ways for facilitators of workplace learning. Increasingly, we are part of work groups, working at times collectively and at times on modules that must eventually come together to be a seamless product. Even more interesting, in a global, virtual context, people want learning that is just in time, and just enough. They want to learn through designs that can be controlled and enhanced by the learner.

Baldwin and Clark (2005) argue for a design architecture that is option-rich and modular. For example, open source coding—where communities of user designers create highly effective products that defy and compete against traditional closed source coding—illustrates a fundamental shift in our thinking about innovation and about who controls the products of our inventions. It is the modularity of the design architecture that permits innovation and collaborative knowledge creation.

These toolkit designs change who can access and use the structural information that underlies much professional work. Novices have access to the same tools as those used by engineers, architects, researchers, financial analysts, even physicians. How many of you have wondered about something, and had someone immediately say "Just a minute—let me Google it."

Creating training and knowledge management programmes that "learn" from users adding examples and prototypes, that branch into multiple training options depending on learner interests and needs, and that can be broken down into discrete units or modules related to steps in a task requires significant skill on the part of designers of workplace learning. On the other hand, they create learning opportunities for the whole organization that can grow with the talent requirements of the organization. These new learning approaches lead us away from a focus on individual competence development to a focus on organizational systems and organization competencies.

Developing core organizational competences

As scholars have tried to clarify what will address organizational capacity development, it has become clear that we need more than broad patterns of competence in individuals. Organizations have core competencies that also can be defined and developed. Garavan and McGuire (2001) say that the starting point of this perspective is that individual competencies are a core, often defining resource of organizations. From a talent development perspective, acquiring and developing individuals with critical talents enriches the core capacities of the organization. On the other hand, one could argue that the capacity to develop and deploy the talents of its members is a core capacity of organizations. The work of Watkins and Marsick (1993, 1997) on developing a learning culture is focused on developing this core competency.

"Clearly the best way for companies to win the talent wars is to turn themselves into learning organizations. The trouble is that few of them know how to do this" (*The Economist* 2006: 20).

Watkins and Marsick's (1993, 1997) work focuses on creating a learning culture, one in which continuous learning is a fundamental strategy of the business. Organizations structured to promote continuous learning have a culture that: values and provides resources and tools for continuous learning opportunities for individuals; ensures opportunities for dialogue and inquiry including capturing suggestions for change and improvement; emphasizes team learning and collaboration to promote cross-unit learning; empowers people to enact a collective vision; creates systems to capture and share this learning; makes systemic connections between the organization and its environment, scanning the environment to learn and anticipate future needs; and provides leadership for learning through managers who know how to facilitate talent development of their employees and who model continuously learning themselves (Watkins & Marsick 2003).

> Core competencies are the collective learning in the organization, especially how to coordinate diverse production skills and integrate multiple streams of technologies. ... it is also about the organization of work and the delivery of value. ... Core competence is communication, involvement, and a deep commitment to working across organizational boundaries. It involves many levels of people and all functions. ... Unlike physical assets, which do deteriorate over time, competencies are enhanced as they are applied and shared. (Prahalad & Hamel, 1990: 82)

In addition to sharing individual skills, "organizational competencies also can include other capabilities such as systems, technologies, or even physical locations or infrastructure" (Kochanski & Ruse 1996: 22). Others believe that a primary component of organizational core competencies are the talents and competencies of its key managers: "the venture's distinctive competencies, which encompass the technical, commercial, and administrative and managerial competencies in which it excels to create customer value relative to competitors" (Burgelman & Siegel 2008: 141).

A resource-based view of organizations

> combines the internal analysis of phenomena within companies (a preoccupation of many management gurus since the mid-1980s) with the external analysis of the industry and the competitive environment (the central focus of earlier strategy approaches). ... The RBV sees companies as very different collections of physical and intangible assets and capabilities. No two companies are alike because no two companies have had the same set of experiences, acquired the same assets and skills, or built the same organizational cultures. These assets and capabilities determine how

efficiently and effectively a company performs its functional activities. ... Valuable resources can take a variety of forms, including some overlooked by the narrower conceptions of core competence and capabilities. They can be physical ... Or valuable resources may be intangible ... Or the valuable resource may be an organizational capability embedded in a company's routines, processes, and culture. ... These capabilities, built up over time, transform otherwise pedestrian or commodity inputs into superior products and make the companies that have developed them successful in the global market. Competitive advantage, whatever its source, ultimately can be attributed to the ownership of a valuable resource that enables the company to perform activities better or more cheaply than competitors.

(Collis & Montgomery 2008: 142)

Competence development at the organizational level stresses creating structures and systems to promote the development of individuals without the limitations of individual competency models that too often become quickly outmoded or overly-specific and that endure even as individuals leave (Wright, Dunford & Snell 2001). They focus on individuals to the extent that they are a core asset to the firm – but also embrace developing broader structures, systems, and organizational capacities. As a result, this direction is more promising and potentially more long-lasting than traditional competency profiling. Another promising direction is a focus on global competence, particularly in terms of developing a global mindset among key personnel as a core organization competence.

Unleashing global capacities: holistic competences and global mindset

Cultural competence and cultural intelligence are often mentioned in the management literature as prerequisites for successful functioning in the ever-changing global business landscape. Walker *et al.* (2003) describe cultural competence in terms of attitudes (e.g., open attitude), awareness of oneself and others, cultural knowledge, and cross-cultural skills. Peterson (2004) presents in very similar terms the concept of cultural intelligence that encompasses the following three components: knowledge about cultures (e.g., facts about the environment—i.e., history, economy, etc.); awareness about oneself and others; and specific skills enabling the fulfillment of a specific task (e.g., behavioral skills). Thomas and Inkson (2003) in their description of cultural intelligence concur with the knowledge and skills component and add the need for mindfulness which they describe as "the ability to pay attention in a reflective and creative way to cues in the cross-cultural situations encountered" (p. 15).

Global mindset is another concept that encompasses holistic competencies that emerged in the past decade in the management literature. Global mindset is frequently associated with the mindset needed in a global business context to make strategic business decisions. Rhinesmith (1996) identified twenty-four competencies that a global leader has to possess and grouped them by responsibility as they relate to the organization's strategy and structure, its corporate culture and its people. Global mindset is associated with both individuals and organizations (Kottolli, 2007). At the organizational level cultural competence requires that organizations 1) have a defined set of values and principles, and demonstrate behaviors, attitudes, policies, and structures that enable them to work effectively cross-culturally; 2) have the capacity to value diversity, conduct self-assessment, manage the dynamics of difference, acquire and institutionalize cultural knowledge, and adapt to diversity and the cultural contexts of the communities they serve; and 3) incorporate the above in all aspects of policy making, administration, practice, service delivery, and involve systematically consumers, key stakeholders, and communities (Cross *et al.* 1989).

At the individual level, Levy *et al.* (2007) concluded that the global mindset is a multidimensional concept and described it as "a highly complex cognitive structure characterized by an openness to and articulation of multiple cultural and strategic realities on both the global and local levels, and the cognitive ability to mediate and integrate across this multiplicity" (p. 244). Global mindset mirrors self-confidence balanced by humility and generosity, and like cultural competence and intelligence encompasses skills such as flexibility and adaptability, collaboration and listening (Werhane *et al.*, 2006; Thorn, 2007).

In a review of the literature on global leadership competencies, Beechler and Javidan (2007) concluded, "the list of effective global leadership competencies are practically endless, to the point in which they become useless" (p. 138). In order to address this issue, the authors identify the following three critical components of a global mindset essential for global leadership: 1) intellectual capital; 2) psychological capital; and 3) social capital. Intellectual capital refers to the knowledge and understanding of global business, cognitive complexity and cultural acumen. Psychological capital is composed of a positive psychological profile (i.e., self-efficacy, self-confidence, optimism and hope, and resilience), cosmopolitanism (e.g., respect for other cultures, openness and sensitivity, flexibility) and a passion for cross-cultural encounters. The three types of social capital (structural, relational, and cognitive) reflect participation in social networks, the nature of relationships in those networks, and the shared meanings derived from them.

In an on-going study that examines critical learning experiences that enabled experienced organization development and change consultants to work successfully across cultures and the competencies they value in their work, Cseh and Coningham (2007) found that the participants were eloquent in expressing their perceptions of needed competencies in a global setting. The most frequently mentioned competency was humility followed by respect of other cultures, curiosity, observation, listening, flexibility, ability to deal with ambiguity and to make immediate decisions, awareness, cultural sensitivity, sense of humor, genuine good intentions, professional knowledge, systems thinking, asking constructive questions, and relationship building. The following quote exemplifies the emphasis on some of the key global competencies:

> Number one is to be humble. Recognize that you don't know everything; you will never know everything about any culture, including your own. So be humble. Be willing to learn and seek learning opportunities and be very quick on your feet. In all the stories I told you I had to remedy immediately. I couldn't sit back and say let me reflect on this for some time. I couldn't say I'm gonna talk to so and so and we'll work this out. I had to make a decision right then about what I was going to do. You gotta be quick on your feet.

Another participant concurred stating:

> So I think there is some receptivity because of who I am and what I do but hopefully it is enhanced by my respect for them, humility that I can't do without them. ... I think being humble and having a sense of humor and being able to handle ambiguity. ... So I think you have to be able to have some ability to tolerate ambiguity and be flexible, if things don't work out, you apologize, you learn from it, demonstrate to them that you have to keep on growing and those are important skills. I think it is the attitude that is probably one of the most important things for a person working in another culture, another country.

The importance of respect and genuine interest in the client's well-being was highlighted by another participant in the following words:

> I think the theories, being well versed in multiple theories and multiple ways of doing things lets me see things that are happening quicker than most people and lets me have ways then to think that are respectful and I think I genuinely care about the people I work with and genuinely want good for everybody and I think that comes across.

Curiosity, observation and listening skills were also considered critical. As one of the participants explained: "... having curiosity and be willing to follow up on it is absolutely essential. If you're not curious you are not going to find your mistakes, you are not gonna want answers."

Although the valued cross-cultural competencies reflect the ones present in the literature and did not constitute a surprise, the high valence attached to humility, respect for other cultures, curiosity, observation and listening, flexibility, ability to handle ambiguity, and ability to make immediate decisions to avoid escalation of misunderstandings was evidenced in the data and raises further awareness of the importance of developing these competencies.

The ability to handle ambiguity and make immediate decisions based on the understanding of the operational context (e.g., the socio-political, legal and economic context and its impact on the functioning of the organization) was also considered critical in the learning of owner-managers of small private companies in Romania to lead successfully in the transition to a free market economy (Cseh 2002). In order to assess the complex situations they faced, the participants highlighted the importance of networking, observation, listening, willingness to learn from others and from mistakes, and understanding the way human relationships affect the conduct of business. The ability to create environments that allow employees and business partners to change their mindset proved to be the most difficult challenge for the study participants. "To change people's mentality is the hardest thing to do ... Time and education is needed ..."

In order to assess the holistic global competencies described in the literature and captured by Beechler and Javidan (2007) and exemplified in the qualitative studies presented above, Javidan, the Dean of Research at the Thunderbird School of Global Management in Glendale, Arizona, and leader of the Global Mindset project, led the development of a 91-question survey (Thunderbird School of Global Management 2008). The survey is used at the individual level to help global managers identify their strengths and weaknesses related to their global mindset and allow for executive training or coaching for needed competence development. At the organizational level, Thunderbird is also using the instrument to measure its own strengths and weaknesses by administering the survey to its students at the start of their studies and immediately before graduation.

Given all of the above evidence, there is an agreement in the literature as well as in practice that the developmental process associated with global, holistic competencies needed for the well-being of individuals and organizations is a lengthy one. Both individuals and organizations are at various levels of awareness, knowledge, and skills along the cultural competence continuum and enabling the development of these levels in time will determine the viability of both protagonists amidst the heightened complexities brought about by rapid worldwide change. Our work is dedicated to ensuring that people, organizations, and society recognize the need and are prepared to nurture these global competencies in order to ensure their global viability and health.

Acknowledgements

This chapter is adapted from an article by Illeris, K. (2008). Competence Development: The key to modern education, or just another buzzword? *Asia Pacific Education Review*, 9(1), 1–4. Reprinted with permission from Education Research Institute, Seoul National University.

The authors would like to thank Rocio Hertig and Rubens Pessanha Filho, George Washington University doctoral students and graduate research assistants, for their help identifying many of the sources used in this chapter.

Chapter 2

Adult education and competence development

From a critical thinking perspective

Moacir Gadotti

In Portuguese and Spanish, competence has three different meanings. It can mean both the function and the faculty attributed by law, relating to disputes, conflicts or opposition. However, it is the other meaning of competence that interests us here, relating to skills, attitude and expertise. We very often find other words associated with competence. We talk about 'competences and skills', 'competences and values', and 'competences and knowledge', always using the plural. In this text, we will concentrate on the development of competences and skills, both in relation to formal and informal education, and vocational training. The subject is current and has been the cause of much discussion, dispute, and contradictory understandings. Often, competence is confused with skill and opposes competition and collaboration.

We recognize that the subject of competences is controversial, that there are purposely distorted views on and caricatures of this subject, and that it needs to be understood beyond the realms of sectarianism. The notion of competences is not new. What is new is a discussion around a certain kind of 'pedagogical competence', that is to say, a new concept of competence that places the notion in the centre of pedagogical practice, while excluding others. That discussion, however, has the merit of confronting an elitist pedagogy, always concerned with intellectual knowledge at the expense of practical knowledge, in other words, the knowledge 'drawn from experience', as Paulo Freire used to say. The competences debate has been positive in terms of the way it approaches the issue of work, and, in particular, the practical intelligence of the workers, irrespective of their diplomas, a positive attribute frequently ignored by academics.

In principle, we cannot talk about a formal opposition between *competence* and *cooperation*. However, we come across this opposition frequently and for a reason, as different and even opposing concepts of competences do exist. Without doubt, the most widespread competences model is associated with an instrumental paradigm that is individualist and educationally non-collaborative.

Therefore, everything depends on our answer to the issue concerning what competences we need to thrive in society, in our nation, and at work.

Companies have worked harder with the competences needed for an individual to triumph in life, so that he or she may be more competitive in the 'market society'. Are competences necessary for an individual to be able to compete? This all depends on the kind of competences we are discussing. Should we only choose those competences that help us the most to compete, or those that are most suited to collaboration?

The notion of competence is not neutral, and is not beyond raising suspicions. There are training *models for* competence. The most controversial meaning of competence is the mercantilistic meaning, which introduces corporate competitiveness models into the educational framework. From an *emancipatory perspective*, it makes no sense to simulate at school, and least of all in teacher–student relationships, the unsupportive relationships that predominate in the free market. When the teacher–student relationship acquires the market form, it results in the teacher losing self-esteem, since he or she becomes a mere mimicker of ideas that have already been talked about and put into practice. With a loss of autonomy comes a loss of creativity, or, 'untested feasibility', as Paulo Freire would say, trying to renounce his ideas and dreams to simulate the ideas of the market. In his book *Pedagogy of Autonomy*, Paulo Freire (1997: 15) denounced that situation, stating the 'permanently present' critic within 'the neoliberal wickedness at the cynicism of its fatalist ideology and inflexible denial of the dream and of Utopia'.

Education cannot be guided by the paradigm of a company formed with the objective of meeting the needs of the market, therefore placing an emphasis on efficiency, and having an objective that does not relate to the human being, but to the needs of the market. For this paradigm, the human being functions only as a pure economic operator. The *pedagogical act* is democratic in its nature, whereas the *corporate act* is orientated around the 'logic of control'.

From a *mercantilistic perspective*, or put more simply, in terms of marketing, the human being is educated to contribute to the reproduction and expansion of its race. It is not without reason that we have the expression 'manpower'. The human is subservient to capital logic. From this perspective, to be proficient is to generate more wealth, even if in doing so it is necessary to be voracious, unsupportive and disloyal, attributes that are a far cry from the most noble of human qualities; companionship, kindness and generosity. That is a concept of the competence that is unconcerned with the *comprehensive education* of the human being. Education, in this sense, is reduced to just the competences and skills required for the market.

In common sense, skill is designated a certain practical domain, while competence may be more associated with its intellectual aspects. Nevertheless, as learning from experience is increasingly less instrumental and more cognitive, it does not seem appropriate to make this distinction.

It is known that education cannot be reduced to skills and the capacity to resolve problems. To be skilful, astute and intelligent, does not mean to be competent. In other words, 'to be capable of,' always demands a complement.

'To be capable of ...' separated from its context, means nothing. To have knowledge, skills or capabilities does not mean to be proficient. And, as no one can say about themselves that they are competent, competence of a subject needs to be recognized by somebody else. For this reason, competence is relative. For me to be competent, I need recognition from another individual who may validate, or 'certify' my level of competence. Skills are only an expression of competence.

As opposed to *individualism*, that type of education promotes *overcrowding*, imposing homogenous and standardized values that are operative, instrumental, and impoverish basic education, rather than enrich it. It is more about training than education, and is a *type of education* that denies the value of the diversity and multiplicity of the situations in which human beings live, both at school, and in the family and at work. As István Mészáros (2004: 48) says:

> without a different concept of education, in other words, the cooperatively managed self-education of the liberally associated producers, inspired by, and orientated towards, the production and satisfaction of their genuine needs, there is no way to escape the vicious circle of the production of scarcity on an increasingly large scale. In the absence of the cooperative self-education of equals who are capable of understanding the true meaning of the word *economy*, all activities will continue at the mercy of the interests invested in the maximum reproduction of *artificial necessities*, inseparable from the lucrative perpetuation of scarcity.

The multitude of meanings of the concept of competences

That said, I would like to speak about another kind of *competence development*, subordinated to another logic, another theory of knowledge, in defence of a learning that is 'significant' (Piaget 1974), 'transforming' (O'Sullivan 2004), and 'cooperative' (Monereo & Gisbert 2005). For Jean Piaget (1974), the integration and cooperation, primarily of the small child with other children of its own age, is a decisive factor in the development of an individual. Cooperative or collaborative learning constitutes a powerful resource for 'reading the world' (Paulo Freire 1997), essential for these times of profound changes that we are experiencing today, at the beginning of the new millennium. Cooperative learning 'transforms heterogeneity into a positive element that facilitates learning (...). Cooperative learning promotes psychosocial and interactive skills, based on values such as collaboration, mutual help and solidarity (...). It is a motor for significant learning' (Monereo & Gisbert 2005: 10–11). Carlos Monereo and David Duran Gisbert warn that learning is not about replacing individual work, or even 'competitive' work, admitting that healthy competition exists that is not aimed at destroying others, but rather is there to test our own limits. When we take part in a football match against another team, the objective is not to destroy the other players, but to compete against them, while testing our own abilities and skills. Mutual competence and competition do not oppose one another mechanically. They depend on a context. In order for collaborative learning to exist, interdependency is necessary, as is individual responsibility, reciprocation and equality in terms of conditions.

Yvon Minvielle (1991: 291) perceives *competence* as 'the system of measures acquired and confronted through practice, and through a game of accumulation and composition, define the professional activities organized within a profession'. Competence is not static. It is something constantly evolving. A person who is competent today may not be tomorrow, if they are not in constant interaction with their environment, or do not pay attention to the changes and obsolescence of the knowledge, techniques and tools of their profession. Therefore, he perceives *profession* (employment, occupation, role) as 'an activity socially defined by its rules, techniques, references, and sometimes even by its rituals'.

Thus, we can talk about political, strategic and professional competence, always in relation to a specific context. Competence is acquired when confronting the challenges of experience. Experience provides us with challenges. To respond to these challenges, we need to build on certain abilities.

The concept of competence is problematic, vast and even ambiguous. It is more about a notion than a concept, a notion quite imprecise, if compared with the *concept of qualification*. The term 'competence', therefore has acquired a number of meanings. It is frequently associated with the ability to control complex situations, ability to utilize information, demonstrate effective use of our knowledge and ability to learn new things. At the same time, it is a significant concept in terms of its association with the ability to lead in complex and unforeseen situations, in different contexts, whether at work, in school, in the family, or in society. As we point out, the problem starts when we reduce school to the dimensions of a company, and introduce, through 'pedagogical competence', a corporate form of logic.

The *multitude of meanings* of the concept of competence, has taken, and is still taking, a long time to discuss. Competence is still a *disputed concept*. Overcoming its ambiguity is both a theoretical and a practical issue. Finally, many other concepts are ambiguous, for example; the concepts of culture, democracy, citizenship, self-governance, justice, and so forth. Many concepts have different meanings depending on their context and the authors who defend them. The abundance of definitions for these concepts does not stop us from considering them an essential part of our lives. We give them the practical context that our principles, social values and policies grant them. This is why we cannot let them remain ambiguous, or adopt them indiscriminately. We need to explain their meaning and significance, in relation to the objectives that we defend, or according to the objectives that we want to achieve.

Recently, my meetings on the subject of the competence development became more high-profile. I have had the opportunity over the last few years to attend conferences and scientific meetings, for different reasons, in different EU countries. At these meetings, I was impressed by the influence of the concept of competence in European education, promoted by the Organisation for Economic Co-operation and Development (OECD 2001). Practically everything is subject to the logic of assessment and performance. While in Latin America, we still have nurtured a certain culture of *weightlessness*, Europe is taking large steps towards another extreme. We have to learn from the European pedagogical way of thinking. The advances in the assessment of performance in learning have been notable. Nevertheless, we cannot stop voicing our concerns over the level of dehumanization that certain educational policies are introducing into our teaching systems. Not everything can be reduced to performance, competences and skills indicators. Education is more complex than that.

UNECE, the United Nations Economic Commission for Europe, has even been insisting on the construction of assessment indicators for competences relating to sustainability. For this, the Germans have developed the concept '*Gestaltungskompetenz*', to refer to the competences and skills relating to Education for Sustainable Development, a concept that seems adequate to me in terms of the objective that is proposed, that is, education for socio-environmental sustainability. According to Gerhard de Haan, professor of the Free University of Berlin, and President of the German National Committee for the Decade of Education for Sustainable Development (DESD), the concept of '*Gestaltungskompetenz*', sometimes translated into English as 'participation skills', 'was formulated thinking precisely in Education for Sustainable Development. *Gestaltungskompetenz* is the capacity to apply knowledge to sustainable development and recognize the problems that non-sustainable development implies' (Haan 2007a: 7). In another context, he translates *Gestaltungskompetenz* as 'shaping competence', and divides that concept into ten parts. He says it is about producing knowledge with an open spirit in contrast to the world, integrating new perspectives, thinking and acting with foresight, acquiring knowledge, and acting in an interdisciplinary manner. He also says it is about having the skills to plan and act in cooperation with other people, participate in decision-making processes, motivate others to be active, reflect on your own principles and those of others, plan and act autonomously, demonstrate empathy and solidarity with those less favoured, and motivate yourself to become more active (Haan 2007b: 12).

According to Alexander Leicht, head of the German Secretariat for the United Nations Decade, *Gestaltungskompetenz* includes:

> thinking with foresight that is orientated towards the future, complex interdisciplinary knowledge, and participation in social decision-making

processes. Therefore, Education for Sustainable Development is not only about the creation of an environmental conscience. In reality, it places a greater emphasis on making people self-sufficient so they can take initiatives that are focussed on viable and long-term development.

(Leicht 2005: 27)

Indicators are important if they are not established just with economic and profitability criteria in mind. Ambiguities and dualisms may also be found in indicators and competences, in relation to the different competence models. Competences in Education for Sustainable Development, for example, cannot be summarized into their cognitive aspects, since they have implications in terms of challenges, behaviour, attitudes and intentions. In addition to the cognitive component, they implicate certain emotional and motivational components. Competences are not limited to an individual's skills or abilities to resolve problems. They implicate the individual's ability to organize their own work, critical thinking, teamwork, feeling united to a human community, as understood by the notion of *Gestaltungskompetenz*.

When dealing with *competences* and *indicators*, relevancy criteria must be established, and we must respect the different contexts and levels of teaching, so as not to hinder searching for some aspects in common. Governments who are committed to include subjects concerning sustainability, need to take into account the different levels of poverty, and the construction of peace, justice and democracy, security, human rights, cultural diversity, social equality and environmental protection, and so forth. This is also useful for UNECE implementation strategies in Europe, states Arjen E. J. Wals (2007), professor of the University of Wageningen, the Netherlands.

It is important to develop new forms of education that recover the actual sense of education that is about acknowledging how to be a better human, learning through different formal and informal methods. Education cannot overvalue the abilities demanded of it by the market or transfer values that legitimate dominant economic interests to the detriment of basic human education.

Competence development and vocational training

Analysing some discussions on this subject (Minvielle 1991; Ramos 2001; Ropé and Tanguy 1997; Perrenoud 2002; Silva 2008), we find that the following *competences* relate in particular to vocational training, but also cover general training. This is the domain of the new technical knowledge associated with exercising the responsibility or occupied role, ability to learn fast about new concepts and technologies, creativity, a broad and global vision of the world, ability to be innovative, ability to communicate, ability to nurture interpersonal relationships, ability to work in a team, emotional self-control, ability to lead in new and unusual situations, ability to lead through uncertainty and ambiguity, action and decision initiative, ability to commit oneself to organizational objectives, ability to generate effective results, entrepreneurial abilities ... these are competences that are more focused on the individual, and the role of that individual.

Competence development refers to the teaching–learning process that can nurture an individual's ability to work in a team, investigate, develop proposals and new ideas, relate and associate, operate in interdisciplinarity, relate, analyse and evaluate situations experienced by companies, apply scientific and operational methodologies, search for information of interest to an organization, exchange experiences between company managers and different departments, and broaden horizons.

All these aspects of competences have been discussed by Brazilian and Latin American educators. The debate has been lively, and is influenced by the educational policies of the region. President of Colombia Uribe Vélez's development plan places the training model for competences as central in the educational policies of that country, without the help of the workers' unions in education. In Brazil, there has also been strong resistance to this concept. Nevertheless, it still exists, particularly in education for professional and technology teaching. That 'pedagogical competence' would emphasize personal professionalization projects at the expense of a more collective approach to vocational training.

This is not recent history. The relationship between vocational training and pedagogical competence, in a corporate framework, started in the 1970s, with the Taylorism–Fordism crisis. According to that discussion, the development of new technologies demanded 'another kind of worker', who was more qualified, and more capable of making decisions. An obedient worker with mechanical skills was no longer enough. An intelligent, self-sufficient worker was required. Corporate demands increased hand-in-hand with technological innovation, and new management and organization techniques: the restructuring of relationships between companies, now more focused on vertical divestiture and the notion of the network, operating changes in their methods and means of production, thus demanding greater adaptability and flexibility of the worker.

The development of competences is associated with *professional qualification*. The notion of 'qualification' is associated with the profile of a more specialized professional, while the notion of 'competence' has been used to define the profile of a more multi-purpose professional, more adapted to different professions. The notion of competence originates, as we have seen, from central countries. The notion of 'knowledge', 'skills' and 'know-how' is more comprehensive, passing beyond the field commonly known as 'professional development'. Competences do not exist without knowledge. Paulo Freire (1997), referring to the professional development of the teacher, preferred to use the term 'knowledge' and not 'competence'.

The relationship between *qualifications* and *competences* has been described particularly well by the Danish researcher Knud Illeris. In his opinion, the concept of qualifications, in its broadest sense

> has been replaced with the concept of 'competence', and this is neither mere coincidence nor an irrelevant terminological novelty. On the contrary, it might be said that this language change constitutes an attempt to take the full consequence of the development in qualifications interest (...). Competence is thus a unifying concept that integrates everything it takes in order to perform in a given situation or context. The concrete qualifications are incorporated in the competence rooted in personality, and one may generally also talk of the competence of organizations and nations (...). The concept of competence does not, like the concept of qualifications, have its roots in industrial sociology, but in organizational psychology and modern management thinking (. . .). The concept of competence also includes the new perception of the relationship between learning and education, where non-institutionalized learning, and not least learning with a direct basis in working life, has come into focus.
>
> (Illeris 2004: 47–48).

Qualification refers more to training in a certain field of knowledge and practice, while the notion of competence is more comprehensive, and is not only associated with a specific professional field. However, if that distinction is perfectly sustainable from a theoretical point of view, in practice, there are different uses with various meanings. Many teachers in Brazil do not accept the concept of competence and prefer to utilize the concept of qualification, in a broad sense of competence, particularly if it concerns vocational training.

Thus, vocational qualification improves the worker's general training. Professional qualification goes beyond updating and expanding upon technical and general knowledge. Today, the working world increasingly demands general vocational training. Therefore, a *professional qualification* must also be a *social qualification*. That qualification must include both *basic skills* – such as the essential knowledge to carry out *work* and to be a *citizen*, and to communicate, read and write, understand texts, security at work, human rights – and *specific skills*, required in terms of worker occupations, including management skills.

The Brazilian Ministry of Labour and Employment's National Qualification Plan, drawn up by President Lula's government, defines qualification as 'a complex social structure, associated with a vision of education that understands that it is the citizen's right to contribute to the democratization of working relationships and to instil a social and participative quality to the development model'(Paulo Friere Institute, 2006–08). *Continuous training* and *self-training* are also the result of the advance in technologies, general access to information, and the need to 'learn by doing' (John Dewey), that a world in a constant state of change is demanding.

Since the second half of the twentieth century, people have been talking about the need to prepare 'a new kind of worker', better educated and more informed, more 'intelligent' and competent, as demanded by industrial development. That demand intensified in recent decades, and a certain 'competence model' was imposed on vocational training that influenced the educational systems. In Brazil, the integration of the notion of competence in educational reform 'was legally initiated with the approval of Law no. 9,394, of 20 December 1996, a new Guidance Law and Basis of National Education (LDB), influencing both basic and professional education' (Ramos 2001: 124).

That vision is present in our National System of Basic Education (SAEB), and particularly, in the concept of our *National Curricular Parameters* (PCNs), which also date from 1996, on the argument that we must adapt education to 'the new demands of the market' and 'basic learning needs' of the worker, so that they are capable of living with the transformations that have occurred in the field of production. Therefore, the worker, rather than just becoming more self-sufficient, would also become increasingly adapted to the changes at work. To sum up, the above-mentioned training would make the worker more 'flexible', gaining the flexibility demanded by the flexible nature of working relationships in the company.

Adult education and popular education

Some people maintain that there is only 'one' education and that there is no need to ideologically label education as 'popular', 'public', 'liberator', and so forth. Education can be a universal process, a 'second nature', as the German philosopher Immanuel Kant (1724–1804) said, even though it is practised in different and even opposing ways. Paulo Freire talks of education of the colonizer, education of the oppressed and the oppressor. Thus, it is necessary to label education and clarify what type of education we are talking about. In one way or another, it has always been labelled throughout its history, for example; as 'aristocratic' in Greece, 'Christian' in the Middle Ages, 'socialist', 'capitalist', and so forth.

The terms 'adult education', 'popular education,' 'informal education' and 'community education' are often used as synonyms, although they do not mean the same thing. The terms 'adult education', and 'informal education' refer to the same disciplinary, theoretical and practical area of education. However, the term 'adult education' has been particularly popularized by international organizations such as UNESCO, in order to refer to a specialist area of education. *Informal* education is a term used particularly in the United States (La Belle 1986) to refer to adult education that is developed in third world countries. In the US, however, internally, the term *'adult education'* is reserved for informal education administrated at local level (Torres 1990).

There are a vast number of paradigms, a combination of theories, investigational logics and action methodologies within adult education or *informal education*. In Brazil, adult education has remained the responsibility of the State, particularly since the Second World War. During that period, informal education was mainly associated with non-government organizations, political parties, churches, unions, and so forth.

Popular education as a general concept of education, normally opposes adult education implemented by the State, occupying spaces where adult education does not reach. One of the original principles of popular education has always been the creation of a new epistemology, based on a profound respect for the common sense that the popular sectors contribute in their day-to-day practice, questioning it, trying to discover the theory present in popular practice, theories that people still do not know, questioning this as well, and incorporating into it a more rigorous, scientific and unitary rationalism.

In August 1985, Paulo Freire was interviewed by the teacher, Rosa Maria Torres, on the subject of *popular education* and *adult education*. In that interview, he expressed his view on that subject, and resolved a frequent confusion that identifies them as equal. He confirmed, in that context, that 'popular education is outlined as an effort in terms of mobilization and organization of the popular classes, with a view to the creation of a popular power' (Torres 1987: 74). To administrate popular education, it is not necessary to work with adults. Popular education is an educational concept that does not depend on the age of the individual who is educated,

> since popular education, in my opinion, [says Paulo Freire] cannot be mistaken for adult education, and is not restricted solely to adults. I would say that the brand, or what defines popular education, is not the age of the students, but the political option, that is to say, the political practice understood and assumed in educational practice.
>
> (Torres 1987: 86–87)

At the end of his life, in the late 1980s and early 1990s, Paulo Freire experienced a period of *popular education recasting*. It was not just the Berlin Wall that fell during this period. Some of the assumptions and significance of popular education were also shattered. The fall of Soviet socialism, the end of the military regimes in Latin America, the recognition of the limit of education, critics of activism and democratism, the lack of systemization of the experiences of popular education, led many popular educators to search for alternative theories and practices that would take into account the new context of change opposing the process of global capitalization. 'Post-modern progressive' popular education, as Freire said, incorporated new themes, for example; an exchange of views on knowledge, civil society concepts, cultural politics, the issue of genre, environmental issues and valorization of subjectivity, and became distanced from a purely classist and reproductivist understanding of education. It is in this context that the *public school* entered into the agenda of popular education, and Paulo Freire started to talk about a popular public school that had an interest in the popular classes. The popular classes recognize the importance of education, and desire a public school that is appropriate in terms of their interests and dreams.

When he took office as the Municipal Education Secretary of São Paulo (1989–1991), Paulo Freire orientated all his educational policies towards the construction of a 'popular public school'. The State was no longer considered an enemy, as it was during the time of the dictatorships. From a highly politicized and unitary viewpoint, popular education became more plural, gaining diversity from theories and practices. As a process of democratization, some popular educators took on government responsibilities, shaping the way the State functioned in favour of the poorest sectors. This involved changing the way that states functioned in favour of those in power, and trying to 'invest in priorities', as Paulo Freire said when he took on the role of Municipal Secretary of Education.

Popular education had already started in Latin America by the nineteenth century. In 1849, General Sarmiento, the president of Argentina, who was also an educator, wrote a book with the title *Popular Education*. He understood popular education to be 'school education', elementary, for everyone, and his aim was to encourage education of the liberal citizen. Popular education began in the interior of the State of São Paulo, as an education to 'shape the people', educating them to become a liberal bourgeois society. Popular education had to be administrated by the elementary public school.

In the twentieth century, the social and unionist movement understood popular education to be education aimed at the interests of the people, not the interests of the bourgeois State. That is why it had to be non-State, non-official education. That concept of *popular education* had different origins: that is to say, the anarcho-syndicalism from the beginning of the last century, self-managed socialism, radical European liberalism, the popular movements to which Paulo Freire contributed, the utopias of the independence that appeared in the nineteenth century, and led to the developmentalism of the twentieth century, and the theories of liberation that also influenced theology.

Popular education is associated with a history of struggles, which we need to remember, mainly against authoritarianism and the Latin American regimes of exception (Rivero 1993). It deals with a history of fights for freedom, autonomy and self-sustained development that values citizen participation and emancipation. The last seventy years have consolidated popular education as a notion of the most important education to originate from Latin America, the greatest contribution from the region to the universal pedagogic way of thinking.

Popular education and *adult education* are commonly perceived to be synonymous. In reality, they maintain a relationship that is strict and singular, yet they are not the same thing. Adult education is specifically targeted at adults. It may be popular or it may not. Popular education, as a notion of education, may relate to any age, level or teaching method.

Until the Second World War, adult education was conceived as an extension of formal education for all people, mainly in rural areas. It was not conceived with its own character, either in its meanings or its methodology. Popular education was conceived as democratization of the formal school.

In the 1950s, as a consequence of the war itself, there was a need for 'basic education', primarily for adults, to shape them towards a culture of peace.

Adult education was associated with *community development*. That concept was particularly supported by UNESCO, the international agency that had recently been created by the United Nations, and was in charge of education, science and culture.

It is in this context that popular education in Latin America became divided between a 'functional', professional notion of education that formed the most productive workforce to encourage 'national development', and a 'liberating' notion (Kane 2001). In the 1960s, these two concepts progressed in opposite directions. The former was more linked to formal, professional teaching, and the latter linked to informal and even clandestine activities (in the Latin American context of dictatorships). Popular liberating education, under military regimes, took refuge with non-governmental organizations and socialist movements. With the democratization of the region, numerous popular education experiences emerged in many sectors (health care, employment, social security, land, housing, genre, religion, and so forth), previously submerged and invisible because of authoritarianism. Popular education lost the *unity* that it had when it was associated with the State, and that it had earned through *diversity*.

Popular education and adult education in Latin America developed in their own way, but this was not completely independent of the *global context*. The world conference on Education for Everyone, held in 1990 in Jomtien, Thailand, agreed that literacy in children and adults would be the first stage of basic education. Therefore, it established the idea that literacy cannot be separated from post-literacy, that is to say, the 'basic needs of learning'. The most recent International Conference on Adult Education, in 1997 at Confintea V, Hamburg, established that adult education was an actual field of formal and informal education, a field encouraged today by the new training spaces created by the new information technologies (Furter 1983).

In May 2009, Brazil will hold Confintea VI. This is seen as another chance for both adult and popular education. This is because the *paradigm of popular education* is without doubt less present today in official international and intergovernmental discussions. Other notions have received much more support and visibility, for example, lifelong learning. The philosophical debate on learning objectives was substituted, through various educational means, by discussions on management, methodologies and evaluation.

People know more about how, rather than why or what, to evaluate. Licínio Lima (2007: 54) says that in this context 'The critical humanist tradition, and liberating and transformative perspectives that characterises popular education, in some cases since the end of the 19th century, have been tremendously hindered. It has given way to the global needs for modernization and productivity, adaptation and employability'. Licínio Lima calls our attention to the democratic and emancipatory potential of the ideal of a life-long learning that is alert to the economist and technocratic deviations of that concept, particularly in the management of human resources.

Education is more than information and learning

We live in a time of information overload. Information has stopped being an *area* or speciality, and become a *dimension* of everything, like the theology of the Middle Ages, profoundly transforming the way in which society is organized. It could be said that an information revolution is now in progress, like in the past when the agricultural and industrial revolutions took place. New technologies create new *knowledge gaps*. As well as the school, company and home, the social environment has now become educational.

In this context, and from a holistic perspective of competences and skills, it is *adult education's* place to select and critically revise information (there is a lot of rubbish being distributed), formulate a hypothesis, be critical, inventive or innovative, be provocative with messages and not just a receiver, produce, construct and reconstruct elaborated knowledge. Similarly, from an *emancipatory perspective*, adult education has to practise all of this in favour of those excluded. It does not discriminate against the poor. It cannot distribute power, but can construct and reconstruct knowledge, know-how, and therefore power.

More needs to be invested in education for young people and adults. This is what UNESCO recommended in its Hamburg Conference (Confintea V, 1997), emphasizing the need to recognize the well-informed educator's indispensible role, guarantee the diversity of experiences, reaffirm the undeniable responsibility of the State towards education, strengthen the civil society and citizenship, integrate the education of young people and adults as a means of basic education, and reconceptualize the education of adults and young people as a permanent process of adult learning.

And it is not just enough to invest in the production of information and data. Education should not be confused with information. There is even such a thing as information overload. We are slowed down by too much information. We need education and knowledge, and we need subjects who may produce knowledge. This is why it is fundamental that we ask ourselves about the *meaning of knowledge.*

What is the purpose of knowledge?

The answer may not seem complicated to us. Primarily, knowledge helps us to find out about ourselves and our circumstances, so we can find out about the world. It helps to provide us with the skills and competences needed for the working world, and to take part in social, political, economic and general life decisions. It helps us to understand the past and predict the future. It helps us to communicate, communicate what we know, to find out more about what we already know, and to continue to learn. Furthermore, it helps to change the world.

Knowledge is humanity's great wealth. It is not just the capital from the transnation that needs education to foster technological innovation. It is a basic need for the survival of all people. For this reason, it should not be *bought* or *sold*, but made available to us all. This is the function of the institutions that are dedicated to knowledge, supported by technological advances. Let's hope that education in the future will be more democratic and less excluding. This is, at the same time, our cause and our challenge. Unfortunately, faced with the failure of the sector's public policies, '*knowledge industries*' have arisen, damaging our human perspective, becoming an instrument of luxury and economic power. To democratize access to knowledge is to democratize wealth and income.

We have not seen that this is the main concern of the intergovernmental agencies dedicated to education. UNESCO is seen to be more concerned with learning than with the meaning of learning. We all agree with the 'Report to UNESCO by the International Commission on Education for the 21st Century' (Delors 1998), which states that for lifelong learning, we need to learn to learn, learn to do, learn to live together, and learn to be. However, one more important aspect to learning also exists, and that is 'Why learn'? UNESCO still needs to debate the political aspect of education.

Education is *information* and *teaching* and *learning*, all at the same time. Paulo Freire states that

> there is no teaching without learning. One requires the other. And the subject of each, despite their obvious differences, cannot be educated to the status of object. People who teach, learn from teaching, and people who learn, teach what they learn.
>
> (Freire 1997: 25)

He does not separate teaching from learning as is done by neoliberal pedagogy.

> Teaching does not exist without learning, and vice-versa, and it was from social learning, historically, that men and women discovered that it was possible to teach. It was in this way, through social learning, and throughout history, that men and women understood that it was possible, and

later necessary, to practice teaching manners, ways and methods. Learning came before teaching. In other words, teaching was diluted into the truly fundamental experience of learning.

(Freire 1997: 26)

We at the Paulo Freire Institute defend the importance of learning. However, when we talk of the *centrality of the learning issue*, we wish to highlight the importance of learning in a country that is not very concerned about the student's right to learn at school. The right to education is not limited to access. Learning, from a neoliberal viewpoint, only highlights the so-called 'useful knowledge' and the individualist and competitive aspects of education. It is not about shifting the educational emphasis towards learning. It is about ensuring, through *education with a social quality*, learning for the whole of society.

The question is not in the act of learning, but in what is learnt. It is about ensuring a 'transformative learning', as Edmund O'Sullivan (2004) maintains, in content and form. In contrast to this perspective, the concept of the learning sustained by neoliberal politics is focused on the individual's responsibility. Solidarity is substituted for meritocracy. As Licínio Lima (2006: 66) states, in neoliberal pedagogy,

> Primarily, the individual is responsible for their own learning, and, at that time, managing their learning process and finding more interesting strategies for themselves, but on an individual, competitive basis. I mean that the citizen gives way to the customer and consumer.

Centrality today, given to learning competences, from a purely competitive perspective, leads to possessive individualism, moving in the opposite direction to the comprehensive education of the human being. In contrast, Paulo Freire brings our attention to our need to observe, in education, the process for the construction of subjective democracy. For this, it is necessary to enhance our capacity for surprise, suspicion, and suspicion of suspicion, as our great maestros of suspicion Marx, Nietzsche and Freud have taught us. We need to take care with the anaesthetics of neoliberal ideology. It is fatalist, and it thrives on a fatalist exchange of views. Also, in itself, it has no amazing reality. Neoliberalism acts as if the current globalization of society was a definitive reality and not a historical category.

Neoliberalism confirms the 'end of history' because it has no interest in history changing. It is interested in history continuing as it is. The liberating adult education, on the contrary, sees the future first, a better future for everyone, a utopia, and proposes pedagogy as a way to reach it. Pedagogy is a guide for Utopia. This is why, when we discuss any educational subject, for example; the subject of competences, we do not lose sight of a society's project, of education for another possible world (Gadotti 2006). Competence development is a subject that interests us. It is fundamental to understand what it is to be competent, and to understand the competence that we have constructed.

Acknowledgements

This chapter is adapted from an article by Beckett, D. (2008). Holistic Competence: Putting Judgments First. *Asia Pacific Education Review*, 9(1), 21–30. Reprinted with permission from Education Research Institute, Seoul National University.

Chapter 3

Competence development in the workplace

Concepts, strategies and effects

Per-Erik Ellström and Henrik Kock

There is today a widespread belief in the importance of devoting resources to education and other forms of competence development as a key factor behind productivity development, innovative capacity and competitiveness. This standpoint is not only an outflow of policy discussions about knowledge or learning economies, but has also received considerable support from research (e.g. Lorenz & Lundvall 2006).

In line with this view on the importance of education for growth and competitiveness, companies have in recent years devoted substantial resources to competence development. The principal arguments for these efforts stem from production economy considerations. These arguments concern the altered and increased requirements on competence that are assumed to follow in the wake of increased internationalization, new production concepts, a wider use of information technology and an increasingly dominant role for knowledge-intensive production in many companies (Brown *et al.* 2001; Adler 2004).

Issues of competence development in working life can, however, also be discussed on the basis of political considerations concerning the distribution of welfare and issues of democracy. Insufficient opportunities for education and on-the-job learning for groups of employees with a limited basic education tend to widen the existing education gaps in society (Rubenson 2006). A further perspective that can be applied in this context, could be derived from work environment research. Studies indicate that a work environment that permits and stimulates learning and competence development may also be of fundamental importance for the employees' health, well-being and personal development (Karasek & Theorell 1990).

What, then, do we know about education and other forms of competence development in companies and other types of organizations? In spite of the expectations that exist regarding efforts to develop competence and in spite of the large amounts of resources devoted to it, there is a marked lack of empirically based research on competence development in companies and other organizations. The purpose of this article is to present a review of research on strategies for competence development in organizations, their prerequisites and effects. More specifically, the following three questions will be addressed: (i) Why do organizations invest in competence development? (ii) What effects can realistically be achieved through competence development? (iii) What characterizes successful strategies for competence development in organizations? However, before addressing these questions, it is appropriate to say something about the concepts of competence and competence development as used in this chapter.

Three views of competence

The concept of competence is often poorly defined in the literature. In fact, a general consensus seems to be lacking concerning the meaning of this frequently used concept. One example may illustrate this point. According to one view, competence is considered as an attribute of the employee, that is, as a kind of human capital or a human resource that can be translated into a certain level of performance. According to another widely held view, competence is defined in terms of the requirements of the tasks that constitute a certain job. This is indeed an important distinction, and in the following we will use the term competence to refer to the former meaning, and the term qualification to refer to the latter meaning.

More specifically, the term competence will be used to refer to the capacity of an individual (or a collective) to successfully (according to certain formal or informal criteria, set by oneself or by somebody else) handle certain situations or complete a certain task or job (Ellström 1997). This capacity may be defined in terms of: perceptual motor skills (e.g. dexterity); cognitive factors (different types of knowledge and intellectual skills); affective factors (e.g. attitudes, values, motivations); personality traits (e.g. self-confidence); and social skills (e.g. communicative and cooperative skills). Using this definition as a point of departure, the notion of qualification may now be defined as the competence that is actually required by the task, and/or is implicitly or explicitly prescribed, for example, by the employer.

As implied by this distinction, an individual (or a collective) may possess a range of competences that are not qualifications, that is, that are not required by the task(s) at hand or prescribed by, for example, the employer. Conversely, a certain job may require qualifications that do not correspond to the actual competences of the individual (or the collective). Thus, the concept of qualification focuses on competences that for one reason or another are valued by an internal or external labour market, that is, competences that have an exchange value.

In addition, it is in many situations necessary to make the following distinctions (for an extended discussion, see Ellström 1997). First, given the view that competence is an attribute of an individual, a distinction can be made between: (i) formal competence, measured, for example, in terms of the years of schooling completed or by the credentials received by an individual and (ii) actual competence as defined above, that is, the capacity of an individual to successfully handle a certain situation or to perform a certain task. Although actual competence differs, by definition, from formal competence and it is, indeed, often the case that one possesses formal competence without actual competence and vice versa, measures of formal competence are often used as an indicator of actual competence (Warhurst & Thompson 2006).

Second, focusing on job requirements, it is important to distinguish between prescribed or actual requirements, that is, between the official demand for competence (e.g. as a basis for recruitment or for the setting of wages) and the competence actually required by the job. Of course, the official demand for competence ideally corresponds to the actual competence requirements of a certain job. However, this correspondence may be disturbed by different factors. For example, official demands for competence are often affected by the demand and supply of qualified people in the external or internal labour market, but also by forces (e.g. professional interests) trying to raise or lower the status of a job.

Third, it might be argued that competence is neither primarily an attribute of an individual (or a collective), nor primarily an attribute of the job. Rather, the focus is on the interaction between the individual and the job, and on the competence that is actually used by the individual in performing the job. Thus, we can talk about this view of competence as the competence-in-use (Ellström 1997). This third view is influenced partly by the competence that the individual brings to the task or the job, and partly by the characteristics of the task/job. Thus, competence-in-use might be seen as a dynamic process of learning mediating between the capacity of the individual and the requirements of the job. This means, among other things, that both factors related to the individual and factors related to the job may facilitate or limit the extent to which the individual may use and develop his or her actual competence. Concerning individual factors, previous experiences and factors such as self-confidence are likely to be of importance (Colquitt & LePine 2000; Illeris 2007). Concerning job-related factors, the formal and informal organization of the workplace with respect to worker autonomy, participation, task characteristics and feedback are likely to have a strong impact on the competence that an individual actually uses to perform his job (Ellström 2006; Kock et al. 2007).

These three views of the concept of competence have different implications for competence development. Both from the perspective of the individual and from the perspective of the firm and society at large, the full use and development of the competences of the employees in the performance of their jobs appear as a rational strategy to pursue. However, this strategy presupposes at least two things. First, that dominant actors in working life (primarily managers and union representatives at different levels) engage in efforts to redesign work content and work organization in order to facilitate increased employee participation in planning, analysis, evaluation and development work. Second, that systems for vocational education and training (VET) and human resource development (HRD) take a more proactive role towards changes in working life. This means that their primary task is not only to adjust to actual or projected changes in competence requirements, but also to provide education and other forms of competence development that will empower employees to engage in developmental work, innovation and continuous improvements in the workplace. We will deal with these issues more fully later in this article. Before that, however, we will, as a next step, ask how the meaning of competence development in the workplace may be conceived.

On the concept of competence development

In this context, competence development is defined as an overall designation for the various measures that can be used to affect the supply of competence on the internal labour market (in individual employees, groups of employees or the whole personnel group). To be more specific, it may refer to measures regarding: (a) recruitment, promotion (e.g. career planning) and personnel mobility (internal and/or external); (b) education or training of personnel, for instance by means of internal or external courses; (c) planned changes of tasks or work organization through different types of measures (e.g. job development, job rotation, team organization) with the objective of furthering informal learning in work.

Competence development can thus refer to one or more of these measures. These measures may be planned, but attention should also be paid to unplanned or unintended functions that a certain action may have. In this regard, it should be pointed out that the term 'competence development' sometimes takes on another meaning, namely to denote the individual learning processes through which competence is acquired. A distinction can therefore be made between an organization-related and an individual-related meaning of the term 'competence development'.

With the definition given above, formal education is only one of several possible measures for competence development in the workplace. Furthermore, it should be emphasized that activities that do not have competence development as their primary objective may imply competence development for the individual as a secondary effect and can therefore be seen as educating/developing. Another important point to emphasize is that different strategies and methods for competence development can be combined. This is probably also often the case in practice. It might even be argued that one *ought to* strive for an integration between two or more of the strategies mentioned in order to facilitate qualified on-the-job learning. In fact, the latter argument received support from a recently conducted study of practices of competence development in the Nordic countries (Høyrup & Ellström 2007). One result of this study was an analytical model for classifying strategies of workplace learning (see Table 3.1 below). The model underlines the fact that formal (curriculum-based) and informal (practice-based) aspects of learning, as well as individual and organizational aspects of learning, are fundamental and indispensable dimensions of learning.

Table 3.1 A conceptual model of strategies of workplace learning

Dimension	Individual	Organization
Curriculum-based	School model	In-service training/continuing education
Practice-based	On-the-job training/ informal learning at work	Organizational learning and development

When using the model to locate the different approaches of promising practices it was remarkable that no strategy could be located in one cell only. All the promising practices had to be located in two or more cells. This finding adds to our understanding of integration and wholeness as basic dimensions of learning opportunities and qualities of workplace learning.

Why do organizations invest in competence development?

Why do organizations devote resources to education and other forms of competence development? Are the investments made mainly an expression of an analytic–rational strategy, or primarily an expression of opportunism and fashion trends? Various theoretical views of competence development give partly different answers to these questions. In the following, we will distinguish between three perspectives of competence development representing different answers to the questions posed, namely what has been called a technological–functional perspective, a conflict–control perspective, and an institutional perspective. We shall then try to shed some further light on these issues on the basis of available empirical research.

A technological–functional perspective

Starting from what we can term a technological–functional perspective (Collins 1979), competence development is emphasized as a conscious and rationally planned strategy for meeting such things as new or increased competence requirements due to altered environmental conditions (e.g. new customer requirements) or changes in the organization. Of fundamental importance in this perspective is the view of education and other forms of competence development as means or tools for furthering competence-increasing learning in participating individuals, that is an instrumental and rationalistic view of education. This learning on the individual level in the form of increased knowledge, increased competence, etc. is seen in the next phase as a means of achieving objectives in the form of increased productivity, growth and developed welfare on the organizational or societal levels.

Further, competence development is seen as a rational goals–means process, which can be controlled without serious problems on the basis of research and other considerations. Starting from certain predefined objectives (e.g. the acquisition of certain knowledge and skills), it is assumed possible, on the basis of pedagogical and psychological knowledge, to design and implement the education process in such a way that it leads to the attainment of the goals set.

This view is represented in whole or in part in several pedagogical research areas, perhaps most clearly in those parts that are based on human capital theory (Becker 1975). Applied to competence development at work, a technological–functional perspective implies the following assumptions, among others: (a) Investments in the education of personnel and other forms of competence development in a company are to a large extent governed by a mismatch between the demand for and supply of qualifications in the company's internal labour market. Such a mismatch can arise through changes in the external or internal context of the company (e.g. an altered competition scenario, technical and organizational changes in the operations). (b) The planning of measures for competence development can be expected to be based on a consciously designed and explicitly formulated policy or strategy for competence development, which in turn is assumed to stem from the company's high-level objectives and business concept. (c) The decision to invest in a certain form of competence development is assumed to be based on rational cost-effectiveness estimates in which the effect of the education is viewed in relation to the costs in the form of wages, loss of production, and the other costs which are associated with the education. (d) The implementation of personnel education and other forms of competence development calls for systematic planning based on analyses of the qualification requirements of the operations, the actual and utilized competence of the personnel and the development requirements derived from these. The measures put into practice are evaluated and revised in the light of the results achieved.

A conflict–control perspective

The perspective presented above is based on the assumption that there is a consensus on fundamental values, norms and objectives in both society at large and individual organizations. On the basis of what is referred to here as a conflict–control perspective, this assumption may be open to criticism. When applying this perspective, it is assumed instead that disagreements and conflicts between different parties and actors in a community or organization (e.g. between employers and employees or between the centre and the periphery) are fundamental to the way in which organizations work. Different actors/parties are assumed to represent different interests and the ideologies that arise from these interests.

Under these conditions, it has been assumed that the activities in an organization can be better understood as political processes characterized by struggle, negotiation and compromise rather than as technical–rational planning and decision-making processes (see, for example, Pfeffer 1981; Mintzberg 1983). This means, among other things, that power and the ability to mobilize power become important resources in the organization. It also means that the structure and orientation of the activities, their objectives and various programmes are not primarily the results of rational decision-making processes based on objective information but of negotiations and compromises whose outcome is determined by internal power relations. The organization is thus seen as an arena in which different actors (individuals and groups) struggle for power and limited resources with the aim of promoting their interests, demands and operational ideas.

From the point of view of a conflict–control perspective on education and other forms of competence development, it is assumed that these processes are determined to a greater degree by the management's or other actors' interest in control, internal disagreements and prevailing power relations in the organization than by economic calculations or humanistic arguments. By extension, this means that personnel training and other forms of competence development can be seen as part of the management's (or another dominant actor's) efforts to control the operations concerned. In other words, competence development in this perspective can be seen as an instrument for ideological control and as a means of replacing or complementing other forms of control, that is, technological or bureaucratic forms of control (Offe 1976; Edwards 1979).

The power relations in an organization in terms of the relative influence of the employer/management, the trade unions and the employees over education and competence development can, in this perspective, be assumed to be of importance with regard to both the content of personnel training (e.g. general versus job-specific competence) and its function (e.g. as an instrument for critical reflection, operational development and changes to unfavourable working conditions). One can therefore expect, in this perspective, all other things being equal, that companies with active and driving trade union organizations will invest more in various forms of competence development than companies where the position of the trade unions is weaker. It can also be expected that organizations with a high proportion of well-educated personnel will offer more competence development (Scott & Meyer 1991).

An institutional perspective

If we start instead from an institutional perspective of competence development, the emphasis is rather on the non-rational processes that control investments in competence development (for general overviews of this theory tradition, see for example Powell & DiMaggio 1991; Scott 1995). Investments in competence development are, roughly, seen as being controlled not by rational goals–means considerations but by a striving towards increased legitimacy (inwards or outwards) by adapting to more or less temporarily predominating ideas (in the form of, say, fashion trends) about rationality, efficiency or modernity in the environment where the organization does business. Putting it another way, one can say that the activities of the organization, in this view, are determined not primarily by rational analysis based on the goals/tasks of the organization, but by institutionalized ideas on what should characterize modern and efficient organizations. With this as our starting point, the organizational structures and operations often have symbolic functions.

In terms of this perspective, then, a company's investments in competence development can be analysed as symbolic arrangements with the function of exemplifying and communicating, inwards and outwards, conformity with the values with which the organization wants to be associated, with the objective of strengthening its legitimacy. In the same way, an increase in the education requirements for a given post can be assumed to have a symbolic-legitimizing function (cf. Collins 1979). The demand for qualifications in an activity is seen largely as a social construction and relatively independent of the 'objective' requirements regarding qualification. With this view, the investments made in competence development can be expected to be reactive, ad hoc in nature and justified by short-term considerations rather than a result of a conscious strategy for competence development.

A series of more specific assumptions regarding the driving forces and prerequisites for an organization's investment in education can be formulated on the basis of an institutional view (cf. Scott & Meyer 1991): (a) Organizations in which a large proportion of the employees have a professional affiliation (e.g. health care) can be expected to invest more in various forms of competence development than organizations with fewer professional people. (b) The stronger and more complex the institutional environment of an organization, the more extensive can the investments in competence development be expected to be. (c) With the increased legitimacy of investments in education and other forms of competence development more types of organizations will invest in competence development, and a weaker coupling is to be expected between the investments made (as regards, for instance, extent and form) and various factors such as job complexity, work organization and competence requirements. (d) With an increased legitimacy of investments in education and other forms of competence development as a means of handling changes in the external or internal context of the organization, it is to be expected that there will follow investments in more general qualifications, and at the same time fewer efforts at systematically evaluating the effects of the investments made.

Empirical research results

What answer can, then, on the basis of available empirical research, be given to the question of why organizations invest in competence development? In an influential article, Tichy (1983) directs our attention to the importance of the environment for the strategy development of companies and authorities, including strategies for competence development. The important factors that Tichy points out are: (a) the technical–economic environment (e.g. automation of tasks, increased importance of information technology, diminishing productivity); (b) the political environment (e.g. increased international dependency, increased demands for influence from various personnel categories); (c) the cultural–social environment (e.g. demographic changes, higher proportion of professionals in the work force, increasing demands and expectations towards the employers).

Extensive studies of companies' investments in competence development have been conducted by Hendry *et al.* (1988), Pettigrew *et al.* (1988) and Hendry *et al.* (1991). One of the main conclusions from these studies is that different external contextual factors can be seen as necessary but not sufficient for companies' investments in education and other forms of competence development. In most cases, the basis for the investments made is increased pressure from the competition, which has led to business-associated (e.g. product development) or technical changes.

In a typical case, these changes have created a skill–performance gap. This gap is usually the factor which can, through fairly complex processes, lead to investment in some form of competence development. Whether or not this is done is decided by the interplay between a large variety of factors in the company's external or internal context. Examples of factors that facilitate investment in personnel training and other forms of competence development include: First, the company's business concept/strategy as regards such things as the extent of technological and product-related changes, and the importance attached to long-term survival. Second, a marked positive educational culture, expressed among other things by the presence of internal actors who push educational questions (e.g. management), the existence of a training/personnel department with sufficient resources and a good reputation, and union organizations that actively participate in the work of change and that push questions concerned with competence development. Third, external demands and support and stimulation for investments in competence development as well as customers' demands for improved quality.

The conclusion drawn by Pettigrew *et al.* (1988) from their data is that the above-mentioned types of factors must be present if competition pressure, no matter how strong, or other external factors are to lead to investments in competence development. Is there, then, no mutual ranking order between all these facilitating factors? If there is such a factor, then according to Pettigrew *et al.* (1988), it is probably the prevalent educational culture in the community and within the company. According to these writers, the most important thing is that the company, so to speak, gets competence development into its bloodstream. However, this can only come about if competence development is seen by all the affected parties in the company as an effective and legitimate way of handling the company's problems.

Several of the results reported by Pettigrew *et al.* (1988) are supported by other empirical research and theory development in the field. A case study of competence development in seven small and medium-sized companies, Ellström and Nilsson (1997), shows that various external factors, and in particular the recession, were important driving forces as regards investments in education. In a typical case, a reduced order intake, with its associated economic problems and risk of lay-offs or shutdown, initiated a search for various ways to maintain and develop the business. In several of the companies, increased demands for profitability, increased customer requirements regarding quality and delivery times or increased requirements concerning the competence of the personnel were among the motives for the investments made in training. Likewise, based on a case study of companies in the business sector, Ram (2000) emphasizes that the nature of the market context and the engagement with key customers are important to the firm's willingness to participate in a programme for competence development.

The importance of internal contextual conditions in the form of a supportive culture is underlined by Spicer and Sadler-Smith (2003), and the authors underline the fact that risk-taking and experimentation are important behaviours among managers in order to support learning within the firm. The importance of how managers of small firms view and evaluate competence development is reported in several studies. Bell *et al.* (2002) show that managers of (small) firms may decide to enter programmes for competence development in order to 'badge', that is to imitate high-profile companies. Similar conclusions are reached by Ram (2000) as several firms used competence development as a marketing device or were under pressure from larger companies to train their staff.

In a recent study based on seventeen small and medium enterprises (SMEs), it was possible to demonstrate that external organizational conditions (e.g. competitive pressure, demands from customers) and internal organizational conditions (e.g. educational 'culture', leadership style) were important factors in determining a firm's willingness to take on competence development (Kock *et al.* 2008). How managers and employees perceived the nature and strength of external and internal organizational conditions was important and these organizational conditions operated as driving forces for the firm's decision to engage in competence development. Moreover, these results also demonstrated that external and internal organizational conditions were related to the strategies for competence development used by the firms. The firms that experienced lower levels of pressure to change in terms of external/internal organizational conditions, used a traditional strategy for competence development – a formal strategy mainly based on internal/external courses for the employees, while the firms that experienced higher levels of pressure to change in terms of external/internal organizational conditions used a more elaborated strategy (an 'integrated' strategy), mainly characterized by an integration between courses and other important ongoing changes within the workplace, for example, a change of the work organization. The results underline the fact that both external and internal organizational conditions are important in understanding why small businesses undertake competence development. However, the importance of external and internal organizational conditions is not limited to *why* the companies participate in a programme for competence development, the results indicate that these conditions also are important for *how* they participate, that is the strategies used for competence development.

However, as in the studies presented above, the external factors alone were not sufficient to explain the decisions on, and the direction of, the investments made in competence development. Instead, the results underline the necessity of taking into account not only environmental factors but also the conceptions and interests held by the owner/management and other actors within the company, and which determine what is seen as the suitable, possible and desirable way to run the company's business, including the investments made in competence development.

Summary and conclusions

To sum up, one can conclude that the research results reported above are fairly unanimous in underlining the importance of various environmental factors for how organizations work with education and competence development. At the same time, it can be seen that no single factor or group of factors (e.g. technology development) can be designated as the most important or, in the final analysis, the deciding factor for the investments made in competence development.

The investments made in competence development can instead be understood as a complex interplay between external factors and the various 'logics' internal to the company that various actors represent. There is also much to indicate that external factors (e.g. increased customer demands or reduced order intake) should be seen as necessary, but not sufficient conditions for companies' investments in competence development. Not least in importance among internal factors is the existence of a facilitating 'learning culture'. It can be assumed that important elements of such a culture are the views of management and union representatives regarding the value of education. Other important factors are the employees' experienced need of competence development and motivation to participate in learning activities. Against this background, it appears that an important task for continuing research is to study in more detail the interplay between external contextual factors and internal factors with regard to decisions concerning investment in competence development, and especially to pursue empirical studies of the 'learning culture(s)' of an organization.

If we examine the reported results in relation to the theoretical views presented in this section, there is no doubt that the technical–functional view with its market-related, technical–economic driving forces for investment in education has fairly strong support (most of the studies discussed here also take this view as their starting point). At the same time, several of the results appear open to alternative interpretation, for instance from an institutional point of view (cf. Gooderham *et al.* 1999).

What effects can one realistically hope to achieve through competence development in organizations?

Research into the effects of education and other forms of competence development in organizations is rather underdeveloped, both theoretically and empirically. As pointed out fifteen years ago by Tannenbaum and Yukl (1992), there is a marked lack of research regarding effects that go beyond measurements of the participants' attitudes. Although more recent research (e.g. Salas & Cannon-Bowers 2001; Alvarez *et al.* 2004) indicates that a number of advancements have been made during recent years, the conclusion made by Tannenbaum and Yukl (1992) is in many respects still valid. Specifically, little progress has been made with respect to the measurement of learning outcomes of competence development.

What is meant by 'effects' and how can they be measured?

The effects of education are taken here to mean a change at an individual, group, or organizational level as a result of participation in some form of educational programme. The changes may apply to knowledge, skills, values, behaviour or some other aspect of human competence. This general and widespread definition of educational effects is based on a view of education as an objective, goal-steered process with certain external, causally determined effects for the participants. Such effects may arise in the long or short term, be general or more task-specific, intended or unintentional, desirable or undesirable.

How, then, can we define and measure the effects of competence development in a reasonable way? A classification of effects, that is still widely used, was proposed by Kirkpatrick (1959; see also Kirkpatrick, 1996) and has been further developed by Holton (1996) and Kraiger (2002). This classification is based on the distinction between four effects or levels of results, namely: (a) participants' attitudes to and evaluation of, for instance, an education and its results; (b) effects on the individual level in the form of acquired knowledge or skills, but also, for instance, in the form of changed attitudes (e.g. attitude to the use of new technology); (c) effects meaning that the individual becomes better at carrying out certain tasks (job performance); (d) effects in the form of improved performance at the business level, for example a work team's performance or performance at the organizational level.

The relations between these levels are complex and of an interactional character. An obvious and rather logical conclusion would be that a positive evaluation of, for instance, an education or its effects on the participants does not really tell us anything about the effects on different levels. Another possible, albeit more general reflection, is that it is of course much easier to achieve positive effects on the first level than on the second, just as it is much more difficult to achieve effects on the third or fourth level than on the second. In general, one must of course issue a strong warning against interpreting effects on the first level (or on any other level) as an indicator that effects also exist on a 'higher' level.

Another more meta-theoretical warning is also appropriate here. The general definition of educational effects discussed here has its roots in what we above called a technological–functional view of education, and can be questioned and problematized both from a conflict–control and from an institutional perspective. Viewed from the latter perspective, it is for instance important to study what an education means and how it is defined by its various actors (management, unions, participants), that is, to take into account the character of the education as a social construction and an ideological–cultural system. Thus, as argued by for example Meyer (1977), the notion of educational effects is both conceptually and empirically linked to education as an institution founded upon socially defined beliefs about the functions of education.

Types of effects of education

What are the effects of participating in competence development? A Norwegian study by Nordhaug (1991), reports varying results of competence development on the individual level. This investigation was based on a sample of individuals ($n=299$). The focus of the analysis is on the benefit to the individual of various forms of education. On the basis of a factorial analysis of the replies to the questionnaire, it was possible in this study to distinguish between three different effect dimensions, namely that participation in the training had provided: (a) motivation for further learning (e.g. increased interest in continued education, increased interest in learning, increased interest in a certain subject); (b) opportunities for career development (mainly promotion, a more interesting job, more independence); (c) opportunities for psychosocial development (mainly increased self-confidence, self-fulfilment, new friends).

As Nordhaug notes, these three factors are interesting, not least with respect to the conventional view of competence development in organizations as a conveyor of more specific, job-related knowledge and skills. This can also be said to be the predominant conception starting from a human capital view (Becker 1975). Education, as a path to career development, as Nordhaug points out, is also interesting in the discussion of education as a sorting mechanism for selection to higher positions or other, more qualified tasks.

Largely consistent with these results, Kock *et al.* (2007), in a study of competence development in small and medium-sized companies, could distinguish the following types of individual effects:

- increased skill in terms of being better able to handle the present tasks;
- increased interest in learning something new in the job, i.e. increased motivation for learning;
- a better overall view of the job;
- greater responsibility;
- greater job satsisfaction.

These results show that, besides various types of cognitive effects in the form of increased knowledge and skills, one can expect various types of effects related to motivation, interest and satisfaction. These last-mentioned effects are interesting, not least in view of the reasoning about education as an instrument for ideological control. An interesting study from this perspective is reported by Tuomisto (1986). In this study, three main types of non-cognitive effects are distinguished, namely: (a) to increase the legitimacy of the job in the eyes of the employees as regards its goals, fundamental ideology and power structure; (b) to increase the motivation of the employees and thus improve their job performance without having to increase their task-related qualifications; and (c) to improve the solidarity, climate and organizational culture of the organization in order to create a spirit of affinity and better support for the goals and values of the business.

This also indicates an intrinsic contradiction in competence development. Personnel education can on the one hand be seen as an instrument for controlling and adapting the employees to the prevailing conditions in the workplace or in the organization: on the other hand, education can at the same time be seen as an instrument for increasing the employees' interest in and preparedness for further learning. These two interpretations of the (latent) functions of personnel education may of course be both correct and fully compatible. An important task for continued research is, however, to clarify these functions and their mutual relations.

Traditionally, the effects of education have been discussed mainly on the individual level. Nordhaug (1991) discusses the effects that personnel education may have at the organizational level. Personnel education can lead to both functional and dysfunctional effects at the organizational level. As an example of the former category, education is assumed to act as a mechanism for such things as:

- selection and mobility on the internal labour market in the company;
- socializing and social control of employees;
- legitimization of goals and decisions;
- improved decision-making ability in the organization:
- development of participative decision making and work environment;
- development of the organization's readiness for change;
- better motivation and learning environment.

Examples of possible dysfunctional effects that are cited include a mismatch between the individual's competence development and organizational requirements (e.g. wrong education, inadequate education, excessive education, brain drain and the development of knowledge monopolies within the organization). This reasoning indicates the importance of also paying attention to unintentional and unplanned effects when trying to measure the results of personnel education. Nordhaug (1991) does not, however, report any empirical data regarding the effects on the organizational level but looks for indirect support for his reasoning in other research. Some empirical support for the occurrence of effects on the organizational level is to be found in Ellström and Nilsson (1997), who report effects such as the following on the organizational level: (a) economic effects (retain personnel, retain customers, improved quality); (b) symbolic effects (inwards: increased motivation, participative spirit; outwards: increased trust by customers or management); (c) effects in the form of organizational learning (competence development comes on the agenda, improved climate for future investments).

What characterizes successful strategies for competence development in organizations?

Few studies have attempted to explore the question of what characterizes successful strategies for competence development. Another way of formulating this question is: Under what conditions can programmes for competence development in organizations be expected to lead to the intended effects?

With the exception of a few survey studies (e.g. Mulder 1998), most of the evidence on this question comes from different kinds of multiple case studies.

Successful results of investments made in education and other forms of competence development in companies depend not only on the strategy and methods used. This is of course an important aspect, but it must not be allowed to obscure the fact that the research in the field indicates rather unambiguously that the effects achieved by means of competence development depend on an interplay between the following factors (cf. Burke & Hutchins 2007):

- prior experiences of the participants (previous experience of education, self-confidence, motivation, competence);
- the planning, content, design and implementation of the programme;
- conditions related to the internal context of the organization, i.e. management, work organization, company culture, etc.
- conditions related to the external context of the organization, i.e. factors such as the complexity and stability of the environment, the competitive situation, the labour market and the rate of technological development in the field.

The latter group of factors – external context – can be assumed to be related mainly indirectly to the effects of investments made in competence development. This group of factors has also been treated fairly exhaustively above, and will therefore not be addressed in what follows.

Prior experiences of the participants

The prerequisites for the participation of adults in education constitute an area that in the past two decades has been in the forefront of adult education research. Preparedness to participate and actual participation in various forms of adult education are very unevenly divided in the community and are strongly linked to living conditions, family background, earlier schooling and present working conditions. It is, for instance, a well-known fact that the readiness to participate in various forms of adult education is related to previous educational level: the higher the educational level, the greater is the readiness to participate in and take advantage of possibilities for further education. It has also proved difficult to affect or compensate for this pattern, other than marginally, by various types of reform (Rubenson 2006).

As specifically regards participation in competence development in organizations, there are a number of studies that show that the more qualified the employee's position in working life, the more usual it is for him/her to participate in various forms of competence development (Rubenson & Willms 1993). This is probably in part, but not entirely, due to the employer offering education mainly to personnel holding key positions in the organization. As shown by Larsson *et al.* (1986), workers without specialist training and with a short formal educational background and jobs that place no requirements on professional competence have a very narrow and instrumental view of education. To a large degree, they lack the motivation to take part in education unless it is directly coupled to job requirements. As a result, there is no demand for education, and the readiness to participate in the education that is offered is probably low in large groups of employees with a limited education and unskilled jobs. In line with these findings, Illeris (2004, 2007) discuss recurrent observations of the basic ambivalence towards participation in educational activities exhibited by people with a short formal educational background. These groups of participants typically have a low degree of motivation for participation in educational activities that do not appear meaningful from their subjective perspective. These findings underline the importance of how an education is introduced and designed.

What, than, can be said more specifically about the factors that affect the motivation of individuals to take part in education? Important factors, which have been emphasized not least in adult education research (Rubenson 2006) and psychological research on training motivation (Colquitt & LePine 2000), include: (a) the participants view of learning and individual development; (b) expected benefits of efforts made; and (c) self-confidence in the sense of belief in one's own ability to learn. These factors are in turn closely related to social background, educational level, previous experience of various types of learning situations, working conditions and economic, political and cultural factors in the community.

Programme-related factors

As regards programme-related factors, one can, on the basis of previous research (see e.g. Ellström & Nilsson 1997; Mulder 1998; Illeris 2005; Burke & Hutchins 2007; Kock *et al.* 2007), point to a range of important conditions connected with the planning, design and implementation of the programme. If we look first at the planning of the programme it appears important that: (a) the motives for investment are problem-oriented rather than opportunistic, that is, that the competence development is seen as part of a strategy, for instance to support an altered work organization or planned new production, and not primarily as a means of getting a share of certain support resources or because, say, competence development is generally 'in fashion'; (b) the personnel participate in some sense directly or indirectly, for instance through union or other representatives, in the planning of the programme at company level (here, of course, different degrees and types of participation can be distinguished).

As regards the design and implementation of the programme, significant factors include:

- the way the participants are recruited to the programme – it is important that the recruitment takes place on a personal basis and through a contact person that makes the potential participant feel safe and secure;
- personal counselling based on a dialogue with the participants, and taking the subjective perspective of the participant as a point of departure;
- the design of the education being based on integration between formal education (course sections) and on-the-job learning, for instance by alternating course sections with practical applications and planning them so that they support on-the-job learning;
- the programme being job-oriented, that is, aimed at deepening or widening the employees' competence as a conscious phase in a more farsighted business or job development (e.g. introduction of goal-steered groups), rather than purely individual-oriented (e.g. aimed at increasing the competence of the employees, but with little or no link to development of the business);
- the education covering a substantial period of time (a month or more) and a large proportion of the personnel (not just key employees);
- the participants having access to competent teachers/supervisors, who in practice have the ability to balance structuring/steering and support for participative working forms on the basis of the participants' needs and qualifications.

Conditions related to the internal context of the company

The term 'internal context' means as used here various factors related to production organization, nature of tasks, management, etc. This group of factors is also treated in a fair amount of detail above. It can therefore suffice to indicate briefly some factors that, on the basis of previous research (Pettigrew *et al.* 1988; Ellström & Nilsson 1997; Skule & Reichborn 2002; Burke & Hutchins 2007; Kock *et al.* 2007), seem to be of special importance for achieving the intended effects of investments in competence development in organizations. First, companies that report good effects of education have also to a greater extent than other companies activities characterized by: (a) more time being allotted to various educational activities; (b) educational activities integrated to other planned changes at the workplace (e.g. changes concerning the work organization); (c) important actors within the company, primarily management and union representatives, seeing education and learning as both an effective and legitimate means of handling the company's problems/challenges, that is the company is permeated by a strong belief in and real commitment to education and learning as being important for its development and survival; (d) the existence of 'idea champions', that is, agents of change (e.g. line managers, foremen, personnel managers or union representatives) who keep the ideas alive, carry them forward and mobilize others to change and develop them.

Second, there are strong indications that the effects of competence development efforts seem to be related to the possibilities for on-the-job learning. In companies that are characterized by a 'good' learning environment (e.g. because the complexity of the tasks calls for continuous learning) effects are reported to a greater extent than in companies where the conditions for on-the-job learning do not appear so favourable (Ellström 1997; Billett 2001; Høyrup & Ellström 2007). The importance of the learning environment is, for example, demonstrated in a recent study on competence development in SMEs (Kock *et al.*, 2007). In this study, a distinction was made between two types of learning environments, that is, learning environments that are characterized as constraining and enabling. An enabling learning environment was defined in terms of high qualification requirements, stimulating potentials for learning at work, a supportive management for learning and a higher degree of cooperation within and between working teams. In contrast to this, a constraining learning environment was characterized by lower qualification requirements, less stimulating potential for learning at work, a less supportive management and a lower degree of cooperation within and between working teams. The results showed that the character of the learning environment was important, as the SMEs classified as having an enabling learning environment reported systematically higher learning outcomes compared to the SMEs classified as having a constraining learning environment.

Concluding remarks

As indicated by a number of studies cited above, investments in competence development in organizations can be understood as a result of a complex interplay between external forces and various internal 'logics' represented by various actors within the organization. Furthermore, it seems as if external contextual factors (e.g. increased customer demands or decreased order intake) are necessary, but not sufficient conditions for companies' investments in competence development. In addition, it is, among other things, required that there is a 'good soil' for such investments within the organization. Not least important in this context is, as has been shown in the studies cited above, the existence of a facilitating 'learning culture'. Such a culture can be assumed to be formed by such things as the views of management and union representatives on the value of educational activities, but also by the employees' subjective need of competence development and their motivation for participating in education. Against this background, it appears that an important task for future research is to study more closely the interplay between external contextual factors and internal 'logics' when it comes to deciding on investments in competence development, and in particular to carry out empirical studies of the meaning and importance of the various 'learning cultures'.

As regards the effects of competence development in organizations, we have, among other things, been able to observe that they are not limited to various types of cognitive effects, for example, increased knowledge and skills. What have been called 'ideological–normative effects' (e.g. increased motivation, increased interest and increased self-confidence) seem likely to be at least as important. This and other tentative conclusions on the effects of competence development formulated above do, however, call for further research in order to be substantiated. What is needed is increased knowledge about the various types of effect that can be achieved, both on an individual level and on an organizational level (cf. Salas & Cannon-Bowers 2001). In both cases, it is important to study both positive/functional and any negative/dysfunctional effects of competence development.

However, what also seems to be required is better knowledge of the circumstances under which it is possible to achieve positive educational effects. In this connection, it is important to study prior subjective experience of the participants (e.g. motivation, expectations and experienced benefit from the education), but also factors related to the programme and to the internal context of the organization.

We may also conclude that a series of conditions seems to be related to the possibilities of organizations to achieve significant effects from the investments made in competence development, but it is far from obvious how these relations should be interpreted. As discussed earlier, one can from both a technological–functional and an institutional perspective give quite different meanings to the concept of 'effect', and the prerequisites for achieving educational effects. From an institutional perspective, the predominant view of education as an activity limited in time and space with certain external and objective effects is also fundamentally called into question. The emphasis is instead on competence development being achieved by means of continuous on-the-job learning, learning that can be encouraged or obstructed by the design of the organization (e.g. the nature of the tasks), by the time available and, not least, by the conceptions of learning and education that guide various actors within the company (personnel, union representatives, management).

Thus, interest is to a great extent directed towards the social and cultural context of the education, including the learning culture existing within the company, but also towards the societal level and the policy-related conditions for investments in education in companies. Against this background, it appears important both to further problematize and analyse what can be meant by the 'effects' of education in companies (and also more generally), and to deepen the analysis of the learning that takes place individually and collectively in a company during and after the implementation of an educational effort. In this connection, it is also important to try to gain a better understanding of the interplay between education as an activity and education as a social institution, or, expressed in theoretical terms: the relations between a technological–functional and an institutional perspective on education in companies.

Acknowledgements

This chapter is adapted from an article by Irwin, P. (2008). Competencies and Employer Engagement. *Asia Pacific Education Review*, 9(1), 63–69. Reprinted with permission from Education Research Institute, Seoul National University.

This study was supported by grants from the Swedish Governmental Agency for Innovation Systems.

Part II

The concept of competence

Chapter 4

Competence

Commodification of human ability

Soonghee Han

Introduction

Competence has developed, as Raven depicted, to meet "the conspicuous irrelevance of much knowledge-based education to occupational performance and the failure of educational qualifications to predict occupational success" (Raven 2001: 253). It was proposed as a parameter that conveys the workplace needs to the area of education and training. When the concept first appeared in the *American Psychologist* in 1973, McClelland asserted that traditional intelligent testing fails to predict the capabilities needed in the workplace or for a successful life, and an alternative concept was necessary (McClelland 1973). The Definition and Selection of Competencies (DeSeCo)'s recent publication, *Key Competencies* inherited the notion of *successful life and a well-functioning society*, according to McClelland, based on the *demand-oriented* or *functional* approach:

> A competence is defined as the ability to successfully meet complex *demands in a particular context* through the mobilization of psychosocial prerequisites (including bothcognitive and non-cognitive aspects). This represents a demand-oriented or functional approach to defining competencies. (Rychen & Salganik 2003: 43) (italics added)

Today, the "demand" that reflects the "particular contexts" goes with the demand of the global knowledge economy that the next generation of capitalism is facing, or *knowledge capitalism*, if you will. As Burton-Jones nicely puts it, "Knowledge Capitalism represents a generic new variant of capitalism, based more on the accumulation of knowledge than monetary or physical forms of wealth" (Burton-Jones 1999: 21). Or, knowledge capitalism under the same regime of capitalism, employed the new ingredients of knowledge supply, exchange, production, and consumption, where competence turned out to be the central indicator of the conjoined body of labor *with* knowledge or the indicator of the "knowledge worker". Naturally most research into competence focused on the issue of "expertise": what kinds of competencies are necessary to fulfill what purposes, etc. The notion of competence was positioned as a "vanguard attractor" to convey the demands of the economy to school. In other words, the world of work began to "demand" what and how schools teach, in which the notion of competence played the role of key parameter.

The urgent issue in this vein, is not to verify the "comprehensive list of successful competencies," since it is impossible and/or unnecessary. Scientific research on competence, rather, should be focused on the investigation of the underlying assumptions, its metaphorical usage, and the structural changes in education that the competence-based education reform might bring about: for example, the purpose of competence-based education reform; the way in which education is handled in the context; methods and standards of new academic and vocational qualifications; establishing a new order of education and lifelong learning, etc.

In this article, I hope to shed light on the nature of competence under the capitalist mode of production, by illustrating several structural changes that the introduction of competence as a new DNA in the world of education will fatally bring about.

First, a critical review on competence will be conducted and this will then be analysed by applying Marx's critical theory. For this, I illustrate the nature of competence as a "commodified human ability" that obtains a standardized monetary value to sell in the labor market. I am going to argue that competence is not merely a particular *tool* to produce commodities, such as knowledge products, but also a commodity *itself*, equipped with the same characteristics of commodities in human experience.

Second, I further explain that the introduction of competence discourse accompanies the new context of the independent global learning economy, within which commoditized competence is produced, exchanged, and consumed. Human Resource Development (or HRD), for example, becomes by itself a key industry in knowledge capitalism. The learning economy represents itself as a crucial *part* or *subsystem* of knowledge capitalism, in which competencies are becoming a key product.

Third, I am going to look into the paradigm shift in the background matrix. For this section, I will demonstrate that competence discourse has something to do with the drastic changes in the educational paradigm from "nation-state education" to the "global learning economy," which is already being observed in some Anglo-Saxon countries and even in Korea: from state-managed education systems to the market-managed; traditional school subject-based curricula replaced by competence-based curricula; academic qualifications integrated into unified forms of qualification frameworks; school achievement being evaluated on the basis of "workplace demands."

Finally, I also argue that human competencies by their very nature have "double-bind" characteristics: They satisfy the partial conditions of knowledge capitalism; however, by their nature, competencies fail to satisfy the full conditions that are necessary to fulfill the capital accumulation process which is accomplished. By analysing the hidden secrets of "implicit knowledge" in human experience, I am going to reveal the "dialectics of competencies" which will empower non-market human learning and help make human life and experience achieve a greater balance between work and life.

Commodification of human ability and alienation of learning

Capitalism as the major context

It was HRD that led the concept introduced in this realm. While HRD investigates the nature of human expertise and its maxim development, human competence is a "displayed characteristic of expertise, not the expertise itself, but very behaviour-specific, definable, and measurable subsets within an individual's domain of expertise" (Swanson 2001: 238). If considering that current HRD presupposes capitalism and market system as the fundamentals, the characteristics of the competence as of the *measurable*, the *definable*, and the *manageable* are directly linked with monetary forms of marketable goods or "human capital" in a capitalist society. These traits define it as its "form" of exchange-value, which is obtained by the characteristics of a commodity and traded in equivalent equations with monetary forms.

In fact, since the collapse of Eastern Europe, capitalism reveals itself as *the* dominant social mode of relationship that captivates the individuality in the social formation, in which the commodified market value turns most of the values in the everyday life world into a part of the system. Competence, in this particular context, takes the form of "commodified human ability." We call "commodities" those things that can be traded, bought or sold in a capitalist system. The competence invented to represent the performance of capital accumulation is put to the process of social exchange with salary, incentives, job status, and other informal rewards.

From Marx's perspective, individuals are social individuals and

> are constituted or rather constitute themselves, as individuals of a particular sort through the social relationships in which they stand to other people. If individuals are social individuals, then the specific nature of their social relationships will be constitutive of the specific nature of the individuals. (Brien 2006: 41)

The relations between men in capitalist society, in this regard, turn out to be that of commodities, or as Brewer mentioned,

> the economic relations between people are carried out by the buying and selling of things. Each individual is concerned only with the things that

are bought and sold. The transportation of social properties onto material things is what Marx calls fetishism. (Brewer 1984: 26)

In this relation, human abilities bought and sold in the capitalist market concern commodified things that can be exchanged in monetary form. Competence is converted into not only a capability to produce commodities, but also a *commodity itself*. The secret of competencies lies beneath the nature of commodity or capital, for example human capital, where human ability is transformed and treated as a form of capital. According to Marcuse, "In capitalist society, labor not only produces commodities (i.e. goods which can be freely sold on the market), but also produces 'itself and the worker as a commodity'"(Marcuse 1972: 10). The nature of the commodity of one's own labor does not come from the work conditions or low payment, but from the nature of the employment itself, or so to speak, from the way one becomes an object of exchange in a labor market and acquires the "nature of commodities of oneself."

Competence is a specifically trained part of human experience that expresses itself as "purchasable goods" with a price tag in the labor market, and is exchanged for social rewards, not to satisfy the need of the learner but rather that of the purchaser: on the one hand, competence is a part of our experience, acquired by learning and doing, which grows or sometimes perishes in us. It is part of *us*, and as such, it holds our own subjectivity; on the other hand, the alienated nature of commodities in terms of competence mutates one's experience, being distorted from one's subjective identity and means that it is dealt with as a form of capital, that is human capital or social capital. It obtains a monetary exchange value through qualifications and is traded in labor markets.

Learning as commodity production

The key issue here is a matter of alienation. The action of selling and buying is mediated by an absolutely quantified monetary form, for example, a quantified form of money in which the natural characters of subjective and personal dimensions diminish. Only the standardized exchange value prevails in this process. In this sense, competence seems still *part of me* but only an *isolated* part of my experience, estranging itself and waiting to be exchanged for another's desire. It becomes estranged, as if it exists outside of oneself, independently, as something alien, or even confronting us. As a term of human resource, competence is no longer the property of lived experience, rather it becomes a commodified experience that controls, estranges, or manages one's life. It is indeed a ridiculous experience, because, although exchanged in the knowledge market, it *is* still an embedded trait of human beings, not separable from body and mind.

To sum up, competence by nature is destined to be detached from the subjective meaning scheme and only prepared exclusively for the purchaser's desire and identity to sell. As soon as one gives up one's subjective identity and meaning scheme for certain competencies, the commodified ability of competencies reifies the possessor, and learning to obtain the competencies turns out to be a form of rote memorization that becomes an estranged experience detached from one's own life. The sole obedience, however, to others' desires comes from the characteristics of alienation that the relations of commodities bring. As Marcuse asserted,

> The alienation of the worker in his product means not only that his labour becomes an object, an external existence, but that it exists outside him, *independently*, as something alien to him, and that it becomes a power on its own confronting him. It means that the life which he has conferred on the object confronts him as something hostile and alien.
>
> (Marcuse 1972: 11)

Or,

> As a result of the 'alienation' of the worker and of labour, the realization of all man's essential powers becomes the loss of their reality; the objective world is no longer 'truly human property' appropriated in 'free activity' as the sphere of the free operation and self-confirmation of the whole of human nature. It is instead a world of objects in private possession which can be owned, used or exchanged and whose seemingly unalterable laws even man must obey – in short, the universal 'domination of dead matter over mankind.'
>
> (Marcuse 1972: 6)

"Human resource" or "human capital," in this respect, follows the same stream as commodified human competence, as a more elaborated stage of its realization. At this stage, an illusionistic misconception takes the power. Just as a capitalist society presumes that "more competent workers get higher wages," so too the exchange values of competence conceivably take the reign of the capital, equivalent to material capital. According to Olssen,

> Becker as a dominant Human Capital theorist, distinguishes two central aspects to such human capital: (1) inborn, physical and genetic dispositions; and (2) education, nutrition, training and emotional health. In this model each person is now an autonomous entrepreneur responsible ontologically for their own selves and their own progress and position. Individuals have full responsibility over their investment decisions and must aim to produce a surplus value. On his quotation, 'entrepreneurs of themselves'.
>
> (Olssen 2006: 219)

However, the workers, though possessing high competence, cannot be autonomous entrepreneurs, or capital holders: because here the word *capital* merely operates as a metaphor. It is necessary to keep in mind that "capital" does not imply stand-alone wealth, like gold or silver, but wealth *put in the capital accumulation process*, which is controlled solely by capitalists. It is simply a mirage that human competence can be transformed into a capital asset. The value of capital or its surplus value can be realized only in a process of capital accumulation that exploits the "competent" workers.

What happens in knowledge capitalism?

Some key questions are waiting for us: more "inbound" than "outbound" questions, such as, what happens to our experience if we equip ourselves with such competencies? Where do competencies stand within the vast organism of human experience, and how is the previous *self* transformed by this equipment of new competence, or this commoditized form of human ability?

Until recently, most competence research focused on the "outbound" aspects of human life, for example, what kind of human ability serves the needs of economic development and salary increases, etc.? However, the research did not raise any serious questions about the *self*. More inbound questions deal with *my* experience, for example, what kind of significant imbalances occur when certain kinds of competencies are secured in us? Put another way, what is the real meaning behind education when it seems to create a situation whereby learning experiences are equated with exchange values, where human experience is reduced to "competencies," to be purchased by others, *especially in knowledge capitalism?*

As Drucker mentioned in his article entitled, "From Capitalism to Knowledge Society", the Knowledge Society has double-bind characteristics: On the one hand, capitalism became "The Capitalism—with a capital C" (Drucker 1998), and the core of competence-driven educational restructuring seems unavoidable, something we simply have to live with; on the other, contradictorily speaking, the trait of "knowledge" as a new leading resource of capital accumulation, fails to satisfy the conditions of traditional capitalism. In an article, I explained the paradox:

> Knowledge economists believe that the fundamental of knowledge capitalism consists of the two modes of knowledge, so-called, *explicit* and *tacit* knowledge (Allee 1997; Wills 1998). Explicit knowledge is 'knowledge as a product' that can be stored and exchanged as a form of knowledge capital. Tacit knowledge instead is 'knowledge as process', learned and produced but not-yet-capitalized, so it is not tradable in any way (Burton-Jones 1999). While explicit knowledge is possessed by companies in the form of intellectual property, copyright, or patents, or 'sold

and bought' from the shelf of the market, tacit knowledge comes with the person who holds it. Quite different from explicit form, tacit knowledge continuously changes, grows, or is extinguished in one's experience. Considering that the 'beauty' of the knowledge economy discourse comes from the discovery of the hidden value of tacit knowledge and its supposed capital value, this non-tradability is nothing but a *paradox of this theory*, and it unsurprisingly considers the theory of learning economy in part.

(Han 2008)

Put simply, Knowledge Capitalism is a "double-bind" with two contradictory trajectories. Knowledge, especially valuable tacit knowledge is the key part of expertise, which in turn cannot be fully objectified and transferred to acquire an exchange-value. Knowledge capitalism has the most important resource of production, knowledge, which by its very nature fails to be entirely compliant in the game of capitalism. Competence, a human ability also exhibits double-bind characteristics: it should translate tacit human ability into quantified, exchangeable, and tradable values to fulfill itself as a form of human capital; it also has the paradoxical characteristic of human experience that cannot be fully translated into a commodity.

Competence-driven education reform in the context of knowledge capitalism

Knowledge capitalism

Knowledge capitalism, without exceptions, locates knowledge and human competence at the centre of the commodity exchange process (Burton-Jones 1999). With regard to this, it is necessary to conceive that the newly emerging concepts of human capital, cultural capital, or social capital are nothing but the mutations of the knowledge capital. Until recently the term knowledge society or knowledge economy had been put to the main stage of debates. Now it is proper time to concentrate on the characteristics of *new* capitalism, fueled with knowledge and human competence as major resources of production: not only to understand the nature of knowledge economy from the eyes of capitalism, but also to understand the nature of *new* capitalism from the traits of knowledge and competence as the major components.

One salient characteristic is that the knowledge economy needs an ever more greatly expanded knowledge and learning market, where the learning economy (or learning society) becomes an essential engine for global knowledge capitalism. In this stream, the competence becomes a prime commodity produced and traded in the new forms of the market (Jarvis 2007). In a traditional society, human learning was perceived as that of the non-market domain, in such contexts as within the family, community, nation states, etc.

Human labor was mostly conceived of as hourly based manpower, while "ability" or "talent" were not marketable concepts, unable to fulfill the role of being fully exchangeable in the market (see how the arts, literature, ideas and inventions have been treated in non-market oriented ways in the era).

Under a new trend of lifelong learning and learning economy as its foundation, "learning" began to be perceived as the main engine of the new economy. As knowledge capitalism established itself, learning as a core processor of producing knowledge was transformed in the new matrix. Human abilities were increasingly "processed" to fit into the labor market's exchangeability, directed to produce "key competencies" that are recognized "qualifications" as explicit value expressions. Now learning is re-designed to produce adequate responses to the specific demands of the business and service industry, or the knowledge economy in general: Learning market, learning industry, learning welfare, and HRD that provide the key domains of the new superstructure of learning economy.

Background: Emergence of "flexible informality"

A society is maintained by the manipulation of the learning process of the members, in accordance with the social code of surveillance and discipline (Foucault, 1977). In fact, a holistic organic system holds many subsystems that are interwoven, and learning as a subsystem plays the key role of managing and handling the societal learning of the members in a given society (Goodson & Dowbiggin 1990; Giroux 1993). The modern nation state has established and managed the formal education system, authorized the uniquely sanctioned position to issue official diplomas or degrees, or otherwise mandated the official knowledge to learn (Apple 1993). Formal education, under the auspice of the state, "disciplined" the upcoming new generations with the "disciplines"(= academic subject) (Young 1998). Indeed, the formal education system has been a pillar for sustaining it, along with the multilayered cultural censorship systems, for example, movies and publications, like the textbook authorization process in the national school curriculum, a part of the process of selecting and screening socially approved knowledge, and putting it in the core of the societal learning management system.

Notwithstanding the economic correspondence theory of Bowles and Gintis, however, modern schools had little to do with what the current meaning of competence implied. What mattered at that time was to discipline the working class, or, put differently, reproducing the *relations of production* or class relations in a capitalist society, not the *forces of production* or competence in human labor. I will place the code of restricted formality to refer to the mode of education at that time. Labor management by Fordism in an industrial society in reproducing the relations of production, represents the restricted formality in education as a code of managing the process of social learning and knowledge at this stage.

However the new, rising megatrends, such as rapid technological innovations, postmodern arts and culture, post-industrial work management, an evolving knowledge economy, and a lifelong learning society, etc., have transformed the code of the education system tremendously. The exploding knowledge and its mantra of value acquisition has urged the dismantlement of the restricted code and has substituted it with the code of "flexible informality" to promote the learning organization and the learning economy to further produce competencies as measurable forms of human resources.

This "restricted formality" is symbolized by the uniform standards of social knowledge and enforcement at school. It was "restricted" because knowledge was rigidly codified as "selected academic subjects" in schools and the stratification of the school diploma classified the class structure of the youngsters. "Official knowledge" was produced at "official institutions" such as universities and affiliated research institutes, where invented knowledge was again put into the process to be compiled to take the shape of "official discipline and instruction." The whole process kept rigidly to the characteristics of "formality" with "hard" subjects, licensed teachers, rules and regulations in schools, explicit evaluation and qualifications to disconnect it from other parts of nonformal and informal learning. It was not important to ask why but what to learn, since this knowledge was codified restrictively and the learning has exclusively dealt with the knowledge that guaranteed upward class mobilization. The notion of competence did not even exist in this context.

On the contrary, "neo-liberal projects for economic innovation and flexibilization" (Stevenson 1999: 311) are moves which significantly change the fundamentals of the educational order (Field, 2002), especially from a school discipline-oriented education system to one of flexible lifelong learning. The technological explosion and the advent of the knowledge economy (Senge *et al.* 1994; Drucker 1998) dismantled the school-centered "restricted formality" and, therefore, schools surrounded by the knowledge of discipline had to find ways out of this transformation. The once useful "restricted code" of social knowledge/learning management no longer advocated adequate functionality. The notion of "disciplined knowledge" faced a new challenge. Instead, the new code of "flexible informality" began to manage the field of social knowledge production and learning: More knowledge began to be produced outside academia, where discipline is no longer the sole method of "processing" and "packing" invented knowledge. The disciplinary rules or the unified code of knowledge are therefore dissolved and diversified, the global economic environment has weakened the political publicity of the state, and the market-driven private realm has advanced to the core of social production and reproduction, instead. The shift from "restricted formality" to "flexible informality" reflects more of the invisible and implicitly useful knowledge which exists within the learning process; it is this which goes beyond the boundaries of the traditional subject-based education system.

Competence-driven changes in the societal learning system

The dominant force of the societal learning system has been slowly relocated from the arena of state politics to that of market exchangeability. Until then, the territory of education kept a certain distance from the "invisible hands" Competence: Commodification of Human Ability of the capitalist mode of production, although positioned as a part of it. While sometimes school credentials have been described as a form of pseudo-commodity (Hall 1979; Liston 1988), the game of education and the game of economics had been clearly distinguished, linked only with blurry connections for school to work transition, at least until neoliberal social policies swept the world of social policies from the 1990s. Under this new trend, major social policies including education, medical services, and social welfare were redirected to fit into this framework. It was the education sector, in particular, that was heavily targeted to reformulate a new learning market as a major carrier of the emerging knowledge economy. The notion of "competence" in this context had the spotlight.

Since the 1990s, the corporate and business sector began to adapt "competence" and use it as a major parameter of practical performance, while educationists of the traditional pedagogy stuck to the notion of "academic achievement" to demonstrate a learner's ability within a school setting. This dualism persisted as long as the two worlds of learning in "childhood" and "adulthood" functioned in an unconnected way, and the concept of competence partially represented the performance of adults who only engaged in work.

However, the lifelong learning concept began to prevail, and the two different worlds of learning slowly met in the early 1990s through the involvement of some intergovernmental organizations, such as the OECD. It was the DeSeCo project of the OECD in particular which introduced the concept of competencies as a universal standard for human achievement including academic and vocational, for the realms of childhood and adulthood, by encompassing the concept of "lifelong learning and the learning society" that strongly linked school and work, academic subjects and work performance, and academic achievement of school subjects and the competencies of the workplace (Rychen & Salganik 2003). Recently, the OECD has redirected the flow of the measurement of international student achievements from the school-stand alone model (e.g. Trends in International Mathematics and Science Study (TIMSS)) to the core competencies model (Programme for International Student Assessment (PISA) and Programme for the International Assessment for Adult Competencies (PIAAC)) that linked academic achievement to competence in a school context.

As a glue to weld the two worlds together, the notion of competence worked as a double-edged sword: On the one hand, it symbolized educational innovation in meeting the new mode of production of capital; on the other hand, it took the role of a "Trojan Horse," dismantling the castle of the modern school and the fundamental meaning of learning at schools. As a new education matrix that combines global knowledge capitalism with lifelong learning was expanding its sphere of influence, the notion of competencies or a stream of "competence-based education" enters into the curriculums of primary, secondary, and higher education. The notion of competence, in this context, was highlighted as a vanguard attractor to change the rules of the game akin to that of the capital accumulation process in education. Now, let me project the five mutually connected policies, easily observed on a global scale recently, and put them together to help make this obscure picture more visible.

First, as seen in the OECD's PISA or PIAAC efforts, competence was chosen as an attractor to measure and compare student academic achievements (OECD 2002, 2004). Additionally, in the United Kingdom, New Zealand, and Canada, competencies became a core feature of the national (or global, if putting it more appropriately) curriculum, by establishing national key competencies standards. This trend significantly undermines the strong foundation of a discipline-based school curriculum (Field 2002; Schuetze 2006).

Second, as the UK's white paper boldly asserted, output-oriented school policies were to replace the input-controlling school administration system. For the new requirement of minimum standards for graduation, the standard of competencies is presented as a major indicator to control the national education system under which non-traditional schools which had evolved differently are treated equally to the traditional academic school. *If standards are a constant, then everything else must be a variable*, and a list of standardized competencies becomes the sole constant that makes other factors variable.

Third, based upon the equivalent value of competence achievements, multiple dimensions of alternative qualifications are developed and slotted into the national qualification framework. Promotion of a non-traditional curriculum and an alternative credit award system are developed to make them contend with each other.

Fourth, greater interchangeability in the competence recognition system is developed so that it bridges the realms of vocational and academic credit (academic competencies are now interconnected with vocational qualifications).

Finally, the learning economy is expanded to support the knowledge economy in general. Education is privatized to be a part of the learning market; the welfare or workfare system turns its concern to the new form of welfare, "learnfare"; the proportion of knowledge workers who mainly serve the learning industry exceeds the number of traditional manufacturing workers; now, and in the near future, the learning market will share the biggest portion of GDP. Learning itself becomes the largest market and industry that produces competencies.

In this context, diverse scenarios are possible related to the competence-driven education changes. For example, if competence achievement is the major key for controlling the quality of education, then the traditional academic subjects will lose their dominant position, since many other practical knowledge sets will satisfy the needs of the designated competence-learning frameworks. Schools will voluntarily adapt and develop new ecologically appropriate competence development programmes outside the traditional subject teaching, which will result in the unified national curriculum being dismantled and diversified. Also, any traditional schools that fail to meet the competence output-requirements will find additional non-formal education resources (financial resources, professional support, or cooperative institutions that work together) to supplement the students to produce better achievements, which will promote interconnectivity between previously stand-alone schools, making them, in effect, "system-schools." In that case, alternative schools will be no longer a "marginal substitution" as seen by the OECD's "Schooling for Tomorrow" project (OECD 2004), rather, they will take a more central place in whole school ecologies.

On the one hand, this new feature will affect the given school system and make it more flexible and adaptable positively, to make them embrace the workplace/civil sectors' needs. Also, according to the standardized competence-based national qualification framework, non-traditional higher education systems, for example, the Credit Bank System, the Self-Examination System, Corporate Universities, and Cyber Universities can all play a more main function in the acquisition of higher education degrees, alongside the traditional universities.

On the other hand, however, the demand-driven school reform will relocate the whole education system in jeopardy. Academic achievement is no longer self-defined by the school and academic knowledge arena. Rather it will be under the control of the demands of the economic environment via the definition of competence, as both the barometer of work expertise and goal of school achievement. Also the characteristics of commodity production in human learning alienate both the work and learning processes.

Conclusion

The reason why we are concerned with the full integration of the capitalist mode of production into the education system is that, as Marx argued, the capitalist mode of production adds mystical characteristics to the elements, or transforms everything into something which is ultimately alienated, corresponding to the value of commodities, in that human ability also takes on the "mystical characteristics" of mere commodities in itself. The nature of commodities is embedded in the mystical process of capitalism, and this is the very nature of exchange values and exchangeability itself.

In this chapter, I sought to analyse the meaning and implications of the notion of competence through a number of steps. First, I tried to analyse the negative side of the concept by employing Karl Marx's theory of capital.

Specifically, I highlighted the way that competence is not merely a particular *means* of producing commodities, such as knowledge products, but also a commodity *itself*. Additionally, I outlined the macro picture of the contextual shift in the education system from one which is state-driven to that of a global, market-driven one. Again, I located the concept in the matrix of knowledge capitalism and HRD industries, and derived a scenario of how the notion of competence will engender a macro education reform in the context of the learning society.

I believe the research into competencies in the future should be balanced between the micro-level functional approach and the macro-level critical approach. Competence is not only a "list of useful expertise" but also a keyword of many grand narratives that initiate the macro changes in education systems for the advancement of knowledge capitalism. It also contains within it a tremendous degree of practicality—it gives us a much needed critical perspective to understand the grand picture of the current changes within education, especially under neoliberalism which promotes knowledge capitalism.

Acknowledgements

This chapter is adapted from an article by Ellstrom, P-E., & Kock, H. (2008). Competence Development in the Workplace: Concepts, Strategies and Effects. *Asia Pacific Education Review*, 9(1), 5–20. Reprinted with permission from Education Research Institute, Seoul National University.

Chapter 5

Holistic competence
Putting judgements first

David Beckett

It's a question of experience. You remember that the past figures were very different. So it raises doubts in your mind. I remember once I was working on a project and there was something I didn't know about it – had something funny about it. At 3 o'clock in the morning I woke and said, 'That's what's wrong with it'. I found it at 3 o'clock in the morning in my subconscious. The decision wasn't a conscious decision. It was working in the back of my mind.

Introduction

Accountancy is a profession traditionally shaped by competence which is readily reckoned: you count, you calculate, you assess and so on. Yet in the little anecdote above, our sleepless accountant is stirred by something else. His technical competence is not in doubt, but his reliance on hitherto strange psychological experiences, is indeed curious. What is he drawing upon to make a professional decision, or judgement? Further, notice the experience is both vivid *and* elusive! He awoke, and something decisive resulted, yet he was not aware of how this worked for him.

This chapter investigates a new approach to professional competence: one that takes such strange experiences seriously, and which tries to build upon recent research initiatives in Australia and elsewhere, to show how workplace expertise, or work performed to standards, is best conceptualized.

First, the traditional behaviourist approach to competence is briefly described, then the 'Australian model' of integrated, or holistic, competences, is set out.

Second, the conceptual underpinnings of this holistic approach are made plain (in three subsections), and an example given of such an approach.

Third, some current aspects of the new attention to these strange experiences – which I address as *phronesis* – such as those our accountant reports, are discussed. Low-status knowledge, typically called 'intuition' or 'commonsense', or 'know how', is receiving long-overdue critical attention. One vivid summary of this epistemological problem is given by Kathryn Montgomery (2006), as part of her detailed account of the clinical judgement of medical doctors: 'Along with "wisdom", "intuition" and "talent", Donald Schon [1987 p13] lists "artistry" as one of the terms typically used as a "junk category" to describe what cannot be "assimilate[d] to the dominant model of professional knowledge' (p. 30). As educators shift their attention to the world of adults' lifelong learning, especially as shown in workplace experiences, it is little wonder that daily life – a 'junk category' of knowledge for the past 2000 years of Western civilization – is found to provide exceptionally rich opportunities for truly educative experiences. Holistic competences are one way to harness these.

Traditional behaviourist competences and moving beyond them

When education and training policy makers push on with competence structures, as they have been doing in many nations since the early 1990s, they typically have in mind an overriding concern with *outcomes*. So their national vocational structures are *technicist*: how to arrive at pre-specified levels of occupational competence is rightly an important policy problem, but its solution has been shaped by showing, through assembling evidence of performance, how an outcome has been reached. Thus, for example, a crane driver can reach 'competence' if, through an assembling of the technicalities of crane driving ('can start the engine', 'can attach the hooks', 'can avoid accidents'), a shipping container is moved across the railyard.

Educators have typically regarded the policy makers' efforts in setting up competence structures with dismay. Reductive, behaviourist and therefore, banal: these are terms that perhaps sum up the criticisms many educators have levelled at competence structures at least in Western democracies over the past decade or so – and in my view these criticisms are by and large accurate, since such structures reduce the work of, say, crane driving, to technical 'atoms' of behaviour. Opportunities for educative experiences, under such a policy regime, are slim and often mind-numbing.

By contrast, there are non-reductive, humanistic structures around where rich opportunities for workplace learning present themselves, perhaps most notably in what Hyland (1997) calls the 'Australian model' of integrated or holistic competence (based upon Hager & Beckett 1995). This has gained prominence through the empirical and conceptual work of several staff at the University of Technology, Sydney across the 1990s (mainly arising in their research for the National Office for Overseas Skills Recognition, e.g. Gonczi *et al.* 1990), which serves as a point of entry to current debates.

In essence, integrated or holistic competence advocates a selective (not exhaustive) assembly of evidence of performative skills and attitudes in a worker from which competence is *inferred*. Central to this inference is a sensitivity to the particularities of the immediate workplace context in the worker, and also to that worker's agency in making judgements about how to proceed in the conduct of the work. So *judgements-in-contexts* are at the heart of this inferentialist account of competence, and are directly linkable to what has become known as the 'practitioner' literature: what is it about the intelligent doing of work which enables performance of it to standards?

Competences notwithstanding, sensitivity to judgements-in-context is now taken to be the hallmark of the successful manager, the nurse, the teacher, the sales consultant, the crane driver and the waiter (for medical doctors, see Groopman (2007) – a best-seller). By this I mean that in these postmodern times, those who can 'read the moment' (or the situation in general) for its particularities and opportunities, are probably those most likely to identify a niche, a hybridity, or an innovation which serves and may even extend prevailing circumstances, thereby reaching new understandings of workplace practices. What is it about the working life of an accountant, one may ask, which generates the 3 a.m. decisional moment? His 'judgement-in-context' brought together extensive technical learning in accountancy, a sensitivity (an *unease*, even) with a particular case, and a relaxed state of mind. And there was an outcome, but it is unlike the usual behavioural competence, which typically looks for an outcome in the form of a specified task or role with a pre-calibrated set of evidence ('performance indicators' or some such).

There is much that is helpful in specified tasks or roles, but such statements of outcome are radically under-determined by experience, or, plainly, what people, such as professionals, actually *do*. Here I take my cue from Mulcahy (2000), where she concludes:

> competence is a complex outcome, or, better perhaps, event. Competence development in its 'richest' sense involves a number of processes – discursive and material – which are only partially assimilable. Rather than regarding competence as something individuals or organisations have, it might be better to regard it as something that they do. (p. 521)

Work is literally embodied in workers, and I want to show how what I call 'inferential understanding' emerges from judgements-in-context. Mulcahy mentions discursive and material processes, and in what follows I want to show the ontological significance of what is 'done' (materially) as a basis for language usage – what is 'done' (discursively).

Conceptual underpinnings of holistic competence

So: what do individuals at work actually *do*? I argue they mainly come to understandings of how to go on, and that they construct these in the 'hot action' of their daily work. In my chapter in Tara Fenwick's book on workplace learning (Beckett 2001), attention is drawn to a reflexivity between, on the one hand, a worker "knowing how" to do something ... that is, what they are drawing upon at work ..., and, on the other hand, the "knowing why" they find themselves drawn to act. Both the "know how" and the "know why" are up for constant renegotiation as, anticipatively, actions unfold – amidst "hot action" in the workplace. (p. 83)

In linking 'knowing how' and 'knowing why' I am exploring *what it is to come to understand something*, at a fundamental level: at coming to understand the achievement of 'understanding' itself, through work experiences for adults. Essentially, *coming to understand something* at and through one's work is very context-specific. Problems, issues, challenges and all manner of 'hot actions' arise in daily work life, and Paul Hager and I have consistently claimed this as the basis for a new epistemology of practice (Beckett & Hager 2002).

This is the place in the analysis to broaden it beyond statements of outcomes (competence), because since the 1990s, much policy attention in Western economies is being given to statements of expectations. What can we expect graduates, for example, to be able to do, in virtue of being graduates of tertiary education as such. How 'employable' are they in this generic sense? These expectations when listed look like holistic competences, since they integrate intelligent action in socioculturally significant ways, and, by definition, they are *contrasted* with the specific skills required in and by the nature of working in particular contexts. One authoritative definition of generic skills (Hager *et al.* 2002), in connecting these to graduates' employability, states:

> The term 'generic skills' is widely used to refer to a range of qualities and capacities that are increasingly viewed as important in higher education. These include thinking skills such as logical and analytical reasoning, problem solving and intellectual curiosity; effective communication skills, teamwork skills, and capacities to identify, access and manage knowledge and information; personal attributes such as imagination, creativity and intellectual rigour; and values such as ethical practice, persistence, integrity and tolerance. This diverse collection of qualities and capacities is distinguished from the discipline-specific knowledge and associated technical skills that traditionally are associated with higher education. (p. 3)

Various forms of testing to do with generic skills now exist in the school and higher education sectors. National testing instruments identify student achievement in the basic or foundation generic skills, 'literacy' and 'numeracy' in the early years of schooling. In Australia, the ACER *Graduate Skills Assessment Tests* have been developed for the higher education sector. The business world is keen to see these skills as markers of 'employability'.

In Hager *et al.* (2002) we claim that the value of such tests in either sector to necessarily capture the holistic nature of the learning involved in acquiring and enhancing generic skills is very much open to question. This is particularly the case in, for example, the use of multiple-choice test formats to test generic skills such as the capacity for teamwork. The assumption is that testing understanding of propositions about teamwork will indicate capacity to perform in a team. The assumed model here is that understandings and skills are discrete, both conceptually and practically. However such dualistic models are highly contested by a more holistic notion of understanding. So my aim in this piece is to argue that, 'inferential understanding', grounded in embodied practice, can provide a strong basis for articulating both statements of outcome (competence), and statements of expectation (generic skills). We get from the materiality of workplace learning, to its discursive nature, not the other way around.

To achieve the construction of the concept of 'inferential understanding', as the basis for renewed attention in adults' workplaces in melding 'knowing how' and 'knowing why', first, inferentialism is laid out, introduced by a case of inference arising in the practice of an organizational psychologist.

Next, judgement as an 'emergent property' of workplace learning is argued, growing out of inferentialism. Finally, the entire argument is summarized and applied to the theorization of competence and generic skills.

Inferring

The case of the corporate executive who couldn't stop talking

An organizational psychologist provides this example of how he melded 'knowing how' and 'knowing why' in making judgements-in-context, involving a stressed client:

> The executive had been made redundant and could not stop talking, so I listened! The main thrust of the story was that this person felt angry – he had given 16–17 hours per day to the job and then had been made redundant. It was important that he had a job as he was the sole bread-winner with family responsibilities.
>
> My first judgement was in relation to when to interrupt and offer a different way of thinking – 'When can I make the decision to interrupt?' – 'this person has a need to "dump"'. From observation of this process I made a judgement that 'this person is not ready for the workforce!' I judged [inferred] that the candidate was emotionally burned out; exhausted; on antidepressants, and possibly in the throes of a life out of control.
>
> Listening was important but I judged that there was a need to intervene at some point.

I made the intervention by asking 'Could you take a break?' in terms of 'How would you feel about taking a month's break to allow yourself to recover?'. My judgement was to manoeuvre the candidate's focus from the 'urgency' of the situation to 'getting back to good health so as to maximize opportunities.'

'Inferential understanding', as displayed in the above case, by the organizational psychologist, is the intertwining of knowing how and knowing why, in specific workplaces (and in 'hot action' at work). The client needed a time of healing, in which new energies, and hopefully a new way forward, could emerge. By 'inferring' from a variety of experiential evidence, the psychologist was able to create such a space, not just in the discourse underway that day (a moment to break in to the conversation), but also to make a material (embodied) difference to the executive's life. The psychologist makes several explicit 'judgements-in-context' to bring these two inferential moments about.

I believe this 'inferential understanding' offers a way to explore how holistic competences can emerge in specific workplace experiences.

What such inferences require for their emergence as holistic competences is simply their public justification. No one expects the psychologist in this case to remain inarticulate over, nor unacccountable for, his professional practice. On the contrary, he should be able (= capable, competent) to state how and why his 'judgements-in-context' are thus-and-so.

To underpin this emergence of new professional competences, amidst 'public justifications', I draw upon the epistemologist Brandom (2000). He locates what he calls the 'genus of conceptual activity' in the pragmatic *expression* of knowledge claims, not in their *representation*. This distinction is crucial so it is worth drawing it out a little.

Instead of grounding knowledge in the representation and refinement of a state of the mind (which fits with Cartesian origins of knowledge), inferentialists like Brandom (and myself) argue for 'a form of linguistic pragmatism that might take as its slogan ... that grasping a concept is mastering the use of a word' (Brandom 2000: p. 6; he acknowledges a Deweyian, Jamesian and Wittgensteinian heritage). Brandom's expressivism – this 'usage' – sees the mind not as a mirror (representing what is inner and is outer), but, similar to a lamp,

> making explicit what is implicit. This can be understood in a pragmatist sense of turning something we can initially only do into something we can say: codifying some sort of knowing how in the form of a knowing that. (2008: 8)

Educators can see the contemporary significance of this – and some of us have gone some way further with it already: workplace learning and especially the Schonian 'reflective practitioner' at work are redolent of this conversion of what is done (acted) into what is said (articulated). My claim is that the psychologist needs to give public justification for his practices – as do we all – and that he is turning what he *does* (such as with a client like the executive) into what he says. This is making explicit what is implicit in his practice; it codifies what we *do* by articulating it – it emerges as what we *say* (to our peers, the public, etc).

Brandom's expressive 'linguistic pragmatism' sits well with certain educational and pedagogical innovation, in adults' workplaces, and supports holistic competences, as these emerge in contexts of 'judgements-in-practice' such as the organizational psychologist occupies. What we know *best* is thus an emergent, publicly justified and therefore accountable achievement. As other epistemologists, DeVries and Triplett (2000), summarize:

> we know first the public world of physical objects. We can extend that framework to include persons and their language. What we know best, however, are those beliefs that are the most well-supported pieces of the most coherent, well-substantiated explanatory framework available to us … our best knowledge will be provided to us by the efforts of science. The picture of knowledge created is that of a communal, self-correcting enterprise that grows from unsophisticated beginnings toward an increasingly detailed and adequate understanding of ourselves and the world. (p. xlvi [emphasis added])

This suggests a way forward for the challenge presented in the last few pages of our book (Beckett & Hager 2002) where we claimed:

> Instead of asking how the learning (through training for example) is represented to the learner – "Has there been a change in the state of the learner?" – the more profound question is: "What inferences can now be articulated by the learner?" (p. 192)

I believe the way forward is to unpack that notion of the public articulation of inferences as a 'communal, self-correcting enterprise' (as DeVries & Triplett stated). Expressive, pragmatic understandings of experience are really *how adults' workplaces are shaped*.

Beckett and Hager (2002) show in some detail what this centring of 'knowing *how*' does to and for traditional education. In a nutshell, 'knowing how' to proceed at work, for most adults, requires a series of decisional actions, some of them articulated, which issue in change, just as we read in the case of the executive who would not stop talking. The psychologist made interventions which discursively and materially changed the client's situation. We may claim that the psychologist's holistic competence, in respect of certain generic capacities, such as problem solving and conflict resolution, for example, *emerged from his practices*.

To give these experiences the epistemological significance they deserve, we need to add the 'knowing why'. The psychologist needs to publicly justify his judgements, thus establishing the competences and the evidence for them in an accountable way. These are fluid and contestable, and a long way from the static, behavioural and reductive competence regimes more common in Western policy arenas. My argument is that inferentialism – the 'communal, self-correcting' justifications given by an individual at and through his or her work of why she or he acted thus-and-so, looks promising as an account of holistic competences.

I now will develop this claim, by dealing with the nature of *competent practical judgements* amidst these public justifications (articulated inferences) in the workplace.

Judging

If we are serious about inferential understanding, then (as Beckett & Hager 2000, 2002 argue) the reflective action of making a 'judgement' is central. Workers do this all day, every day, and I have claimed, right from the accountant's 3 a.m. decision making, that these adult learning experiences are central to a new concept of holistic competence.

Frequently, what humans find themselves doing – even at 3 a.m. – is making decisions (judgements) about what to do next. Workplace learning is increasingly shaped by this sort of fluid experience ('knowing how' to go on), but it needs to be *made explicit* (as in Brandom's 'expressive approach', above). The 'making explicit' is what the best adult teachers and trainers can do, in facilitating, even revealing, adults' experiences for educational purposes. Mentoring schemes are an example.

Judgements under this latter, inferentialist, model, are *practical* in that they are expected to be efficacious: they deal in what is thought to be good (that is to say, appropriate) *in specific contexts in which they are embedded*. There has to be this pragmatic point to it all, especially for coming to understand practice through the emergence of holistic competences. 'Problem-solving' for lawyers will carry inferences for and from practice differently than for masons, or accountants, or psychologists.

Earlier, we noted that Brandom locates inferentialism in the *pragmatic expression* of knowledge claims. He means to move the achievement of understanding beyond static representationalism (such as traditional behaviourist competences display) into a more dynamic, process-focused mode – what I am calling 'inferential understanding'. He unpacks this when he states:

> According to the inferentialist account of concept use, in making [an explicit truth] claim one is implicitly endorsing a set of inferences, which articulate its conceptual content. Implicitly endorsing those inferences is a sort of doing. Understanding [sic] the conceptual content to which one

has committed oneself is a kind of practical mastery: a bit of know-how that consists in being able to discriminate what does and does not follow from the claim, what would be evidence for or against it and so on. (p. 19 [emphasis added])

In expressing this personal mastery – this competence – at and through work, adults find themselves committed to and bound up in sociocultural expectations, specific to their practices, that thus-and-so (whatever the course of action is) will be justifiable – and can be justified. That is the 'public' requirement for 'justification'.

This directly affects education and training. Now, workplaces that are serious about the productive exercise of generic competences and skills are keen to support them in favour of novel, unexpected outcomes, albeit those that contribute to strategic as well as individual purposes. My inferential understanding thus provides a theoretical underpinning for the making of a judgement ('knowing how and why' to go on). Such 'judgement-making' is a form of doing, where there are distinctive reasons articulable in that process of doing. These reasons can be distinctively novel, and unexpected. They provide the raw material for a claim on creativity. Thus the inference of understanding is perhaps *creatively* generative for others, as well as to the individual: 'I/She did x, because I/we/they can justify it like this …'.

The model of holistic, or integrated competence, which has been developed in Australia in the 1990s (outlined above) instantiates this theoretical analysis. To reiterate: this model is explicitly based on the *inference* of competence from an array of performative evidence, and is sensitive to the 'contextual' nature of generic skill formation and development.

The Australian model fits with the judgement-driven nature of workplace learning, and it invites a diversity of assessment evidence in support of judgements – inferences – of competence. Furthermore, this model can generate novel and distinctive outcomes: the competent practitioner, whose practice is defensibly competent, by reference to the public standards of a work-based peer group (such as profession, or occupational association or industry), can create new practices.

Such a process is an example of what Brandom called the 'communal self-correction' of individuals' actions – and even of identities. It also appears that holistic and generic competences, if these were to have any purchase on particular workplace experiences (that is, in the case of graduates, enhancing their 'employability'), would need to make available opportunities for this 'communal self-correction'. Group-based project work would be a workplace-specific example of this communal self-correction, where a new graduate or someone on field placement (whilst still in tertiary studies) could endeavour to display her or his generic skills in real life with real peers. Without such a context for the claim to possess or to have acquired generic skills, they float off the planet.

'Communal self-correction'

The case of the lawyer who reflects on what he brings to workplace judgements

This practitioner acknowledges the technical aspects of his competence as a lawyer – broadly, these are compliance requirements, then he launches in to less clear waters, where the ethic of legal practice is his standard of account-ability for his 'judgements-in-context':

> First of all you've got to comply with the rules – that's the rules laid down by the court, and the government, and the Law Institute, or what-ever professional body governs the actions of lawyers in this state.
>
> Then you've got to live with your own conscience and then you've got to live with your client, and what your client thinks is right and appropri-ate. And maybe what is right for the client's pocket. So you have to think about all those matters. That is you have to think about the legality of it, the ethics of it, and the client's interest. It's usually pretty obvious what the client's interest is because that's a minimal payout or resolution on the best commercial terms possible, or the best way of settling it in someone's interests. That's usually pretty clear. The legality is usually pretty clear – you usually know whether something's legal or illegal.
>
> Whether or not it sits with you morally can be a problem, but I have difficulty in thinking of ... I think you know what's wrong and what's right. And I would be instinctive in that. And if people put propositions to me on the phone ... you'd instinctively say, 'No that's not right'. Or, 'I don't think you can do that'. Or, 'You shouldn't do that'.

Notice how embedded the lawyer is in his commercial and community con-text, and how receptive he is to what his instincts tell him. This ability to take community and personal ethical standards as the catalyst for such instincts marks out expertise, as is now more widely recognized. Gigerenzer (2007), taking a research perspective on 'gut feelings', indicates how the expertise of experts is shown in the speed with which they cut to the deci-sional moments, discarding the psychic and experiential scaffolding that has defined their competence in the past. We may say that having climbed the ladder (of competence), we kick it away.

Montgomery (2006), in analysing the clinical judgements in medicine, puts the same point this way, in drawing upon the landmark 'novice to expert' work of Patricia Benner, for nursing: 'The acquisition of a clinical skill is a process that goes beyond mastery of rules ... to a stage where the rules are no longer recalled: each case is comprehended wholistically'. She acknowl-edges that Benner drew upon Dreyfus and Dreyfus, who 'maintain that experts reason not by methodical inference but "holographically" ...' (p. 35).

Montgomery, just a few pages earlier, states that clinical judgements are marked by 'practical reasoning necessitated by an absence of certainty' (p. 42), and, central to this analysis, what practitioners bring to such reasoning is '[d]escribed as intuition ... essential to good practice, those "gut feelings". This is 'a sort of know how: as nonscience, this must be art' (p. 30).

So our lawyer, like our psychologist, and before that, our accountant, work as much on their hunches, gut feelings, instincts and intuitions as much as on their technical or theoretical knowledge, in making competent, even expert 'judgements-in-context', through this capacity in inferential understanding.

The lawyer goes on:

> I'll discuss intuition, in a sense. Because I work in a very limited area which involves largely insurers, you get the feeling or the sense sometimes that some people are better than others at working out what the correct facts are. ...
>
> Now it is very difficult to know whether someone is telling the truth, has told the truth, or will tell the truth. And it's very hard to prove anyone wrong. But after a while I think you become more – stronger in your views. You work out that that's more likely than not to have happened. I don't know how you do it sometimes, except to say it's intuition. I guess it's something that just happens because people will ring me up on the telephone and put a particular fact situation to me, and I'll just say I don't believe it. Now why don't I believe it? I suppose because it's just something that I consider to be incredible. But I have to concede that sometimes I might be wrong.

Here is an explicit admission of the 'absence of certainty' Montgomery notes as a characteristic of clinical practice. The professional is casting about for communal self-corrections: he is embedded in the ethos of his profession, and in the public articulation of his decisionality – his judgements. How can we conceptualize this new epistemology of practice? I revive Aristotle's approach to the art of balanced judgement – and I am not alone in doing so.

Phronesis revived

The implication of the theorization outlined above for the epistemological 'junk categories' I named in the Introduction is profound. As Bent Flyvbjerg (2001) puts it;

> Regrettably, the pervasiveness of the rational paradigm to the near exclusion of others is a problem for the vast majority of professional education, and especially in practical fields such as engineering, policy analysis, management, planning and organisation. . .

This has caused people and entire scholarly disciplines to become blind to context, experience and intuition, even though these phenomena and ways of being are at least as important and necessary for good results as are analysis, rationality and rules. (pp. 24–25)

Flyvbjerg, however, directs us to the way forward, which I share:

The person possessing practical wisdom (*phronimos*) has knowledge of how to behave in each particular circumstance that can never be equated with or reduced to knowledge of general truths. *Phronesis* is a sense of the ethically practical, rather than a kind of science. (p. 57)

Aristotle's *phronesis* is indeed helpful (as Beckett & Hager 2002 claim) in making sense of this reliance upon strange experiences. Flyvbjerg goes on:

Phronesis goes beyond both analytical, scientific knowledge (*episteme*) and technical knowledge (*techne*) and involves judgements and decisions made in the manner of a virtuoso social and political actor. I will argue that *phronesis* is commonly involved in social practice ... (p. 2)
... and is [the] most important because it is that activity by which instrumental rationality is balanced by value rationality, and because such balancing is crucial to the sustained happiness of the citizens in any society, according to Aristotle. (p. 4)

And throughout his chapter entitled 'Rationality, body, and intuition in human learning', Flyvbjerg (2001) refers for support to the 'Dreyfus' model of competences and skill formation, suggesting that old traditional models of learning skills are unhelpful:

Practical experience consists precisely in an individual's ability to readily recognize skill and virtuoso experience. [In relating an experiment with paramedics and experienced teachers of paramedics ...] 'The teachers attempted to identify a competent rescuer by looking for individuals who best followed the rules the teachers themselves had taught their students in CPR. The teachers concept of "good" resuscitation technique was simply to follow the rules ... .Being novices, the students could do little else'.

Again, Montgomery (2006) articulates a similar way forward, for her, based on research in to how our contexuality frames our practices:

Bourdieu's habitus and Geertz's common sense are useful concepts because, like Aristotle's phronesis, they characterize a kind of knowing that is not hypothetico-deductive, not scientific, but nevertheless deserves the label 'rational'. Those who possess this rational capacity or virtue in great measure are often regarded as wise …

Because competent clinicians embody a habitual and "automatic" commonsense method of responsive knowing, the idea of a rationality that is both deeply ingrained and largely unaware of itself is essential to understanding their enculturation, the formation of the professional self.

(pp. 165–166)

Conclusion

I have tried to show how 'inferential understanding' gives due significance to the dynamics and realities of adults' workplaces, and to the processes now acknowledged in many workplaces – whether these be competences or generic skills – as advancing this 'communal self-correcting' of claims to know something expertly, or proficiently. This self-correction is the public articulation of reasons for acting.

The emergence of inferential understanding at work will take any number of forms depending on the variables in particular workplaces. This should guide the way generic skills and holistic competences are manifest: are there public ways workers (or learners, still in formal studies) can articulate their judgements about 'know how' which is by definition, located in 'local, personal and the particular' workplace experiences? This supplies the 'knowing why'. Teamwork, and other forms of socially reflective practice (for example, 360 degree appraisals, 'retreats', role plays, simulations, project- and problem-based groups) are some ways these articulations are made public, and similar activities should be pedagogically central in formal studies, especially in tertiary education.

In summary, an adult's learning at and from work through inferential understanding requires two things. First, a prior commitment to undergoing diverse experiences from which one can learn, and, second, a continuing commitment to the public articulation of reasons for one's judgements at work – one's daily business. I claim that lists of holistic competences and generic skills make no sense unless they show they are grounded in practical judgements and that the reasons practitioners can give for their judgements are publicly articulated among their peers.

Holistic competence based upon 'inferential understanding' requires not only one embodied practitioner but indeed a whole community of them, because the practices are public practices. Justifications of how one proceeded, or intends to proceed, or (more commonly) finds oneself proceeding are articulable in justifiable ways, depending on the values and norms of one's community. There will be a range of these, all overlapping, from the community of a workplace, of a profession, of a citizenry, and even up to the general level of humanity itself. Crane drivers will have these, of significance in railyards where containers are to be moved. Western education and training policy makers have not been able, or willing perhaps, to tap into these rich sources of knowledge. Rather than write off these 'knowings', as 'junk categories', my argument is that now, in this era of lifelong learning, on educational if not political grounds, we ignore them at our peril.

Let Montgomery (2006) have the last words here: our holistic competences are fluid, tentative and dynamic since they are, she states, 'bottom up rules of practice or maxims ... hedged and qualified, layered in memory with skepticism':

> What experienced clinicians possess ... is an immense and well-sorted catalogue of clinical cases and the clinical judgement to know how to use it, and that store of knowledge is activated by seeing, touching and questioning the patient. Such knowledge is varied and extensive enough so that the bottom-up rules of practice or maxims that the cases collectively embody are hedged and qualified, layered in memory with skepticism about their applicability to any particular patient. (pp. 34–35)

Acknowledgements

This chapter is adapted from an article by Han, S. (2008). Competence: Commodification of Human Ability. *Asia Pacific Education Review*, 9(1), 31-39. Reprinted with permission from Education Research Institute, Seoul National University.

Part of this chapter is based on Beckett (2004). Quotations are data from a University of Technology, Sydney, project on professionals' workplace learning, directed by Paul Hager and David Beckett (2000–1).

Chapter 6

Competence, learning and education

How can competences be learned, and how can they be developed in formal education?

Knud Illeris

From qualifications to competences

It is not so very many years ago that the concept of competence was mainly a formal and legal matter, something that gave a person a legal right to make decisions in a certain area, especially in terms of public administration. However, over the last two decades, the use of the word has permeated the areas of education, working life, management and politics as a modern expression for what a person is actually able to do or achieve.

During the 1990s, this led to a pronounced change in language usage in relation to the intended results of education and the human resource demands of the labour market, implying that the concept of 'competences' to a great extent was being substituted for that of 'qualifications'. Moreover, this was not just an incidental or trivial language renovation. It should rather be understood as an attempt to take the full consequences of the change in the types of abilities that were demanded.

The concept of qualifications has its roots in industrial sociology and fundamentally relates to labour demands for concrete knowledge and skills. Most significantly, it was used in relation to the so-called de-qualification of labour demands as a result of industrialization (cf. Braverman 1974). However, this was gradually accompanied by a trend towards an increase in demand for a range of personal or generic qualifications such as flexibility, reliability, responsibility, creativity and independence.

Conversely, the concept of competences was first taken up in organizational psychology and modern management. Here, the point of departure is on the personal level, referring especially to the individual ability and readiness to meet the changing challenges of a job. Precisely such competences as the above-mentioned personal and generic qualifications are needed for this purpose, while the more definite qualifications take on the character of something that can be drawn in and contribute to implementing the competences in specific situations.

This could also be expressed by saying that the concept of competences attempts to include different types of qualifications in an understanding which spans a person's potential and practical abilities at one and the same time, that is a holistic concept integrating all that is necessary to manage a given situation or challenge: the concrete qualifications are integrated into the personal competence in relation to a specific task. Whereas the qualification approach started with the single elements and gradually developed in the direction of a more coherent understanding, the competence approach starts with a whole – such as the type of person who will be able to manage a certain task – and from this position, eventually identifies different qualifications that must be available or acquired.

A definition of competences

When dealing with the concept of competence, however, it soon becomes very apparent that there is great uncertainty about and great variety in interpretations of what precisely is meant. Many very different definitions have been proposed and none of them can be said to be authoritative or generally accepted. In accordance with the considerations above I think, however, that the following proposal points to the most important and far-reaching qualities of the concept:

> The concept of competence refers [...] to a person's being qualified in a broader sense. It is not merely that a person masters a professional area, but also that the person can apply this professional knowledge – and more than that, apply it in relation to the requirements inherent in a situation which, in addition, may be uncertain and unpredictable. Thus competence also includes the person's assessments and attitudes, and ability to draw on a considerable part of his/her personal qualifications. (Jørgensen 1999: 4)

This definition is – as I see it – adequate primarily because it includes the central condition that competences involve the ability to deal appropriately with future and unforeseen situations. Australian David Beckett and Paul Hager accordingly regard the crucial quality of a competence as the ability to immediately make the professionally proper judgements and decisions in all the new situations that constantly arise in working life (Beckett & Hager 2002; Beckett in this volume). It is precisely this quality that makes competences so important and attractive in this modern, ever-changing world, and at the same time constitutes an immense challenge to education and training of any kind. How can people be educated or trained to function appropriately in situations that are unknown at the time of the acquisition?

This is actually a question that undermines a great deal of traditional educational thinking that takes as its starting point the formulation of precise objectives and then tries to deduce educational measures from these. Fundamentally, it must be realized that competences are not something that can be produced like commodities, but must be developed in and by the person, hence the concept of 'competence development'.

The orientation towards development and future situations is the central quality placing the concept of competences so much more in line with modern demands than the concept of qualifications. In this regard, it must, however, be noted that competences (as a concept) are sometimes connected with an air of trendiness, which may contribute to the popularity of the concept in management and policy circles but makes it problematic in academic discussions.

In general, it is obvious that the concept of competences captures something that is essential in relation to education and learning today, precisely because it relates to how a person, an organization or a nation is able to manage in a constantly changing globalized market society. Thus, the societal changes that fostered this concept and other linked concepts such as 'the learning society', 'the learning organization' and 'lifelong learning' imply a new conception of the relation between learning and education/training with an increased focus on informal learning possibilities outside the educational institutions in daily life and in working life especially.

However, to capture the impact of this change of perspective it is not enough just to refer to 'practice learning' or 'learning in working life' as has often been the case. It is obvious that the school and education system will still be the 'State Apparatus' which is constructed to be the fundamental public means of providing the competences demanded. Moreover, it will inevitably – also in the future – be in the practical and economic interests of both the private and the public sector that as many competences as possible should be developed outside working life and without placing a strain on the economy and daily working conditions of companies and organizations.

Therefore competence development cannot be a means of making savings on public education budgets, something that some politicians seem to imagine to be the case. On the contrary, it is a challenge demanding increased cooperation between education and training institutions and private as well as public workplaces. In all likelihood, this will lead to increased costs for both parties if the promises of adequate and up-to-date competence development are to be met – which is regarded as a key factor in future competitiveness.

Finally, it must also be stressed that a decisive factor in all this will be that competence development programmes are set up in accordance and cooperation with the persons and groupings that are to implement the competences. Whereas qualifications to some extent could be understood and dealt with as 'objective' qualities, it is inherent in competences that they include personal and collective motivations, emotions and engagement, and their practical value to a great extent is dependent on a positive interest and attitude. From this point of view, competence development could be an important democratizing factor in working life and society in general. However, this is by no means always the case.

Therefore, a persistent question is whether the great commitment to the idea of competence development will be able to meet the positive prospects that it most certainly implies. Like other keywords from the same vocabulary, the concept of competence development seems to have a double impact and to demonstrate tension between a very promising and useful interpretation of very real and significant demands of modern societies and a mere buzzword, which, behind the tempting surface, hides new and 'clever' means of human and economic exploitation of labour.

As competence development is an advanced kind of learning, a more serious and practicable understanding of the concept could perhaps be achieved by resorting to a basic and comprehensive learning theory to see what specific qualities are required in order for a learning process to obtain the nature of competence development. In the following I shall therefore briefly explain some fundamental features of the learning theory which I have fully developed in my recent book, *How We Learn: Learning and non-learning in school and beyond* (Illeris 2007), and relate these features to the issue of competence development.

The dimensions of learning and competence development

The first important condition to realize is that all learning implies the integration of two very different processes, both of which must be active if learning is to take place. The two processes will usually be integrated and experienced as one and the same, but in certain situations, especially in the case of what we call reflection, there may be a displacement.

The one process involves the external interaction between the learner and his or her social, cultural and material environment, which takes place whenever we are awake but can be more or less intensive and conscious. The criteria of this process are of a historical, geographical and societal nature, dependent on time and place.

The other process is the internal psychological process of elaboration and acquisition, which connects the impulses and impressions of the interaction with the results of prior learning and thereby forms the learning outcome. It is important to realize that this is always a linking of the new to the knowledge, skills, understandings, attitudes and behaviour patterns etc. that have already been developed, and is thus a most individual construction. Even if several learners receive the same impulses as, for instance, in a traditional teaching situation, the learning outcomes will be different, because to some extent the broad scope of individual preconditions involved will always be different. The criteria of the acquisition process are biological and psychological – depending on the very complex learning potentials developed by the human species and the prior learning and experience of the individual learner.

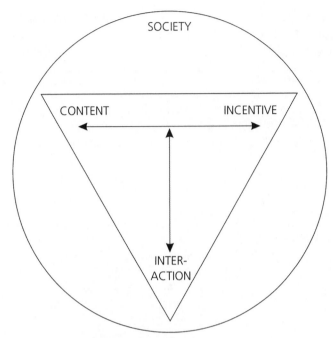

Figure 6.1 The processes and dimensions of learning.

Further, the acquisition process has the nature of integrated interplay between two equal psychological functions involved in any learning, namely the function of managing the learning content, and the incentive function of providing and directing the necessary mental energy that runs the process. There is always a learning content – it is impossible to learn without learning *something* – but there is always an incentive also, a mobilization of energy, and the nature and strength of the incentive force is decisive for the nature and validity of the outcome. What is learned with strong engagement is generally learned in a more differentiated way and is easier to remember and apply.

The fundamental processes and dimensions of learning can be depicted as in Figure 6.1. The fundamental processes of interaction and acquisition are depicted as two double arrows spanning out a triangular field between the three angles that constitute the three dimensions of learning. It is the core claim of this understanding of learning that all learning will always involve these three dimensions.

The content dimension concerns what is learned. This is usually described as knowledge and skills, but many other elements such as opinions, insight, meaning, attitudes, values, ways of behaviour, methods, strategies etc. may also be involved as learning content and contribute to building up the understanding and the capacity of the learner. The endeavour of the learner is to construct *meaning* and the *ability* to deal with the challenges of practical life. An overall personal *functionality* is thereby developed.

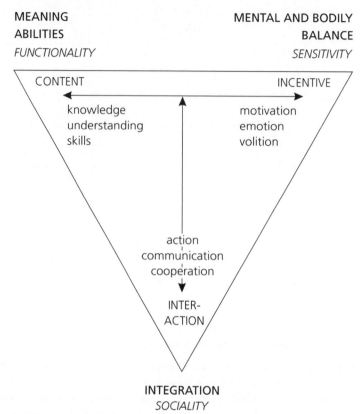

Figure 6.2 The structure of learning as competence development.

The incentive dimension provides and directs the mental energy that is necessary for the learning process to take place. It comprises such elements as feelings, emotions, motivation and volition. Its ultimate function is to secure the continuous *mental balance* of the learner and thereby it simultaneously develops a personal *sensitivity*.

These two dimensions are always initiated by impulses from the interaction processes and integrated in the internal process of elaboration and acquisition. Therefore, the learning content is, so to speak, always 'obsessed' with the incentives at stake – for example whether the learning is driven by desire, interest, necessity or compulsion. Correspondingly, the incentives are always influenced by the content, for example new information can change the incentive condition.

The interaction dimension provides the impulses that initiate the learning process. This may take place as perception, transmission, experience, imitation, activity, participation etc. (Illeris 2007: 100ff). It serves the personal *integration* in communities and society and thereby also builds up the *sociality* of the learner. However, this building up necessarily takes place through the two other dimensions.

Thus the triangle depicts what may be described as the tension field of learning in general and of any specific learning event or learning process as stretched out between the development of functionality, sensitivity and sociality – which are also the general components of what we term *competences* (see Figure 6.2).

In relation to competence development, it is very important to emphasize that precisely these three qualities of learning – functionality, sensitivity and sociality – are the basic building blocks of competences. It is the strength of these qualities that is decisive for the extent to which learning takes on the nature of competence development. The holistic demand that this concept implies can adequately be specified into a claim that functionality, sensitivity and sociality must be involved with considerable weight in relation to the area in question. Therefore, for learning to have the quality of competence development it must include all three learning dimensions in ways that are important and relevant in relation to the required competence.

The four types of learning

What has been outlined in the triangle model and the discussion above is a concept of learning which is basically constructivist in nature, that is it is assumed that the learner him or herself actively builds up or construes his/her learning as mental structures. These structures exist in the brain as dispositions that are usually described with a psychological metaphor as *mental schemes*. This means that there must be some organization of the learning outcomes in the brain since when we become aware of something – a person, a topic, a problem etc. – we are able to recall in a fraction of a second what we subjectively and usually unconsciously define as relevant knowledge, understanding, attitudes, reactions and the like. But this organization is in no way a sort of archive and it is not possible to find the different elements at specific positions in the brain. It has the nature of what brain researchers call 'engrams', which are traces of circuits between some of the billions of neurons that have been active on earlier occasions and therefore are likely to be revived, perhaps with slightly different courses because of the impact of new experiences or understandings.

However, in order to deal systematically with this, the concept of schemes is used for what we subjectively tend to classify as belonging to a specific topic or theme and therefore mentally connect and are inclined to recall in situations that we relate to that topic or theme. This applies to the content dimension in particular, whereas in the incentive and interaction dimensions we speak rather of *mental patterns*. But the background is similarly that motivations, emotions or ways of communication tend to be organized so that they can be revived when we are oriented towards situations that 'remind' us of earlier situations where they have been active.

In terms of learning, the crucial thing is that new impulses can be included in the mental organization in various ways, and on this basis it is possible to distinguish between four different types of learning that are activated in different contexts, imply different kinds of learning results, and require more or less mental energy. (This is an elaboration of the concept of learning originally developed by the Swiss biologist and epistemologist Jean Piaget (e.g. Piaget 1952, Flavell 1963)).

When a scheme or pattern is established, it is a case of *cumulative* or mechanical learning. This type of learning is characterized by being an isolated formation, something new that is not a part of anything else. Therefore, cumulative learning is most frequent during the first years of life, but later occurs only in special situations where one must learn something with no context of meaning or personal significance, for example a pin code. The learning result is characterized by a type of automation that means that it can only be recalled and applied in situations mentally similar to the learning context. It is mainly this type of learning that is involved in the training of animals and which is therefore also referred to in the concept of conditioning in behaviourist psychology.

By far the most common type of learning is termed *assimilative* or learning by addition, meaning that the new elements are linked as an addition to a scheme or pattern that is already established. One typical example could be learning in school subjects that are usually built up by means of constant additions to what has already been learned, but assimilative learning also takes place in all contexts where one gradually develops one's capacities. The results of learning are characterized by being linked to the scheme or pattern in question in such a manner that it is relatively easy to recall and apply them when one is mentally oriented towards the field in question, for example a school subject, while they may be hard to access in other contexts. This is why problems are frequently experienced in applying knowledge from a school subject in other subjects or in contexts outside school (Illeris 2009).

However, in some cases, situations occur where something takes place that is difficult to immediately relate to any existing scheme or pattern. This is experienced as something one cannot really understand or relate to. But if it seems important or interesting, if it is something one is determined to acquire, this can take place by means of *accommodative* or transcendent learning. This type of learning implies that one breaks down (parts of) an existing scheme and transforms it so that the new situation can be linked in. Thus one both relinquishes and reconstructs something and this can be experienced as demanding or even painful, because it is something that requires a strong supply of mental energy. One must transcend existing limitations and understand or accept something that is significantly new or different, and this is much more demanding than just adding a new element to an already existing scheme or pattern. In return, the results of such learning are characterized by the fact that they can be recalled and applied in many different, relevant contexts. It is typically experienced as having understood or got hold of something that one really has internalized.

Finally, over the last decades it has been pointed out that in special situations there is also a far-reaching type of learning that has been variously described as significant (Rogers 1951, 1969), expansive (Engeström 1987), transitional (Alheit 1994) or *transformative* learning (Mezirow 1991). This learning implies what could be termed personality changes or changes in the organization of the self and is characterized by simultaneous restructuring of a whole cluster of schemes and patterns in all the three learning dimensions – a break of orientation that typically occurs as the result of a crisis-like situation caused by challenges experienced as urgent and unavoidable, making it necessary to change oneself in order to move on. Transformative learning is thus both profound and extensive, it demands a lot of mental energy and when accomplished it can often be experienced physically, typically as a feeling of relief or relaxation.

As has been demonstrated, the four types of learning are widely different in scope and nature, and they also occur – or are activated by learners – in very different situations and connections. Whereas cumulative learning is most important in early childhood and transformative learning is a very demanding process that changes the very personality or identity and occurs only in very special situations of profound significance for the learner, assimilation and accommodation are, as described by Piaget, the two types of learning that characterize general, sound and normal everyday learning. Many other learning theorists also point to two similar types of learning, for example American Chris Argyris and Donald Schön have coined the well-known concepts of single and double loop learning (Argyris 1992, Argyris & Schön 1996), Swedish Per-Erik Ellström speaks about adaptation oriented and development oriented learning (Ellström 2001), and Russian Lev Vygotsky's widespread idea of transition into the 'Zone of proximal development' may also be seen as a parallel to accommodative learning (Vygotsky 1978).

However, the descriptions of the four learning types immediately imply that while traditional school learning and education predominantly promote assimilative learning, competence development demands that accommodative and in some cases also transformative learning are involved to a considerable extent. This means that if formalized education is to result in more than incidental competence development, it must include learning activities that are aimed at and adequate for these types of learning – such as, for example problem solving, investigations, projects, and practice of various kinds (e.g. Olesen & Jensen 1999; Illeris 2004; Illeris *et al.* 2004).

Barriers to learning

Another problem in relation to learning is that much intended learning does not take place or is incomplete or distorted. In schools, in education, at workplaces and in many other situations, people very often do not learn what they could learn or what they are supposed to learn. Therefore I find it important also to discuss briefly what happens in such cases.

Of course, it cannot be avoided that we all sometimes learn something that is wrong (cf. Mager 1961) and something that is inadequate for us in some way or other. In the first instance, this concerns matters such as mislearning, which can be due to misunderstandings, lack of concentration, insufficient prior learning, unclear or inadequate teaching and the like. This may be annoying and in some cases unlucky, but simple mislearning due to 'practical' causes is not a matter of great interest to learning theory as such mislearning can usually be corrected rather easily, if necessary.

However, today much non-learning and mislearning are not so simple, but have a background in some general conditions that modern society creates, and in some respects the investigation and understanding of such processes are definitely as important as more traditional learning theory to understand what is happening and how to cope with it in practice.

The central point is that in our complex late modern society what Freud called defence mechanisms – which are active in specific personal connections (cf. Anna Freud 1942) – must necessarily be generalized and take more systematized forms because nobody can manage to remain open to the gigantic volumes and impact of influences we are all constantly faced with.

This is why today people develop a kind of semi-automatic sorting mechanism vis-à-vis the many influences, or what the German social psychologist Thomas Leithäuser has analysed and described as an *everyday consciousness* (Leithäuser 1976). This functions in the way that one develops some general pre-understandings within certain thematic areas and these pre-understandings are activated when one meets with influences within such an area, so that if elements in the influences do not correspond to the pre-understandings, they are either rejected or distorted to make them agree. In both cases, this results in no new learning but, on the contrary, often in the cementing of the already-existing understanding.

Thus, through everyday consciousness we control our own learning and non-learning in a manner that seldom involves any direct positioning while simultaneously involving a massive defence of the already acquired understandings and, in the final analysis, our very identity. (There are, of course, also areas and situations where our positioning takes place in a more target-oriented manner, consciously and flexibly.)

However, not only the volume but also the type of influence can be overwhelming. For example, on television we are faced every day with so much cruelty, wickedness and similar negative impact that it is absolutely impossible to really take it in. People who cannot protect themselves from this are doomed to end up with some kind of psychological breakdown. Other new forms of similar overloading are caused by the endless changes and reorganizations many people experience at their workplaces, social institutions etc. or the helplessness that can be felt when consequences of the decisions of those in power encroach on one's life situation and possibilities.

In the most important cases, for instance when a change to a basically new situation in a certain life area must be overcome, most people react by mobi-lizing a genuine *identity defence* which demands very hard work of a more or less therapeutic character to break through, usually by a transformative learn-ing process. This happens typically in relation to a sudden situation of unemployment or other fundamental changes in the work situation, divorce, death of closely related persons, or the like, and it is worth realizing that such situations happen much more frequently in the modern globalized market society of today than just a generation ago.

Another very common form of defence is *ambivalence*, meaning that in a certain situation or connection one both wants and does not want to learn or do something. A typical example is that of people who unwillingly and through no fault of their own become unemployed. They are, on the one hand, fully aware that they must engage in some retraining or re-education, but, on the other hand, strongly wish that this was not the case. So they go or are sent to some courses but it is difficult for them to concentrate on the learning and they use every possible excuse to escape, mentally or physically.

In all such defence situations learning is obstructed, hindered, derailed or distorted if it is not possible for the learner to break through the defence, and the task of a teacher or instructor will often be to support and encourage such a break-through before more goal-directed and constructive training or edu-cation can take place. But teachers are usually not trained for such functions although these functions quite frequently are necessary if the intended learn-ing is to be promoted.

Another psychological mechanism that may block or distort relevant learning is mental *resistance*. In itself this is not so very time-specific, as all human beings in any society will experience situations where what they try to accomplish cannot be carried through, and if they cannot understand or accept the barriers they will naturally react with some sort of resistance.

In practice it is sometimes quite difficult to distinguish between non-learn-ing caused by defence and non-learning caused by resistance. However, psychologically there is a great and important difference. Whereas the defence mechanisms exist prior to the learning situation and function re-actively, resis-tance is an active response caused by the learning situation itself. Thus resistance contains a strong mental mobilization and therefore also a strong learning potential, especially for accommodative and even transformative learning. Often when one does not just accept something, the possibility of learning something significantly new emerges. And most great steps forward in the development of mankind and society have taken place when someone did not accept a given truth or way of doing or understanding things.

In everyday life, resistance is also a most important source of transcendent learning although it may be both inconvenient and annoying, not least for teachers. In any event, today it should be a central qualification of teachers to be able to cope with and even inspire mental resistance, as precisely such per-sonal competences which are so much in demand – for example, independence, responsibility, flexibility and creativity – are likely to be developed in this way. This is why raising conflicts or dilemmas may be included as effective, but demanding techniques in some particularly challenging educational situations.

Learning defence plays a very big role today in terms of competence development. The steadily more pressing demands for learning and personal development in all sorts of situations imply that to a growing extent everybody has to develop comprehensive defence systems. In this way it becomes problematic how individuals can develop consciousness and self direction concerning which influences and impulses to allow through the defence and in which situations a higher degree of openness is appropriate. Psychologically this is a very complex matter closely connected to such issues as the development of positive learning environments and space for reflection – two areas which in this way become decisive for learning to take on the nature of competence development.

Another and similarly demanding psychological issue of great importance for competence development is how to make room for the transcendent potentials involved in learning resistance. In this context it is important both to be able to recognize resistance and to permit it to be expressed and help it be qualified and transformed into changes and development.

Learning requirements for competence development

The most essential conditions that are crucial for learning in different situations to take on the nature of competence development can be summarized as follows:

- The three dimensions of learning – content, incentive and interaction – should all be activated in significant, conscious and relevant ways in relation to the desired competence development.
- Learning processes should be arranged and practised in ways that make room for assimilative, accommodative and also transformative learning, if applicable.
- The learning environment should include possibilities for the reflectivity that is necessary to overcome learning defence and for learning resistance to be expressed and transformed into development.

It is not the intention of this chapter to delve deeper into how these conclusions can be transformed into practice. Conditions and traditions are extremely different in different countries and settings and it is always important to observe local possibilities. In Denmark, experience over almost 40 years has pointed to two main roads. One is, inside the education and training system, to apply problem-oriented and participant-directed project work and project studies. Since this was introduced at Roskilde University in 1972 it has spread in a lot of different ways to almost all parts of the educational system, including primary and secondary school, vocational education and training and most professional training and retraining programmes (Illeris 1991, 1999, 2007; Olesen & Jensen 1999). The other is to carry further the traditional exchange programmes between workplaces and schools that have been used in connection with apprenticeship and some professional training programmes for more than a century (Illeris *et al.* 2004). Another important contribution to mention here is the work on the issues of 'situated learning' and 'communities of practice' as described in various publications by American Jean Lave and Etienne Wenger (see e.g. Lave & Wenger 1991; Wenger 1998).

However, in general it is obvious that traditional, institutionalized education and training activities do not fit in with the conclusions above. These activities are characterized by a dominating focus on the content dimension of learning, assimilative processes and a quite insufficient understanding of learning defence and resistance. Even in cases where much has been done over many years to overcome these restrictive conditions, for example by means of group work, more reflective procedures, new forms of assessment etc., traditional classroom teaching and exams tend to persist and occupy the major part of the time. Moreover, political attitudes towards new pedagogical and educational ideas have generally been ambivalent, if not hostile.

But when these limitations are observed from a perspective of learning theory and the conditions for competence development, it also becomes obvious that moving the learning activities outside the institutions is not in itself sufficient to change the picture in any decisive way.

This is because even when the three learning dimensions are involved in practice in a much more direct way than in the institutions, even when the chances that all learning types are involved are considerably better, and even when in practice there often seem to be better possibilities to counter defence and qualify resistance towards relevant learning, there is absolutely no guarantee that all this will actually function as hoped or expected.

On the contrary, at many workplaces, public as well as private, there are lots of reasons why, for example, learning motivation is low, transcending processes are blocked by routines and traditions, there are heaps of defence mechanisms related to work pressure, stress, unprofitable resistance due to power conditions and the like. For these and many other reasons the learning environment is often very restrictive – even if a 'learning organization' is what is aimed at and asserted and a favourable learning environment is what the management is trying to establish.

Finally, it is fundamentally important to realize and take into account that workplaces basically exist to produce goods and services and not – like the educational institutions – to produce learning and competence development. This implies that as soon as there is pressure of time and it becomes difficult to consider everything, the immediately productive activities will tend to be prioritized – and in modern working life such pressed situations seem to be the rule rather than the exception. Or put in a different way: at many contemporary workplaces workers and employees experience work pressure which is so massive and work demands which are so heavy that this in reality stands in the way of anything but very hasty, superficial and incentive learning processes. And it is of no use deceiving oneself by claiming that many things are learned better under pressure. One can perhaps learn to wriggle out of trouble and cope but very often such adjustments are precisely what postpone and stand in the way of proper competence development.

Decision making and power conditions

In addition to the general discussion of learning activities, learning environment and the problematic conditions of traditional education and training in relation to the need for competence development, to complete the picture some other important topics should also be addressed.

One of these topics is about direction of the learning activities. Of course, authorities and institutions are responsible for the more general decisions about educational programmes. But the need for competence development strongly implies that as much as possible should be left open to be decided by the participants at floor level, that is the students, teachers and instructors who are actually involved in the everyday activities.

This is because a core quality of competences, as previously mentioned, is the ability to make qualified professional judgements and decisions. As a consequence of this, it is obviously important that as part of their competence development students are involved in and get used to taking part in relevant professional decisions, not least about the professional content and nature of the learning activities. This makes it both appropriate and necessary that there is as much latitude as possible to allow participants to involve themselves in essential decision-making processes about their own competence development, making it worthwhile for them to engage in these. Being involved in rather indifferent decisions produces no competence development.

This is important, not least because many countries are currently tightening the frame conditions of the educational and training systems. This implies, on the one side, increased institutional direction and control of the content and exams and, on the other side, that institutions are made independent and thus become regulated by the market economy. Both sides seem to result in a higher degree of top-down management so that students come to take general conditions and power structures for granted and adjust to adaptation. In this way they do not get used to reflecting on how things are decided and organized – which clearly contradicts the essence of competence development.

Another quite different issue to consider is the situation of the low skilled and others for whom daily, ordinary learning demands involve genuine problems and defeat. To some extent freer and more practice oriented learning

activities can form an opening for these students – who in Denmark constitute approximately 20–25 per cent of the population. But they will also quite
often experience having to make a lot of decisions about their own activities
as another threatening demand on them. They are usually the first to ask for a
clear framework of rules and teacher directed activities so that they know
what to do and what is expected from them. However, this does not result in
much competence development – as I have defined and used this concept here
– and therefore in the long run they are let down if they only learn to do as
they are told.

Thus the answer to this must be that teachers and instructors take on the
task of helping these students to gradually take responsibility for themselves
and to join the common discussions and decision making processes. This is
actually quite a challenging task, partly because it is often a hard process for
these students to come through – even though they will usually want to do so
if they have been brought to see its importance – but also because what is
actually demanded of the teacher in this situation is to take responsibility for
gradually transferring power and influence from him or herself to students.
This demands a certain degree of insight and self-discipline, because in general we are not used to deliberately relinquishing power and influence (Illeris
1998, Weil *et al.* 2004).

Some concluding points

The last point not least makes it clear that the issue of competence development implies some very complex challenges to different levels of the
education and training systems:

- Generally, the first demand is to move the concept out of its current status as a buzzword, take it seriously and openly analyse the conditions and
  challenges it generates in the various parts of the system. The considerations above can only be taken as a point of departure in this connection,
  and more concrete considerations must be taken up by those who are
  involved in the different areas.
- Next, it must be taken seriously that effective and goal-directed competence development implies that stringent top-down direction of
  educational and training activities leaves very little space for adequate
  experience making at floor level. A general rule of thumb should be not to
  decide and direct more than absolutely necessary at any higher level and
  accordingly leave as much as possible to be decided by the students, teachers and instructors who are actually involved in the learning practices.
- Finally, it must be observed that competence development demands
  active learning patterns that are problem- and practice-oriented and
  involve relevant judgement and decision making as well as individual
  and social reflection. As competence is in the nature of the potential to

think and act adequately in unknown future situations, it is important that education and training for this purpose should involve problem solving, individual and social self-direction, relevant professional decision making and systematic reflection about what to learn and how to learn it, and how learning activities have contributed or not contributed to the development of desired competences.

Competence development is not a production process that can be planned and directed from the outside. It is rather a personal and social endeavour to grow to deal with a complex world by taking part in important and complex professional activities. If there is no room for the engagement and participation of those who are to develop their competences, there will hardly be any adequate competence development. Thus, trying to bring about competence development by force and direction is as hopeless as trying to make things grow by restricting them.

Acknowledgements

This chapter is adapted from an article by Hjort, K. (2008). Competence Development in the Public Sector: Development, or Dismantling of Professionalism? *Asia Pacific Education Review*, 9(1), 40–49. Reprinted with permission from Education Research Institute, Seoul National University.

Chapter 7

Learning to be an expert

Competence development and expertise

Peter Jarvis

An expert is one who 'has extensive skill or knowledge in a particular field' or someone who is 'skilful or knowledgeable' (Collins English Dictionary 1979). Perhaps the dictionary should also have offered the possibility that an expert is both skilful and knowledgeable. Yet it would be true to say that for a number of years the word 'expert' has fallen into something like disrepute as terms such as 'competence' have dominated the vocabulary of political correctness. On the other hand, in the circles of Human Resource Development, 'expertise' seems to be more centrally placed than 'competence', at least in the USA (Swanson 2001).

But we have all been witnesses to deskilling as the world of technology has intruded into the worlds of production and service. It has changed the nature of work and, therefore, of work preparation. Even Lyotard (1984: 48) wrote about higher education and the higher professions:

> In the context of delegitimation, universities and institutions of higher learning are called upon to create skills, and no longer ideals – so many doctors, so many teachers in a given discipline, so many engineers, so many administrators, etc. The transmission of knowledge is no longer designed to train an elite capable of guiding the nation towards its emancipation, but to supply the system with players capable of acceptably fulfilling their roles at the pragmatic posts required by its institutions.

But, despite this emphasis, we have not destroyed the need for experts, although we have wrongly downplayed it in recent years, as I want to argue here. If we carefully examine the new workforce, we can see that there are many who have been deskilled, those whom Reich (1991) called the routine production workers, whose employment involves operating technology that has removed the skill from the production processes; they can be trained to operate the machinery and with every new piece of technology they can be updated and once they have learned it, then they go and operate it. They are the flexible workforce since they can be trained to operate almost any piece of machinery. In addition, those who do the routine manual and service but nontechnological jobs also need to be competent and can be trained to be so. But there are still other types of workers who have just as great a need of expertise (both knowledge and skills) as they have ever had, and there are at least three types of worker who fall into this category: the professionals, the crafts and trades people and those who work with people (managers and sales people). This is not a matter of dividing the workforce into those who need knowledge and those who need skills – it is about dividing it between those who need expertise and those who need competence. Both of these may be understood as a potential – for work and for life in general, but whereas competence has more the nature of a general potential in a broader field, expertise is rather involving specific knowledge and skills in a specific subject or area. My concern in this chapter is with those who need expertise and I want to focus on three aspects underlying the process of becoming an expert – the nature of knowledge, practice and learning – and in the final section I want to examine some implications of this for vocational education.

The nature of knowledge

Knowledge has been traditionally regarded as theoretical, objective and an unchanging truth, but in recent years this has been recognized as misleading. Objectively, there are data and information but they are not necessarily unchanging. They are objective in as much as they can exist outside of and beyond the knowledge of those people who do not know. Data and information are the knowledge of those who propound them but they only become other people's knowledge when they have been learned subjectively. Then they become knowledge and as knowledge develops through experience and practice it might assume the form of wisdom – knowledge and wisdom are learned – much is actually learned by doing rather than just by thinking. We will return to the nature of learning below – but in the first instance, we see that the transmission of data and information are part of the curriculum of vocational education but knowledge and wisdom cannot be taught, only learned. This distinction between objective and subjective knowledge is fairly recent and traditionally scholars have not separated objective and subjective knowledge in this way but rather just referred to it all as knowledge – but not all knowledge carries equal status or significance.

But as early as 1926 the German sociologist Max Scheler (Stikkers, 1980: 76) began to classify knowledge into seven types based upon their speed of change:

- myth and legend – undifferentiated religious, metaphysical, natural and historical;
- knowledge implicit in everyday language – as opposed to learned, poetic or technical;
- religious – from pious to dogmatic;

- mystical;
- philosophic-metaphysical;
- positive knowledge – mathematics, the natural sciences and the humanities;
- technological.

Scheler regarded his final two forms of knowledge as the most artificial because they changed so rapidly, whereas the other five are more embedded in culture. We might dispute with Scheler about many aspects of this typology, including the fact that the humanities are coupled with mathematics and the natural sciences – indeed, I would place them in the same category as philosophical and metaphysical knowledge. While his analysis was over-simple, he did make it nearly one hundred years ago. Nevertheless, he makes the point clearly that many forms of positive and technological knowledge change rapidly – he suggested 'hour by hour' – but that was in 1926 and now it might be minute by minute! Consider how quickly the mobile phone or the personal computer, for instance, get out of date and how often there is pressure to purchase a new one in order to get up to date, even though we may not need it. Think of the amount of research and new knowledge necessary to produce these new commodities for this knowledge economy. Not all scientific knowledge changes rapidly: the speed of light, for instance, has not changed, whereas our understanding of the nature of light has changed. Hence, Scheler's typology, while useful for our discussion only represents some aspects of our understanding of the complex nature of knowledge itself. While he was not totally correct, his artificial forms of knowledge are related to the dominant forms of knowledge in the knowledge society and it is these that workers have to know, even to produce.

It is those societies that are at the centre of economic globalization that might be seen as knowledge societies: it is these that Daniel Bell (1973) first called the post-industrial societies. For him, knowledge is the fundamental resource for such societies, especially theoretical knowledge (Bell 1973: 14) and, as Stehr (1994: 10) pointed out, when these societies emerge they signal a fundamental shift in the structure of the economy, since the primacy of manufacturing is replaced by knowledge. It is not knowledge per se that is significant to the knowledge society but scientific – including social scientific – knowledge (Stehr 1994: 99–103) since it underlies production of new commodities and services and, consequently, has economic value. Knowledge in itself has no intrinsic value; it is only its use-value as a scarce resource which is significant. Indeed, certain forms of new knowledge are a scarce resource and usable in the production of goods and services for the market of consumption. Every marginal addition to the body of scientific knowledge is potentially valuable in the knowledge economy.

If some forms of knowledge are changing so rapidly, the question needs to be asked, how do we know that they are true? It was Lyotard (1984) who answered this question when he referred to performativity, that is that useful knowledge works – it has use-value. Knowledge then is not just something that exists in the mind, it has got to work in practice. Practical knowledge has become a dominant form of knowledge in the work place – and this again is something that is learned rather than taught, although teaching can play some part in the process. Since there is a great emphasis on practical knowledge, curricula have to be more practical than in previous years, although universities especially have not traditionally concentrated on the practical aspects of the knowledge that they have taught, and so when they are teaching practical subjects they need to recognize that they should teach not only *knowledge that* but also *knowledge how*. But even *knowledge how* is not the same as *being able to* and there is no conceptual relationship between the two – *being able to* is learned in practice while neither *knowledge how* nor *knowledge that* are learned exclusively in practice.

However, Stehr's assertion about the knowledge economy utilizing artificial, or rapidly changing, knowledge is correct and it has at least two implications that concern us here: first, these artificial forms of knowledge soon become out of date so that initial vocational preparation must focus on the short term and, second, there is a tendency to omit those other cultural forms of knowledge, such as moral knowledge, from our considerations as insignificant for vocational preparation since they apparently have no use-value. We will return to both of these points, but before we move on we can see that each of these three types of worker needs a practical knowledge base in order to function in practice, even though the new worker remains a novice at the outset. However, it must be emphasized that the knowledge economy demands, even if it does not need such, highly qualified novices when they embark upon their careers (Livingstone 2002). I do not want to discuss this point here, but it is one of the un-debated discourses of the knowledge economy that requires more consideration.

The nature of practice

Traditionally, it was assumed that the knowledge learned in the classroom could be applied to practice and we used to talk about practice being the application of theory. But gradually over the past two decades we have learned that there is a major gap between theory and practice and when I wrote *The Practitioner Researcher* (Jarvis 1999), I assumed that practice preceded the practitioners' own theory – or rather their own practical knowledge. Practice is the process of transforming *knowledge that* and *knowledge how* into *being able to* – itself a process of learning. We all learn by doing – doing is an indication of being and intention.

However, the process of learning to be able is a much more complicated process than merely applying theory to practice as Nyiri (1988: 20–21) made clear:

One becomes an expert not simply by absorbing explicit knowledge of the type found in text-books, but through experience, that is, through repeated trials, 'failing, succeeding, wasting time and effort ... getting a feel for the problem, learning when to go by the book and when to break the rules'. Human experts gradually absorb 'a repertory of working rules of thumb, or "heuristics", that combined with book knowledge, make them expert practitioners'. This practical, heuristic knowledge, as attempts to simulate it on the machine have shown, is 'hardest to get at because experts – or anyone else – rarely have the self-awareness to recognize what it is. So it must be mined out of their heads painstakingly, one jewel at a time.' [All quotations from Feigenbaum and McCorduck 1984]

As the years go by the experts not only gain knowledge and skills, they gain wisdom, which can be regarded as:

> the ego's increasing capacity to tolerate paradox. This same capacity characterizes the mature defenses, which can maintain a creative and flexible tension between irreconcilables and allow conscience, impulse, reality, and attachment all to have places at the center stage.
>
> (Vaillant 1993: 328)

But this process of gaining expertise and wisdom is not something that happens in a short period of time. Through these complex learning experiences, novices might move gradually towards the status of expert, a process which was first discussed by Dreyfus and Dreyfus (1980). They posited that a learner goes through five stages in becoming an expert: novice, advanced beginner, competent, proficient and expert (cited from Benner 1984: 13; see also Tuomi 1999: 285–340). But it was Aristotle who focused on this practical knowledge – which he called practical wisdom – something that could only be learned with the passing of years. In precisely the same way, more experienced workers might continue to learn and continue to develop new knowledge through the process of practice. But there is no short timescale on this process – Benner (1984: 25) suggests that competence in nursing (the field of her own research) might come after two or three years of practice, and proficiency between three and five years (p. 31). However, this raises quite major questions when we recognize the speed of change of artificial knowledge – some of the knowledge learned in the classroom might already be out of date before the practitioner has become an expert. Indeed, practice itself is not static but rapidly changing so that practitioners are not simply using knowledge gained in the classroom or in any form of initial vocational education. Indeed, they may reach a stage where they have to innovate within their own practice or, in other words, where they create new knowledge and new ways of doing things and their expertise means that they also need to be creative – they become experts. There

are at least two implications of this: first, we have to be aware, not every practitioner moves through this progression – for some, each procedure is the mere
repetition of the previous one so that we can say that some practitioners have
twenty-five years of experience while others have one year of experience twenty-
five times; second, the expert can become frustrated by the rules of bureaucracy
and job satisfaction can decline if the expert practitioner feels frustrated (Jarvis
1977) and this can be especially problematic in a litigation-orientated society.

Practitioners also have to gain that wisdom that Vaillant (1993: 328) wrote
about in order to practise in this type of situation – the ability to 'maintain a
creative and flexible tension between irreconcilables and allow conscience,
impulse, reality, and attachment all to have places at the center stage' of practice, since these go with expertise. Immediately we see that practice is no
longer just a matter of knowledge and skill, it is about the practitioner being
confident, creative, having the right impulses, commitment, and so on. But
more than this – in practice, practitioners work with others – patients, clients,
colleagues and so on. It is a social activity and while expertise is very important, Maister (cited in Daloz *et al.* 1996: 25) wrote that 'Your clients don't care
how much you know until they know how much you care'. In other words,
practice is a moral undertaking; it is about trust and respect for others.
Practice is ultimately about the nature of the practitioners themselves. Practice
is about the person – as practitioner. This points us to a broader understanding
of vocational education since it is about developing the person as well as teaching knowledge and skills. But before we examine this, we see one other thing
– *being able to* is not something that can be taught, it has to be learned but it is
even more than this – *being able to* is about *being* itself, but before we turn to
this we now need to look at the nature of human learning.

The nature of human learning

Being able to is not something that can be taught, neither is expertise nor wisdom – but neither it nor they can be learned and learning is not something
that is restricted to the classroom or the lecture theatre – learning is something that can happen anywhere and at any time. Consequently, at the heart
of our concern lies the understanding of the learning process, which is itself a
very complex process – but one that we take for granted. Learning is as *the
combination of processes whereby the whole person – body (genetic, physical and biological) and mind (meaning, knowledge, skills, attitudes, values, emotions, beliefs and
senses) – experiences a social situation, the content of which is then transformed cognitively, emotively or practically (or through any combination) and integrated into the
person's individual biography resulting in a changed (or more experienced) person.*

This is a much more complex definition of learning than usually suggested and
more complex than the one that I posed when I originally sought to understand the
learning process (Jarvis, 1987) and even different from the one which I used when

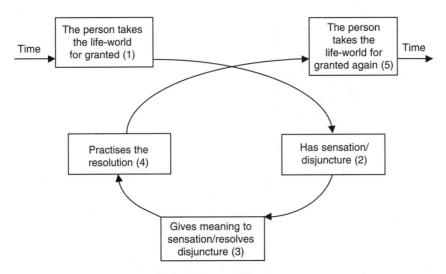

Figure 7.1 The transformation of sensations in learning.

I examined learning much more fully elsewhere (Jarvis, 2006). It is the one which I have later developed further (Jarvis, 2008). Basically, however, four things happen during the learning process: a sensation (physical, emotional, attitudinal, etc.) is changed into 'brain language', the experience that the person has on receiving the stimulus is transformed, the person is changed from one state to another and the person's relationship with the life-world is changed from harmony to disjuncture and gradually back to a new harmony provided the external world does not change (which is debatable). I have depicted this process in the two diagrams above and below.

In Figure 7.1, following Schutz and Luckmann (1974), we take our life-world for granted (box 1), and we live in the flow of time (what Bergson called *durée*) but when we cannot take our world for granted we experience disjuncture or have some sensation or stimulus that causes us to experience disjuncture (box 2). Through the learning process we transform the sensations (box 3) and then we seek to practise the resolution (box 4) which may be much more than just performance since we are not mindless individuals, and this may, after many attempts, lead us to a new harmony with our life-world – provided other factors in the life-world have not altered.

Learning, however, is still more complicated than this first diagram suggests, as the second diagram illustrates because it involves the person of the learner (see Figure 7.2).

In this second diagram, we can see the other aspect of the learning process that occurs simultaneously with the first – the learner is transformed: the learners in the life-world (box 1_1) have an experience (box 1_2) – that can occur

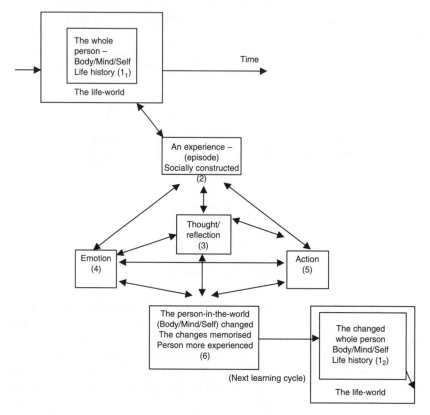

Figure 7.2 The transformation of the person through learning.

in the classroom or the workplace, or elsewhere – which is constructed as a result of our perception of the situation and our previous learning, and it is the content of this experience which is transformed, and we undertake learning (box 6) through our thinking, our doing and our emotions (boxes 3, 4, 5) and as a result of this learning the whole person (body, mind, self, life-history) (box 6) is changed. It is this changed person (box 1_2) who has future experiences and continues to be changed as the practitioner gradually becomes an expert.

When we move from the classroom to the field of practice we actually move from the taken for granted to a new situation (box 1) which is disjunctural since it is another situation and we do not know precisely what to do in it and so we try to resolve the disjuncture by utilizing the *knowledge that* and the *knowledge how* that we have learned, and by so doing we begin to learn *to be able to* – but this is a new learning experience. Through practice (boxes 3, 4 and 5), we gradually learn the necessary knowledge, skills and attitudes, etc. necessary to be able to take our practice situation for granted (box 6). This is where the danger occurs in practice – we can then just take our practice situation for granted and perform our practice unthinkingly, or else we can see each situation as unique, each differing slightly from the last, and so we make each one disjunctural and we adapt our practice accordingly, or as Nyiri says 'through repeated trials, "failing, succeeding, wasting time and effort ... getting a feel for the problem, learning when to go by the book and when to break the rules"' we learn to perfect our practice, even to innovate upon it and produce that new knowledge and skill that we discussed earlier. During this process, we are changed (box 7) and perhaps we grow in wisdom pre-consciously during the process.

Competence is, in a sense, when the practitioners acquire the necessary expertise to fit into the social situation and begin to take their situation and practice for granted. Becoming an expert is when they continue to create their own disjuncture in the practice situation in order to enhance their expertise beyond that of merely 'fitting in'. It is this trying to reach beyond the 'taken for granted' that distinguishes the expert from one who merely has competence or expertise – this is when creativity begins and it is built upon the solid foundation of expertise. Once they reach this state they begin to realize just how much more there is to learn – the beginning of wisdom is the realization of ignorance. But the significant point is that it is the whole person – body and mind – who is changed and who acquires expertise and wisdom as a result of all that trial and error learning in practice, especially if it is coupled with continuing vocational education – but both wisdom and this level of expertise cannot be taught – they can only be learned in practice.

Some implications for vocational education

Thus far we have looked at the nature of knowledge, practice and learning and we can see that this analysis has certain implications for vocational education: I want to look briefly at four here: the short and the long term; the learner; learning in practice; preparing the manager/supervisor.

Short and long term: Traditional vocational education has a short-term end-product only for the routine production workers who can acquire competence to operate technology or to perform their routine roles within the employing organization. For all other workers, vocational education should be seen within a longer time frame and this means that we have to recognize not just the demands of the occupational role but the demands of the practice within which that role is performed. Once we do this we have to look at the wider types of knowledge and skill that are necessary. We have, for instance, highlighted the need for moral knowledge for those who deal with people either as clients or as colleagues and this demands more than mere instrumentality. But this is only an illustration of the way that we need to think about the breadth of initial preparation and prepare workers to be able to learn beyond competence.

The learner: Many approaches to learning are concerned with the way that the information is processed or the behavioural outcomes of the learning process, but in the model of learning that I have suggested I have focused on the learners themselves. Most theories of learning are, I believe, quite deficient in this in a number of different ways, as I have argued in *Towards a Comprehensive Theory of Human Learning* (Jarvis 2006) where I have focused on the person of the learner. The learner is both mind and body and in learning and in practice the one does not operate without the other. This also calls into question the emphasis on the concept of competence with its behavioural implications and also information processing with its emphasis on the brain as a glorified computer. The expert is more than a functionary responding to the demands of the system – the expert is a significant person in society using expertise and knowledge to transcend the system and enrich the lives of all who live in society. We need to understand the nature of personhood and learning if we are to be of service to those with whom we work; we need to value the person of the learner and this is more than human resource development – it is about personal growth and development. At the heart of our concern is respect for the personhood of people as we help them develop all of their abilities. Ultimately, we are all involved in *learning to be* as well as *learning to do* and *learning to know* – this chapter is about *learning to be an expert*.

Learning in practice: We have to recognize that if we want experts, and wise ones at that, we have to prepare workers to understand that the practice into which they are going is a constantly changing one where new demands are being made on them all the time and that they also have to make new demands upon themselves so that they have to be prepared to learn new practices, to learn to enhance their existing ones, and so on. They have to learn how to learn, which means that new types of teaching and learning techniques have to be incorporated into the vocational training programme. New knowledge, new skills, new teaching and learning techniques – this points to the fact that vocational education needs itself to be undergoing continuous change and the importance of work-based learning needs to be recognized and, in addition, we have to help educational institutions to recognize and accredit such work-based learning programmes. However, programmes of this nature require higher educational institutions to continue to adapt their understanding to accreditation and place even more significance on the relationship of practice to theory. We have to recognize the complex process of learning in practice and help those who are undertaking it.

Preparing the manager/supervisor: Since the workplace is a site of learning, those who supervise need to be involved in the workers' learning. Consequently, managers and supervisors should to be taught how to be mentors of work-placed learning. This then is part of their continuing professional development and the concept of management needs to undergo some transformation as we develop teams who need to learn to work together.

Conclusion

Vocational education is now far removed from training and the old debates about knowledge and skill, and the policy implications of these changes have to be taken into account from the outset. In this depersonalized society, we need to re-emphasize the place of the person and we need to re-conceptualize learning away from the rather sterile debates about lifelong learning that occur in policy documents and learn what it really means for whole people to learn. Perhaps the focus of our vocational education needs to come from the UNESCO report *Learning: The treasure within* (Delors 1996) in which there are four pillars of learning – to be, to do, to know and to live together. Here we begin to grasp what it means for people to learn – primarily learning to be, so that we can also learn to know, to do and to live together wisely and with expertise.

Acknowledgements

This chapter is adapted from an article by Sawchuk, P. (2008). Labour Perspectives on the New Politics of Skill and Competency Formation: International Reflections. Asia Pacific Education Review, 9(1), 50–62. Reprinted with permission from Education Research Institute, Seoul National University.

This chapter was originally presented as a paper at the Hong Kong Council for Vocational Education and has subsequently been revised for this publication.

Part III

Competence development in different contexts

Chapter 8

Competence development in the public sector

Development, or dismantling of professionalism?

Katrin Hjort

For more than a decade competence development has been a key concept of modern management in both the private and the public sector, but to some extent its meaning and practice have been different in the two sectors. In the public sector in particular, it has been closely related to a number of other buzzwords characterizing the dominant neoliberal political conceptions, such as Lifelong Learning, New Public Management, Market Orientation and Decentralization.

From an idealistic point of view, competence development is intended to promote professionalism, understood as knowledge creation, self-management and the ethical commitment of civil servants. However, the development has increasingly involved elements of supervision, declining flexibility and time-consuming evaluation, which may have contributed to the de-qualification and demotivation of the civil servants. It is therefore a basic question whether the learning activities labelled as competence development are part of a developing or a dismantling process in relation to professionalism in the public sector.

The competence development discourse

The Danish Welfare State has been reformed in many ways over the last ten years. Like many other public welfare systems in the world, the Danish model with free – or tax paid – access to education, health service and social security, has been criticized as being expensive and inefficient. The influence of global neoliberal discourses has become increasingly visible, and the public service institutions have been challenged by the implementation of market-like incentives based on new combinations of competition and political control (contract management). Welfare in Denmark is primarily financed by public money at present, but an increasing number of welfare institutions are being transformed into self-owned or private enterprises, and the fate of the welfare state is still unknown.

The concept of competence development played an important role in these transformation processes. The concept has been adopted from international discourses and integrated in new ways of governing the human service organizations, but it has also played an extremely significant role in the professionalizing strategies of the Danish 'semi-professions'. Among nurses, teachers and social workers, for example, it has been widely assumed that competence development is the path to a better job, more influence, higher wages and higher status. A great number of individuals have engaged in further education and research and development activities at public workplaces. Trade unions have incorporated competence development into their political strategies, and a number of collective agreements concerning competence development have been signed between civil servants and public employers. When it comes to practice, however, the concept of competence development has referred to everything from a three hour IT course to extensive, experimental development projects.

The first part of this article will analyse the construction and popularity of the concept of competence development in Denmark over the past ten years as representing a number of holy and less holy alliances between at least three different strategic interests:

1   *Lifelong Learning* – new understandings of learning and new educational policies on the national and transnational level (OECD, EU).
2   *New Public Management* – new government strategies implemented as part of the transformation of the public sector in Denmark and the other Nordic welfare states.
3   *Professionalizing* – new labour market strategies among public servants in Denmark.

The second part of the article will link different understandings of competence development to different strategies for professionalizing, and describe a process in which a wide variety of decentralized, self-administered and directly user-orientated competence development activities have changed into activities aimed at meeting narrow goals that are politically defined at a central level. The third part of the article will discuss the basic question of *whether the learning activities labelled as competence development are to be seen as part of a developing or a dismantling process in relation to professionalism* in the public sector in Denmark. Have the competence development activities actually contributed to increased professionalism, understood as an extended scientific knowledge base, enlarged scope for decision making and the greater social legitimacy of civil servants (Abbott 1988; Freidson 2001)? Or have the competence development activities – as parts of the general reform processes in the Danish public sector – contributed to reducing the jurisdiction, the autonomy and the ethical commitment of 'People working with People' within the welfare organizations or human service enterprises? Finally, the chapter raises the question of whether, in their choice of strategies, public servants themselves have been so focused on *professionalizing*, understood as increased social status and legitimacy, that they have ignored the risk of decreasing their own *professionalism*, their own ability to 'do a good job' in relation to the human beings – patients, students, clients etc. – they encounter at work (Goodson & Hargreaves 1996).

Competence development – a floating signifier?

In a theoretical perspective, the concept of competence development could be defined as a 'floating signifier' – a term the discourse theorists Laclau & Mouffe (1985) took from Michel Foucault (1977). Like many other key concepts in the discourse concerning public transformation – modernization, development, quality, learning, efficiency etc. – competence development may be understood as a phrase the most important meaning of which is that it does not mean anything. Or more accurately, the concept's 'reference to reality' has not been fixed but is still floating. This characteristic has made it the ideal subject both for struggles about how to define the world and for alliances and compromises between many different parties, each of whom have wanted to inscribe it into *their* version of reality, *their* rationality, *their* perspective. The concept has been sufficiently vague or 'empty' enough to act as a starting point for negotiations, in spite of – or merely because – the various stakeholders involved not necessarily having the same understandings of the term or the same reasons for supporting it, at least as long as no side had conquered hegemony, that is had been able to freeze *their* definition, *their* discourse as the only valid and legitimate one, *doxa*. In this way the existence of floating signifiers such as competence development may be understood as signalling the dynamic character of the power relations in the field during the period in question, that is the turn of the millennium. As already mentioned, at least three strategic interests, political, administrative and professional, have been competing and cooperating.

Holy and less holy alliances

At the turn of the millennium competence development – regarded *both* as formalized adult education *and* as recognition of the informal learning in the lives of the employees – was viewed as a method of strengthening the competitiveness of individuals, enterprises and nations on the global market. Within *educational policy*, competence development was viewed as a centre of motion in the strategy for lifelong learning and related to the new narrative of the knowledge society, which became – if not hegemonic – then at least dominant in Europe after the death of the great narratives and the fall of the Berlin Wall (European Commission 1995, 2000). However, the idea of people learning through their own activities throughout life is not new. As is well known, its roots are in the European Enlightenment, and in the twentieth century the idea legitimized a diversity of liberation or self-regulation projects with very different political signatures (Weber 2002). The present conceptualizing of lifelong learning appeared for the first time in 1972 in UNESCO's programme for social justice, local sustainability and literacy in the Third World. The Organisation for Economic Co-operation and Development (OECD) officially recommended lifelong learning in 1996, and in 2000 the European Union put lifelong learning and life-wide learning on the agenda in order to increase economic effectiveness, organizational flexibility and the employability of the workforce (Greenwood & Stuart 2002). In Denmark, lifelong learning was formulated as a general policy of education, initially in 1998 by the private organization, 'The Competence Counsel', later on in 2003 by 'The National Competence Accounts', set up by the Danish Ministry of Economic and Business Affairs.

In this way competence development as a concept or phenomenon in the Danish public sector was part of very extensive strategic efforts, and not limited to educational policy but linked to overriding finance, industry and labour market policies. The standards for the competence development of the public employees were not only set by local or national agendas, but to an increasing extent by supranational objectives. A concrete example was the reform of the Adult Education System that contained new master's programmes for experienced adults, including the highly educated professionals and semi-professionals in the public sector – and incorporating the efforts towards a synchronization or integration of the European systems of education (The Bologna process 2001).

In a political perspective competence development was a question of economic growth. In *an administration perspective*, competence development was rather a question of implementing new methods of management and control in the public sector. The New Public Management (NPM) trend in Denmark over the past ten years can – as mentioned – be described as an attempt to readjust the big public sector wholly or partly to the market without surrendering political control. The core ambition in the currently dominant Contract Management System is to use the market or market-like economic incentives to implement politically established, centrally defined objectives. On the one hand, the single organization (hospital, school etc.) must act as an independent strategic unit framed by broad regulations. On the other, it is obliged to give increasingly more detailed accounts of its results according to central standards (Bregn 1998; Klausen & Ståhlberg 1998). Within this context, competence development has been a management tool, an integrated part of staff policy linked to the differentiation of wages in order to motivate each employee to deliver a work output that supports the organization's main strategy and objectives (Kompetencerådet 1999; Ministeriet for Finans, Industri m.fl. 2003; Andersen *et al.* 2003; Evetts 2004).

In Denmark, the trade unions of the employees in the public sector have chosen to be co-players in the transformation process from traditional welfare state government to quasi-market management. For this reason, the specific Danish model for public transformation has been labelled 'negotiated modernization' (Pedersen 1998). For example, in 1997 CFU, the main trade union for public employees in Denmark, and the Danish Ministry of Finance entered into the first collective agreement on systematic and strategic competence development with the explicit objective of ensuring both the single organization's needs for flexibility *and* each employee's need for professional and personal development. The specific content of the agreement, however, remains to be negotiated locally (Andersen *et al.* 2003).

In *the perspective of the professionals or semi-professionals*, competence development was a part of a changing labour market strategy – from wage labour politics to professionalizing efforts. Caring for others is, as known, traditionally women's work. For one thing, the majority of women are employed. Secondly, the work consists to a great extent of tasks that historically have been taken care of by the women in the families – if these tasks have been performed at all. In the light of history, it can be appreciated as obvious progress that 'caring and developing work' in the Nordic Welfare State model has been defined as paid work in public settings, that is as work that is not only carried out just for love or as a vocation, but defined as work that gives entitlement to wages and acceptable work conditions. However, the result of the wage labour strategies of the semi-professionals in Denmark in the 1980s left many of the public servants themselves with a certain feeling of discomfort. To hold on tightly to one's rights as a wage labourer chafed against both the specific character of the work and the fundamental values of the professions. The work supporting human life and learning processes is, obviously, in principle or by nature (!) unpredictable, uncontrollable and permanently alterable. The idea that the work initially is carried out for the good of 'the other', for the benefit of 'one's neighbour' was, moreover, still a central element in the professional ethos, constituent for the internal field-discourse and professional identity, as well as for the external social legitimacy of the semi-professionals. Traditional wage labourer weapons such as strikes or 'work to rule' therefore fundamentally disputed their basis of legitimacy, however justified these fights might have appeared, considering the wage level and work pressure of the public servants (Hjort 2001, 2005).

In Denmark at the turn of the millennium, professionalizing seemed to be a solution to these dilemmas: The 'semi-professions' or 'wannabe professions' wanted to be 'real professions' just like the 'classic professions': clergymen, doctors and lawyers. They wanted to be recognized for their real knowledge, skills and ethics, and they wanted salary and status according to their merit. More men had to enter the trades to avoid their stigmatization as female occupations and competence development had to be emphasized (Nielsen 2003). From this point of departure, the public servants and their organizations entered the scene in order to influence and enter alliances with the strong competence development discourses represented in European policy and Danish Public Management.

However, how did the public servants interpret the term 'competence development' and how exactly did they understand the relations between competence development and professionalizing? What actually happened when the idea of competence development had to be implemented at public workplaces in the welfare institutions?

Competence development and professionalizing

The concept of competence development was able to function as a common denominator in the negotiations between the many diverse interests because initially it was kept floating. It was not defined precisely but 'kept in the air' as an ambiguous term, and it could refer to a multitude of different forms of practice: on-the-job training, formal education, participation in research activities, ethical profiling, documentation projects aimed at making the work of public servants visible to the outside world etc. While the discursive landscape that the public employees and their professional organizations were to acquaint themselves with when they wished to join in the discussion was tense and a source of confusion, on the other hand it offered a wealth of opportunity for creating new positions by reframing, interconnecting and recreating discourses in a creative manner. The same could be said about the term 'profession'. In connection with the strategies of public employees, many different understandings of professionalizing have appeared which have hooked up to or been hooked up to different types of competence development activities. The inspiration was obtained from an everyday understanding of professional work as well-paid or good work, but it was also obtained from the classic sociological theories of professions. It could be the more *profession-sceptical* theories which, with Max Weber (1905), stress that the creation of a profession is a question of power relations and the strength to monopolize knowledge, education and occupational areas. But it could also be the more *'profession-friendly'* theories which, with Talcott Parsons (1968), emphasize the professions' actual functions and social legitimacy in a highly specialized society. More recent theories about professionals' learning and learning in professional practice have, however, gained particular popularity – both the *rationalistic* versions (Dale 1989; Jarvis 1999; Hargreaves 2000) and the more *holistic* versions which, like Polanyi (1966) and Lave and Wenger (1991), stress practical or 'tacit knowledge' and the collective, social and cultural aspects of learning and competence development (Illeris 2004, 2007).

According to the choice of the framework for understanding, competence development has thus, with Max Weber, been understood as a question about acquiring *formal competences* (degrees, titles, authorizations) with the purpose of strengthening the profession. Or competence development has, with Parsons, been understood as a question of developing *real competences* in order

Table 8.1 Perspectives on professions and understandings of competence development

	External perspectives on professions		Internal perspectives on professions	
	Max Weber 1905	*Talcott Parsons 1968*	*Polanyi 1966, Rolf 1991, Dreyfus & Dreyfus 1986, Lave & Wenger 1991, Wackerhausen & Wackerhausen 1993*	*Dale 1989, Argyris & Schön 1996, Jarvis 1999, Hargreaves 2000*
Professionalizing	Some workers have conquered access to and been able to monopolize a specific area of occupation based on a specific monopoly of knowledge linked to a specific education.	Some workers have acquired a specific function in society because they have developed specific expertise that makes them capable of performing certain difficult and important tasks.	Some workers have developed practical, bodily and social knowledge and a work place culture that enables them to make discretionary decisions in emergent situations.	Some workers have been able to account for the results of their work within a discourse that is accepted as legitimate by external stakeholders.
	Authorization Focus on exclusion of others, high salary and social status.	*Autonomy* Focus on self-management, space for decisions and quality control among colleagues.	*Discretion* Focus on tacit, collective and culturally embedded knowledge and ethics.	*Documentation* Focus on accreditation and accountability, efficiency and effectiveness.
	Social closure	*Social contract*	*Social trust*	*Social legitimacy*
Competence development	Increasing formal competences (degrees, ranks, grades).	Increasing real competences by education and scientification.	Increasing work quality by engaging in (trans-) professional development projects at the workplaces.	Increasing legitimacy by making work and work results visible.

to substantiate professional autonomy, the right to manage, plan, execute and evaluate own work, exercise professional discretion and exercise collegial self-management. Competence development activities have been *directed inwards* as (trans-) professional quality development projects in cooperation with the direct users of schools, health care etc., and they have been directed outwards, aiming at documenting and legitimizing the civil servants' competences vis-à-vis the outside world: consumers, authorities, politicians, etc.

In other words, the picture of competence development and professionalizing has been multifaceted (see Table 8.1).

From broad to narrow definitions of competence development

In spite of the multifaceted picture of competence development in the Danish public sector, it is possible to describe a process that has altered the concept over the past ten years. It is obvious that the understanding of competence development through the years has narrowed from ambiguous and broad definitions to a steadily more unambiguous and narrow definition of what the term is to refer to (Drevsholt *et al.* 2001). This may be illustrated by two examples from 1997 and 2000, respectively:

> Competence is understood as the individual person's knowledge and ability, motivation, commitment, will, learning and development *potential*, relations between employees and between employees and managers as well as organizational relationships. This means that competence development is the strengthening of the *abilities, opportunities and motivation* of employees and managers as well as the *development of organizational structures* in which employees and managers can use their competence.
>
> (Debate: Competence Development in the Health System; in Krag 1997 – emphasis added)

In this definition, competence development is understood broadly as the development of human resources and potentials, individually and collectively and as a question of arranging organizational structures that can support this development. The discourse may be characterized as *holistic or idealistic* based on metaphors of organic growth and on narratives that tell the story about development from force to freedom.

The next quote is from an agreement between the Danish Ministry of Finance and the Danish Central Federation of State Employees' Organisations. Competence development is here defined much more narrowly:

> Strategic Competence development means that the employees' development is anchored in the institution's daily and in particular future task solution (…) This means that initially *an overview of the institution's need for competence development* must be created. It is only when this has occurred that a decision can be made about which goals will be set up for the individual employee, i.e. which competences must be developed so the employee can contribute to the overall goal. This results in an appraisal interview where actual agreements are made about the competence development activities that are to take place in the future. In connection with the interview, *actual development goals for the individual employee* must be set up.
>
> (The Danish Ministry of Finance 2000 – emphasis added)

The discourse in this quote from the Ministry of Finance is quite different from the discourse of the Health Authorities three years before. The overall goal is defined as organizational effectiveness of the public organization and the individual employee's competence development is understood as the means to this goal. *Functionalism and rationalism* have taken the place of idealism and holism. The belief in organic growth into the realms of freedom and the future has been replaced by a technical-instrumental approach – the ambition of being able to manage in a chronically changing world.

Is competence development about creating broad human development opportunities or narrow contract or result management? Should competence development be created from the bottom up or managed from above? Does competence development involve individual or collective processes? Is competence development about imagination, creativity and innovation, or about rationalization, standardization and control? Are the clients to be defined as citizens participating in – and co-responsible for – quality improvement or as customers demanding service and guarantee certification? How can we measure competence development? Do we only value competence development if it is exactly measurable here and now?

These have been the two outermost poles in the Danish competence development debate, but if a winner is to be identified in the last ten years' battle about defining the term competence development, then this is clearly the Danish Ministry of Finance and its narrow – or precise – definition of competence development. Correspondingly, the losers are the broader competence development concepts based on local development work conducted in cooperation between professionals and clients. In the same movement, the understanding of professionalizing has shrunk from being a question concerning the development of employees and organization, individually and collectively, to a question that first and foremost is about how public employees, via formal merit and (more or less) scientific documentation, can generate evidence to prove the effect of their work and thus legitimize themselves (Hjort 2008).

Professionalizing or de-professionalizing?

To explain the process of the movement from broad to narrow understandings of competence development, the last years' general political development must be taken into consideration. The process has been embedded in important contextual, cultural and societal changes. During the years in which competence development has been popular, a number of decisive professional and political changes have occurred in Denmark as well as the rest of Europe. These changes have placed a new form of re-centralization or re-bureaucratization on the agenda as a supplement to or replacement for the decentralization strategy on which the reform projects in the welfare states were initially based. The 'openings' related to the idea of decentralization or self-administration have been replaced by new forms of central control, influenced by the current neoliberal/neoconservative government alliance in Denmark, but not only confined to this.

First of all, the traditionally broad 'success criteria' of the welfare state (better education, health and social support for *all* without regard to standing), and the traditional public ethos based on universalistic and, in principle, client-oriented standards, have been challenged by new criteria defining success as effectiveness and efficiency and new standards related to 'objective', that is measurable, quality goals. The combination of more market surveys and strengthened contract and performance management has meant that the public organizations, to an increasing degree, have been caught in the crossfire between daily, practical and economic operational necessities on the one hand, and political legitimating efforts on the other. Despite all formulated intentions about independent profiling and consideration for local stakeholders, it has become increasingly difficult for the organizations to manoeuvre independently, including determining their own competence development policy (Petersen-Testrup 2004). In step with this, the opportunities for public employees to impose *their own* fingerprint on the decentralized agreements have been reduced. In this context a new kind of practical reasoning has been introduced, new internal and external necessities that have caused all parties – including the public servants and their trade unions – to see not the locally self-administered and development oriented, but the formalized and standardized as the most serviceable, the most easily adapted, or the lesser evil. Apparently, the power relations in and around the public institutions have been such that it might gradually have appeared more and more reasonable or 'natural' to all involved to regard the questions of learning and competence development as a question of adapting strictly to the market and the new forms of public governance. It can be argued with Foucault that new government regimes, new management techniques and new practices of self-management have been developed and installed. This is a process actively involving the civil servants themselves (Foucault 1997; Rose 1999).

Empirically, the consequences of this process cannot simply be described as professionalizing – interpreted as expanded knowledge, increased professional autonomy and higher ethical standards. It can equally be described as de-professionalizing, that is in the form of polarization between A) employees with opportunities for new management and development tasks, and B) employees whose jobs to an increasing extent are de-qualified, intensified and depersonalized. This process has had major (unintended and unexpected?) consequences – at least seen from the point of view of the majority of the public servants themselves. For example, absence due to illness has increased tremendously and today it is very difficult to recruit employees for jobs within the health sector. The process has correspondingly given rise to extreme dissatisfaction among the users of the public services in Denmark, even though there is no political agreement about whether it is the new forms of political control and exposure to the market that are the *reasons* for the problems in the welfare institutions or the *solution* to the problems within welfare in Denmark (Hjort 2004, 2008).

Dismantling the Welfare State?

The last question to be raised here is the extent to which the public employees within the Danish welfare institutions, through their choice of labour market strategies, including competence development strategies, have actively contributed to their own de-professionalizing.

From one point of view it can be claimed that individuals' and organizations' enormous focus on formalized individual merit in the further/higher education system – in a context where personal payment or the institution's co-financing plays an increasing role – has strongly contributed to the increased A/B polarization. Some employees have the family or institution-linked network resources that are necessary to gain access to more education and thereby – potentially – new career paths, while others do not have this opportunity. Some employees have got a chance to obtain new knowledge monopolies and new forms of influence and decision-making competence in this way. But to an increasing degree, the work of others is reduced to unskilled or low qualified routine work which is executed according to 'manuals', directed and evaluated by others. Viewed in this light, the competence development engagement has proactively contributed to the increasing hierarchization and taylorization of human service.

Correspondingly, it could be claimed that in their eagerness to legitimize themselves and their own work through documentation activities, reports and accounts – and other forms of confessions – the public employees have willingly supplied the upper layer in the contract control pyramids with all the information that is necessary to develop new *management sciences* and *managerial technologies*: evaluations and impact measurements, benchmarking systems, contract management agreements, etc. They have thereby actively contributed to the reduction of their relative professional autonomy and this way personally contributed to the rationalization, intensifying and streamlining of their own work!

In another perspective it might be asked what could have happened if the public employees, via their professionalizing efforts and commitment in competence development had *not* tried to *oppose* some of the negative consequences of the transformation of the Danish Welfare State?If they had not focused on education and documenting the effect of their work, how could they have safeguarded themselves against being disqualified and potentially made superfluous in step with the advance of processes of change? This includes safeguarding themselves against a scenario where work with people is reduced to 'serving customers, who are always right', that is work not performed by trained and experienced professionals, but by 'servants'.

If the positive aspects and the potentials are examined, it may be claimed that by focusing on competence development on a large scale, the public employees have succeeded in legitimizing their own professionalizing efforts by – creatively – joining the powerful international discourses within New

Public Management and Lifelong Learning. By taking the knowledge and competence term at its word, the Danish public employees and their professional organizations have been able to position themselves so strongly that they have succeeded in foiling the intentions of 'removing the professionals from the helm', which was formulated at the start of the public reform project (Dich 1973). In line with the transformation of the Danish Welfare State, teachers, nurses and social workers etc. have become increasingly more important agents in the economy. If the Danish economy is going to depend – not on agriculture or industry – but on knowledge and services, the groups of workers within these areas must be of growing importance and potential societal influence.

From a third angle, the question posed about the (semi-) professionals' contribution to their own de-professionalizing can be answered not with a 'yes' or a 'no' but with a 'both/and' or a 'neither/nor'. With Foucault it could be claimed that precisely by subjecting themselves to new government strategies, the professionals are subjected in new ways. By exposing themselves to new forms of government regimes such as team work and contract management, by using new government technologies, such as electronic calendars, and by engaging in new self-management activities such as personal career planning, they also obtain opportunities to construct and position themselves in ways that represent new power relations – and thus new possibilities for knowledge creation about 'work with people' and its conditions in 'expanding modernity'.

Whether this form of knowledge creation will come to represent a key political perspective, a profession perspective – or perhaps simply different perspectives on how different people's needs for help, care, support, teaching, healing, etc. can best be accommodated in various ways – is still unclear or, more correctly, a question of power relations and the power of definition.

Acknowledgements

This chapter is adapted from an article by Parker, B. & Walters, S. (2008). Competency Based Training and National Qualifications Frameworks: Insights from South Africa. *Asia Pacific Education Review*, 9(1), 70–79. Reprinted with permission from Education Research Institute, Seoul National University.

Chapter 9

Labour perspectives on the new politics of skill and competence formation

International reflections

Peter Sawchuk

Introduction

> Governments, employers and trade unions increasingly face a need to prepare workers for a new and more flexible labour market, and the prospect of a working life which involves a variety of occupations and skills ... a *new politics of skill formation* has emerged, facilitating and regulating the development of workers' competences and transferable skills ...
>
> (Martinez Lucio *et al.* 2007: 323; emphasis added)

While the politics of skill/competency formation may not be as 'new' as some believe, the fact is that the new millennium has appeared to have crystallized momentum for attempts at such approaches. In this regard, it has become clear that the pressures of globalized trade, production and inter-capitalist competition, technological and demographic change (Martinez Lucio *et al.* 2007) have produced a willingness for experimentation.

The skills/competencies approach, as has been recognized, is not neutral. The discourse of skill/competency formation belies the fact that recognition, classification, regulation and the legitimacy and resources to shape activity in ways reflecting particular material interests represent deeply political questions. Given the embeddedness of this issue in industrial relations, organized labour – while battered, bruised and in decline in most, but not all advanced capitalist countries – represents a relevant standpoint from which to investigate the skill/competency question. The goal of this chapter is to address the complexity and inner contradictions of this formation from the standpoint of organized labour to show how concerns over 'actual skill/competency' are marginalized in relation to traditional modes of economic struggle. As we shall see, however, labour perspectives on this issue are hardly monolithic, either within or across countries.

Below, I begin with a brief review of existing critiques of the skills/competency approach specifically. I then supplement this literature with a consideration of the skills debate from the field of sociology of work which is more generalized in nature. Across these two traditions we see the relevance of discerning interwoven orientations to 'actual skill/competency' as opposed to matters of 'power/control'. This review sets the stage for a profile of labour perspectives on skill/competency including a comparative analysis of recent initiatives in Norway and Canada. It is demonstrated that, in distinct ways that express national differences, both Norway and Canada have seen the politics of 'new' skill/competency formation overtaken by traditional forms of industrial relations struggle.

Existing critiques of skill/competency frameworks

Skill/competency approaches to workplace and economic policy have emerged based on a range of perceptions which are shared internationally. Stakeholders across virtually all advanced capitalist countries perceive a need for greater mobility of employees across economic sectors. Governments now assume that the new economy brings a need for new forms of skills and competencies linked, for example, to an emphasis on 'soft', transferable skills, the validation of non-formal and informal learning, and access to learning for workers with low formal skills. Within both North America and Europe, many countries have generated policy frameworks, see for example the Lisbon Council proclamations, which seek to use innovations in training and learning to develop dynamic knowledge-based economies. It is unquestioned in such policy frameworks that transferable skills and competencies are necessary for the development of a more competitive economy, while it is also presumed that such approaches are the best means of supporting workers in an increasingly competitive global economy (Martinez Lucio et al. 2007).

Among most OECD countries, state-driven policies targeting individualistic, skill/competency intervention as a form of industrial policy are nothing new (cf. Boreham 2004). Recognizing that theories of macro-economic management have consistently shaped the development of training as well as education in all advanced capitalist countries, we can nevertheless see that skill/competency frameworks have in some ways helped crystallize the centrality of education and training as economic policy (e.g. Brown et al. 2001; Olsen et al. 2004). As we shall see later on, a variety of countries including Norway and Canada have recently made sustained attempts at their own versions of this policy. And, central to virtually all such attempts are prescriptions to tighten the linkage between all forms of learning (education, training and informal learning) and organizational competitiveness.

Critical analyses of skill/competence frameworks are as well established as the policy frameworks themselves. From this perspective, researchers have addressed the inequities that tend to be reproduced in such skills/competencies approaches (Jackson 1991; Rainbird 2000; Heyes & Stuart 1994; Atkins 1999; Mojab 1999; Payne 2000; Shah & Burke 2005). Others have noted how skill/competency frameworks reflect a rejection of the wider, social goals of life-long learning in terms of broader personal development and deepening forms of collective participation in work processes as well as society (e.g. Coffield 2000). More generalized is the critique that lies at the centre of the question of political economic legitimacy of skill/competency approaches. As Rikowski (e.g. 2001) points out, employers who do not recognize the nature of 'labour power', its uses, abuses as well as its relationship to learning, skills and competencies under capitalism are likely to be unable to understand, much less articulate, their training needs. In fact, as a variety of researchers have noted: 'skill' and 'competency' has, by now, become the epitome of a 'floating signifier' – danger-ously close to, as Lafer (2004: 118) puts it, 'nothing more than "whatever employers want"'. Or, as Payne has so consistently explained for a decade now, skills and competencies are:

> ubiquitous ... being applied to such diverse phenomena as reading, writ-ing, problem-solving, learning, team work, salesmanship, marketing, presentation, perseverance, motivation, enthusiasm, attitude, corporate commitment, customer-orientation, stress management ... mean[ing] whatever employers and policy-makers want it to mean.
>
> (Payne 2000: 361)

Critics have also been particularly persistent in their challenge to skills/competency approaches in terms of conceptualizations of learning itself. As Fenwick summarizes (Fenwick *et al.* 2005):

> '[s]kill' is an illusion that floats according to the prevailing knowledge politics and observer bias identifying bits of performance spied among joint action, and marking it as some capability possessed by this or that person immersed in the communal flow.
>
> (p. 2)

In fact, applications of skill/competency are in practice, if not by definition, unable to appreciate the situated or contextualized nature of performance. Such critiques offer a portal to discussions of the way the skill/competency frameworks may in fact reproduce forms of social exclusion which at the same time valorize the types of hierarchical 'knowledge politics' that Fenwick speaks of above. This is the case whether we are dealing with culturally specific forms of knowledge, immigrant credentials, or more generally in terms of the traditionally upheld divisions between mental and manual labour, vocational and professionalized knowledge, and so on. Research evidence shows that hier-archical ordering of capacities are presumed and often directly embedded in skill/competency policy initiatives. And, from here it is a simple extrapolation to understand the skill/competency approach as a mechanism for producing (and then attempting to resolve) the notion of 'worker deficit'.

It is of course no mere coincidence that individualized notions of learning, skill and credentialization predominate in a capitalist political economy (e.g. Sawchuk 2003a). Individuation in the learning processes – both organized and informal learning processes – ratifies the commodification process as well as the ethos of privatized market exchange. Skill/competency policy, naturally and pragmatically follows the prevailing winds in this sense.

Referenced as a skill/competency approach, what is really at stake is the locus of control of learning; a redirection of people's energies from engagement in educational institutions, vocational training systems as well as collective bargaining processes, towards the direct and immediate mediation of learning by the needs of the firm, the sector, and capital in general. Herein lays a gap that simply cannot be ameliorated from an organizational standpoint, even in the case of critical Human Resource and Development (see Vince 2005). It is a situation in which, as Paul Thompson (2003) has recently commented, 'employers are finding it harder to keep their side of any bargain with employees' (p. 361). That is, skill/competency approaches contain a tension in which, on the surface the possibility of more engaged, meaningful, flexible and productive forms of work are offered while at its core the danger of intensified forms of exploitation, instability and vulnerability lurk. The shift to skill/competency, in short, places a vastly larger number of cards in the hands of employers who can utilize processes of recognition, designation, support and direction of learning activity in keeping with interests that are often antagonistic to those of the learner/worker.

A view from the de-skilling/up-skilling debate in the sociology of work

Up to this point, we have summarized literature that is widely available, both in this collection and elsewhere. What is less often linked to the critical assessment of skill/competency approaches, however, is the tradition of skills discussion in the field of the sociology of work. I argue that this field offers additional clarity to our comprehension of the politics of skill/competency formation. A review of the skills debate in terms of the sociology of work shows that over the last three decades discussion has produced what can be called the 'up-skilling/de-skilling impasse' (Sawchuk 2006). The roots of this impasse are found in two opposing sets of theses: the 'industrialism' and 'post-industrialism' theses on the one hand, and the Marxist labour process theory or 'capitalism' thesis and its subsequent branches on the other.

Briefly summarized, emerging in the post Second World War era, the industrialism thesis projected that work was to progressively become more skilled, less physically demanding and less monotonous producing what has come to be known as the up-skilling argument (e.g. Spenner 1979; Nonaka & Takeuchi 1995; Frenkel et al. 1999). As Wood (1982) persuasively established early on, skill is not only a label used by management to divide and reduce the power of workers or the product of workers' collective resistance as Marxists suggested; it is at the same time a discourse of effective operation within a prescribed framework of capitalist organizations and economy.

In response to the industrialism/post-industrialism theses generally, came the work of Braverman (1974) which paid close attention to the organization of work (and specifically Scientific Management), seeking to recover a Marxist approach. Braverman Labour Process Theory analysed the effects of the separation of conception and execution and argued these to be an expression of management's war with (craft and office) workers for control and through it heightened profitability. Skill and competency, in this sense, was the medium through which power, control and exploitation were enacted as well as contested. Specifically, Braverman tried to demonstrate that, on an aggregate level, the Taylorized technical division of labour – fragmenting jobs into minute actions and rearranging activity based on management prerogative – sought to break down knowledge forms and the power that skilled workers exercised within the production process. Others since Braverman have built on the approach (e.g. Burawoy 1979; Zimbalist 1979; Littler 1982; Baldry, et al. 1998). Followers expanded upon Braverman's thesis, either implicitly or explicitly, through greater attention to the subjective dimensions of the labour process (such as worker consciousness, resistance and consent) and later sought to address Braverman's exclusion of gendered divisions, the need to deal with more than simply manufacturing sites, the need to develop a more detailed understanding of command/control structures as well as macro-economic factors, and eventually the need to address issues of globalization and the effects of advanced technology.

Summarizing these literatures, Warhurst et al. (2004: 5) have concluded that through these debates some basic forms of 'consensus' around skill and work have emerged. Here it was argued that researchers mutually acknowledge several key principles: i) skill includes internalized capacities resident in the individual worker; ii) skill includes job design, divisions of labour, technology and control; and iii) skill is socially constructed. This list of points of consensus in many ways parallels the principles attended to by a range of scholars writing two and three decades ago. Complicating matters, however, has been the explosion of skill types – most recently 'emotional' work/skill, 'articulation' work/skill, or 'aesthetic' work/skill: a trend that has deepened the debate over distinctions between 'personal traits' and 'learned skill' or 'competency'.

On the surface, this anticlimactic arrival at general principles defining skill that mirror so closely principles established decades ago, paired with the rampant expansion of categorization of virtually every human capacity as a skill/competency, do not suggest much of a contribution to our understanding of the new politics of skill/competency formation. However, upon deeper consideration, in fact the de-skilling/up-skilling debate has produced some important clarifications. We can see, for example, that the sheer difficulty of quantifying skill and competence has stimulated a variety of important questions: not simply the fundamental question of why we need to quantify skill/competence exactly, but also what this widely held need implicitly says about what we see as relevant and legitimate? Answers to these types of questions help to reveal the unarticulated presumptions that frame both past and current analysis of skill and competence. That is, clearly, the motive is embedded in the need for productivity, but productivity of a profitable kind; it is embedded in the need for competitive national firms, but competition under certain auspices; it is embedded in the need to engage and reward people, but people constructed *as individuals* vis-à-vis a labour market; and, ultimately the motivation is embedded in matters of control and social struggle.

The de-skilling/up-skilling debate has also encouraged researchers to address how it could be that the arguments for widespread 'up-skilling' as well as 'de-skilling' could *both* remain as persuasive as they each do. In other words, reconciling this apparent contradiction has forced deeper considerations of the meaning of skill, competence and working knowledge itself. This consideration has begun to join the vastly superior assessments of the *work processes* from the field of sociology of work with the equally superior assessments of *learning, skill and knowledge development processes* available from fields addressing adult learning, training and education specifically.

What becomes clear from this multidisciplinary comparison is that up-skilling must be understood in a dual sense, as including both those skills that management hopes for and legitimizes through skill/competency orientations, and the wide variety of 'skills' and 'competencies' (e.g. of disengagement, resistance, class consciousness, labour organizing, sabotage, etc.) that it does not. Against this observation, the de-skilling thesis must be understood on a conceptually different plane; a process revolving around autonomy, power, control and exploitation rather than skill per se. It is a thesis, therefore, that meaningfully theorizes forms of disempowerment and appropriation, as old skills are displaced and the new ones that emerge are frequently both limited and limiting in terms of anything but exchange-value generation. The up-skilling and de-skilling debate in the sociology of work – much like the current stand-off between advocates of skill/competency approaches and their critics – is therefore frequently fuelled by researchers referring to fundamentally different frames of reference and presumptions.

Labour perspectives on skills/competence frameworks

I argue that the critical orientation to skill/competency frameworks that has been developed thus far helps us to understand the series of failures that plague such initiatives to date: the failure to recognize the socially situated and collaborative nature of all skill performance, the failure to openly address the imbalances of power and thus the tendencies to reproduce inequities, the failure to recognize economic, sectoral, organizational dynamics, and finally the failure to address the conflation of 'actual skill/competency' versus relations of 'power/control'. Despite these shortcomings, what is clear is that organized labour across different national contexts has not infrequently supported skills/competency frameworks. Building on the recent analyses in Forrester (2005) and Martinez Lucio *et al.* (2007), we can in fact discern four, interrelated interests that have tended to draw different labour movements into national skill/competency framework participation.

First, there is an interest in skill/competency frameworks among labour movements which is oriented by a general belief that access to training enhances workers' lives: narrowly in terms of the work process, but also more broadly in terms of a member's labour market value. In fact, adult education participation research (e.g. Courtney 1992; Sawchuk 2003b) has demonstrated that virtually any form of engagement with training or educational programmes does tend to increase worker participation in the workplace and also increases participation in further education. Skills/competency frameworks would conceivably fit into such dynamics, achieving the types of goals that many labour organizations desire in these terms.

Second, labour movements are increasingly attentive to the matter of legitimacy. As the recent review of the status of organized labour internationally by Pencavel (2005) has shown, in many advanced capitalist countries, union density is in decline (see also Peetz 1998; Kelly 1999; Waddington and Kerr 1999; Martin & Ross 1999; Waddington 2000, 2001; Hurd 2001). These declines are most sharp in the USA, the UK and Australia but also identifiable in other countries including Japan and France. However, in countries such as Germany, Italy, Norway and Canada, union density has tended to remain relatively stable. For those national labour movements in some form of decline, there is often a concern for the broader legitimacy of unions as social and economic actors. Skill/competency frameworks in this context appear to offer an opportunity for renewed involvement in an economic policy which, in turn, offers the opportunity for increased legitimacy.

Closely related to this second point is a third one: practical recruitment potential (i.e. building membership). The labour movement in the UK is perhaps the clearest example of a national organized labour federation actively supporting a skills/competency approach with this purpose in mind. The UK's Trade Union Congress has actively supported 'employability' programmes focused on skill/competency approaches, an expression of which is the 'Union Learning Representative' programme (see Forrester 2005) which has as one of its goals to increase the relevance of unions in the lives of members as well as to support drives for increasing membership levels.

The fourth reason that organized labour has had for engaging with current skills/competency frameworks is the most basic. It is based on the widespread optimism that increases in skill and competencies among their membership will help companies compete effectively in global markets, in turn, increasing employment security for the membership, stabilizing wage levels and so on. Virtually every national labour movement that has supported skill/competency initiatives (e.g. the UK, Germany, Spain, Norway) has included this as its rationale either implicitly or explicitly.

Commenting on the broader, but closely linked 'lifelong learning' agenda, researchers (e.g. Green 2002; Cooney & Stuart 2004; Payne 2006) have noted that policy-in-practice varies significantly across countries, and that much depends on the interrelations between the state, employers and trade unions. However, even when national labour movements are in agreement with a specific skill/competency framework, practical challenges remain. In this regard, Martinez Lucio *et al.* (2007), in their detailed comparative case study of Germany, Norway and Spain, summarize several examples. The authors note the challenges of inter-institutional coordination for effective implementation of skill/competency frameworks. In terms of the three countries they analysed this meant re-orienting national and sectoral collective agreements, vocational education systems, and required the development of a functional framework of regulation at a broader political level. Particularly in countries such as Norway and Germany, forms of tripartite (state, employer, labour) bargaining were seen to be as much an impediment to new skill/competency initiatives as a support. The authors go on to note that, in addition, there was the contradiction of applying national policy to firms that operated internationally.

This brief indication of the challenges of implementation of skill/competency initiatives begins to emphasize the limitations of a generalized list of 'labour perspectives' such as the one provided above. A general list of interests, as useful as it may be, obscures the complexity where skill/competency frameworks are concerned. In particular, it obscures the differences within specific national contexts and within national labour movements. Moreover, to adequately understand the meaning of labour perspectives in relation to the adoption of and/or cooperation within national skills/competency frameworks, it is necessary to more deeply assess the meaning of these interests in relation to both issues of 'actual skill/competence' as well as matters of 'power/control'. When we take a close look at specific national cases, what we see is that much of labour's (and employers') interest in skill/competency frameworks has little to do with learning and skill per se. Understanding how and why this is so requires us to move beyond general themes to look at the contingencies of specific national contexts.

A comparative analysis of labour responses to the new politics of skill/competence formation

To respond to the issues highlighted above, we turn in this final section to a comparative analysis of labour response to the politics of skill/competence formation in Norway and Canada specifically. From a labour movement perspective, a focus on Norway and Canada offers a great deal. Of course, while it may be of value to study labour movements in decline, it is arguably of equal or greater value to attend to the cases in which it is not. Second, while it is important not to take the comparison too far, the Canadian and Norwegian economies share a number of important similarities which shape skill/competency needs. Both countries rely heavily on natural resources including petroleum and hydroelectric power as well as mining, timber, pulp and paper; both have sizeable public sectors; while in addition both have experienced similar declines in manufacturing. Productivity growth has been similar in the two countries over the last decade (2.5% for Canada; 2.8% for Norway); and both feature comparable levels of unemployment. Both have roughly comparable trading relationships to larger economic blocs to their south (the USA and the EU). While Norway's population is obviously smaller, it has a comparable educational infrastructure: in fact, Canada and Norway lead the world in post-secondary educational attainment, and each country features among the highest rates of participation in work-based training (OECD 2002, 2004; Livingstone 2004). In terms of labour relations, both countries have relative stable union density. At the same time however, there is an important difference that bears directly on the national experimentation with skill/competency frameworks. As we shall see below, Norwegian industrial relations are based on a more centralized, tripartite, social partnership governance structure; whereas Canada features a decentralized industrial relations system more similar to those seen in the USA and the UK. It is this final point that is perhaps most salient for understanding their distinct responses to skill/competency frameworks. Despite the difference, however, I argue that the labour movements in both countries have struggled with a similar contradiction: a contradiction rooted in a failure to clearly distinguish between 'actual skill/competency' development and 'power/control' dimensions endemic to the politics of skill/competency formation.

Labour and 'Competence Reform' in Norway

According to the recent case study by Payne (2006), Norway is regularly seen as an example of positive progress and engagement in terms of the skill/competency question. Its comprehensive programme of 'Competence Reform' (the *Realkompetanse* project), however, would seem to have hit the natural limits of engagement (Teige 2004) – what Payne (2006) refers to as the end of a cycle of policy and academic thinking' (p. 477). From the perspective of labour, Competence Reform has proven relatively ineffective in improving either work–life balance or productivity. Norway, as mentioned, is an example of strongly regulated, centralized national social bargaining structure involving employers (represented by such groups as the Confederation of Norwegian Business and Industry), labour (i.e. the Norwegian Confederation of Trade Unions), and the state.

However, according to Skule *et al.* (2002) the origins of the skill/competency initiative lie initially in the efforts of the Norwegian labour movement in the 1990s. Labour's chief concern at that time in addition to national competitiveness and employment, was the growing divide between high and low skilled workers and the potential negative effect on solidarity, quality of work–life balance and work participation. Here, as in many instances of application we see an example of the 'floating signifier' of skill/competency: quality of work life, participation and concerns over membership unity are addressed through the amorphous skill/competency discourse. Indeed, idealized discussion of Competence Reform in Norway quickly descended to earth when specifics were discussed, and rapidly turned into a traditional negotiation over such matters as the financing of educational leave. Important in the negotiation was eligibility of different training topics with employers dismissing programmes that did not directly meet the immediate needs of existing production systems, and labour expressing concerns that narrow forms of training and re-training might result in an overall de-skilling process. As Teige (2004) notes, ultimately employer groups would not be party to agreements that threatened managerial control.

Within the Norwegian labour movement itself, the skill/competency framework was accepted by those in some sectors and contested by those in others, while additional fragmentation appeared between executive and rank-and-file union members as well. In fact, according to Teige (2004), a large proportion of rank-and-file members preferred to drop the agenda of skills, training and quality of work–life balance in favour of reversing the wage restraint agreement signed by the Confederation several years earlier. Most pointedly, as Payne (2006) notes in this quote from a former union official, 'the attitude of the members tended to be one of why do we need more competence?... The Competence Reform came to be seen as just another excuse not to give us more wages' (p. 482). Rank-and-file workers appeared to remain unconvinced by the national competitiveness arguments (unlike their union executive): in many ways this represented a refusal by rank-and-file workers to confuse issues of 'actual skill/competence' with those of 'power/control'; a matter in which they had little faith in the former's ability to deliver the latter. In turn, union executive officials lamented the lost opportunity of having Competence Reform serve as a path towards greater say over the work process and technological change, despite the evidence that employers remained intransigent about ceding any form of workplace control.

What is easily lost in much of this is a point noted earlier. Norway, like Canada, already has the most educated adult populations in the world. Short of an indictment of the entire Norwegian educational and vocational training system, it is therefore not hard to see how Competence Reform might be perceived as having more to do with issues of power and control, rather than 'actual skill/competence' needs. Indeed, in practice Competence Reform seemed to have included significant numbers of employers continuing to prefer the certainty of keeping a lower-skilled employee to the uncertainty of losing one with more advanced skills and thus broader labour market appeal (Payne 2006).

This contradictory conflation of skill/competence and power/control issues expressed itself in other ways as well. As a representative of the Norwegian Federation of Manufacturing Industries put it succinctly enough: '[w]hat you will see is low skill, labour intensive jobs and mass production steadily moving out of Norway to Latvia and the Baltic states. The reality is that if you want to stay in a job in this sector then you have to develop your competence' (Payne 2006: 490). Here we see an example of 'skill/competence' as a signifier for wage competitiveness.

What were the actual successes of the Competence Reform programme? The Competence Reform initiative resulted in significant levels of the documentation of non-formal learning, with many using this documentation to gain advanced standing in existing secondary educational programmes and higher education. The initiative resulted in the delivery of some additional training, though there remained no pay for educational leave. What is striking perhaps is the degree to which the lofty rhetoric of skill/competency devolved into such conventional, long-standing education and training concerns.

The impasse reached in the Norwegian case, in fact, was shaped from the beginning by matters of control rather than competence. Indeed, this realization among employer and labour representatives alike has appeared to have led to shrinking interest. What may hold some promise, however, is the tentative emergence of support for turning attention towards the workplace itself. Nordic countries, and Scandinavian countries in particular, long renowned for their attention to technological change, work–life studies and the labour process itself (cf. Skule & Reichborn 2002), would appear ideally positioned to undertake this next step in the new politics of skill/competency formation. What anecdotal evidence there is suggests the possibility for gains in skill/competency as well as power-sharing and trust when changes at the level of day-to-day work processes are the focus of efforts. Here again many other employers remain sceptical, viewing such experiments as 'an extra cost and time out of production' (see Payne 2006: 493).

Labour and 'Essential Skills' in Canada

Like Norway, a skill/competency initiative has also emerged in Canada. However, unlike Norway, the process does not have roots in the labour movement beyond a basic shared concern for adult basic education (literacy and numeracy). Indeed, reflecting the absence of social partnership the initiative finds its origins in federal state efforts primarily; predictably this has led to low levels of acceptance and application.

One explanation of these low levels of acceptance is Canada's decentralized industrial relations regime where labour negotiation is found mostly at the firm level, though with some instances of sectoral agreements through what is known as patterned bargaining and some limited attempts at social partnership agreements through Canada's sector councils. Inhibiting comprehensive experimentation further is Canada's constitutional structure which features a division of responsibility between the federal government (with responsibility for work-based training matters) and provincial government (with responsibility for educational provision including vocational education and apprenticeship certification) making any attempt at comprehensive reform unlikely.

Nevertheless, in 2004 the Human Resources and Social Development Canada (HRSDC) department of the federal government introduced the 'Essential Skills' programme (2005a, 2005b). The Essential Skills programme revolves around occupational profiling rooted in a traditional attempt to identify and track the incidence of nine competencies: reading text; document use; numeracy; writing; oral communication; working with others; thinking skills; computer use; and, continuous learning.

What is clear, is that in terms of a labour perspective, the basic approach to skill/competency within this programme is limited and limiting. The Canadian Labour Congress (CLC) has made it clear that such approaches have the potential to increase surveillance, to increase the intensity of work, training and education, and to establish accountability frameworks built on a foundation of competitiveness and profitability rather than genuine skill development (CLC 2005, 2006). The CLC response to the Essential Skills programme appears to recognize its narrow conceptualization of skill and competency themselves: as outlined earlier in this article, often individualized, cognitive capacities are central while the collective, situated nature of competence is marginalized resulting in a 'deficit model' of worker capacities. These and many other elements, according to the CLC, form the implicit infrastructure of HRSDC's stated goals of producing a 'more productive workforce'. Thus, the labour response in Canada is – on the surface – markedly distinct from that seen in Norway. In contrast to Norway, the CLC has taken a rejectionist stance.

Understanding the fragmented and contradictory orientation within the Canadian labour movement is difficult due to decentralization. The CLC report, in fact, recognizes this fragmentation even while producing its recommendations. For our purposes here, this fragmentation can be understood most easily through a basic three-part framework that describes the different forms of Anglo-North American trade unionism: 'business unionism', 'service unionism' and 'social unionism'.

Business unionism is an approach that forefronts a partnership between capital and labour in terms governed by capitalist production, circulation, distribution and consumption as pre-given and sacrosanct. It is somewhat difficult to distinguish business unionism from the range of participatory management/human resource practices currently available, but nevertheless, a business unionism perspective of the Essential Skills framework seen in Canada is largely positive, not unlike the orientation of Norwegian labour executive members. In the case of Canada, this approach has been expressed at the individual firm level. Overall, it is an orientation to the skill/competency question that aims at skill and knowledge development that best facilitates the competitive power of the firm. In Canada, examples of this are found in individual employers introducing the Essential Skills framework in individual workplaces as an expanded Human Resource programme aimed at more effectively advertising, sorting and hiring, and, in a small number of cases, anecdotally related, which have resulted in support for educational upgrading. What is clear is that even among labour representatives oriented by a business unionism approach, there is no evidence of incorporation of Essential Skills orientations into collective agreements. Here the distinction between 'actual skills/competency' and 'power/control' remains unaddressed.

Service unionism is an approach that forefronts a relationship based on conflict between capital and labour; however, it is also an approach that orients almost exclusively to wage/benefits bargaining in the absence of a concern for participative control in the labour process. This approach seeks to maximize the wages and benefits that accrue to union members. A service unionism perspective on the Essential Skills programme in Canada would not be expected to challenge who controls the assessment and recognition of the basic skill/knowledge sets. Additionally, it is doubtful that such an approach would challenge the relevancy of the skill sets themselves. To the degree that skill/competency frameworks such as the Essential Skills programme have been initiated in Canada, it is through this type of negotiated model that has, as in the case of Norway above, typically led to conventional bargaining over issues such as paying for educational leave, and so on.

Finally, social unionism is an approach that is highly variegated, prone in the last two decades as well as in the inter-World War period in North America, to have been understood through a variety of additional subforms and strategies. It is summarized generally as forefronting social change by including as part of organized labour's interests, the needs of the broader

working classes under capitalism. As such, it has taken on a range of additional titles such as 'campaign unionism', 'organizing unionism', 'community
unionism' and 'social capital unionism'. Here we are most likely to see an orientation to 'actual skill/competency' as individual and collective organizing
capacities separate from production learning which is, in keeping with labour
relations law in Canada, ceded to managerial control. That is, the
'power/control' dimension of the skill/competency question is forefronted;
'actual skill/competency' is taken seriously but only in the context of the
needs of labour organizing and the skills necessary for the functioning of the
union with little reference to production competencies. From a social unionism perspective, at the centre of a critique of the Essential Skills programme
is an interest to build practical capacity to transcend current labour processes,
job and technological design for greater economic democracy. Examples of
where, in fact, a genuinely new politics of skill/competency is emerging from
a labour perspective is found among unions actively campaigning in the service sector such as the UNITE-HERE union in the hospitality industry
(Sawchuk 2007). 'Power/control' issues are forefronted, 'skill/competency' is
understood internal to union goals, and changes in labour processes including
production skill/competency are viewed as an unproblematic outcome of
broader changes.

Beyond these different ways that labour has taken up the skill/competence
agenda in Canada, it is relevant to note that serious discussion of the Essential
Skills has, for all intents and purposes, been limited to state policy personnel
and, occasionally, human resource professionals. With minor exceptions,
labour in Canada has largely kept its distance beyond their (limited) participation in sector councils which benefited from an associated cash injection early
in the framework's initiation (Anonymous 2004). However, what has become
clear is that employers, within and outside of sector councils, have maintained
an orientation to motives not unlike those seen in Norway. As Hayes (2005)
reports, employer motives remain fixated upon dealing with 'the process of
improving productivity and performance, and finding solutions to labour
shortages' (p. 7). She goes on to forecast the emergence of an approach that
'effectively avoids targeting individuals and encourages organizations to create
conditions allowing for strong cultures of learning' (p. 7): a prediction that has
turned out to be grossly misguided. In Canada, like in Norway, the
skill/competency approach has spiralled into virtual irrelevance; stranded on
the shores of issues of power, control and the distribution of resources.

Conclusions

I began this article with a review of the standard critique of skill/competency
frameworks. As these scholars have noted, skill and competence as it is taken up
in such frameworks is a floating signifier that obscures context, inequities and
the social nature of the learning process itself. 'Skill is an illusion', according to

Fenwick, subject to the prevailing 'knowledge politics'. The upskilling/deskilling debates in the sociology of work added further clarity to the distinctions between 'actual skill/competence' and issues of 'power/control'. Thereafter I sought to add an appreciation for industrial relations negotiation from the standpoint of organized labour. It is in this context that we see the degree to which the skill/competence rhetoric is perpetually on the brink of sliding into the push and pull of traditional negotiation. In practice, skill/competence became a proxy for struggles over power and control.

In turning towards a review of organized labour perspectives specifically, I outlined four pragmatic interests in skill/competency initiatives that labour has regularly expressed. Here again we saw that these interests had relatively little to do with genuine 'up-skilling' or raising the competency levels of either workers or work processes.

The more detailed profile of Norwegian and Canadian initiatives demonstrated the ambiguity and unevenness of labour's perspective on the skill/competence question in practice. Norway with its tripartite, social partnership governance structure saw the labour movement initiate a Competence Reform programme only to find the emergence of a traditional negotiation over the funding of educational leaves, accompanied by increased documentation of workers' learning and some moderate increases in educational access. Employer intransigence was matched only by rank-and-file worker rejection of Competence Reform in favour of traditional wage gains. In Canada, a rejectionist stance was maintained by the central labour federation while some small-scale engagement occurred at the individual firm and sector council levels. By far the bulk of the labour movement in Canada deemed the Essential Skills programme irrelevant to their concerns, in some cases eclipsing the skills/competency approach with their own development of organizing cultures.

In both cases – in countries that one might predict fertile ground for new initiatives to take root – the spiralling irrelevance of the so-called 'new politics of skill/competence formation' has been deeply shaped by something that both employers and labour seem to have implicitly understood: in the absence of gains in their respective power and control there is little reason to invest energies into skill/competence frameworks. This confirms the critique of at least a subset of scholars who have maintained that political economic questions remain the fulcrum over which the politics of knowledge pivot. Indeed, it appears likely that, until the matters of 'actual skill/competence' and 'power/control' are simultaneously taken up within the labour process itself, motivation among either employers or labour for participation in such initiative will continue to be elusive.

Competences and employer engagement

Pam Irwin

Defining competences

Although the terms 'competence' and 'competences' are widely used in management, employment and education, they are challenging to define. Initially coined by Boyatzis (1982) to mean 'an underlying characteristic of a person...motive, trait, skill, aspect of one's self-image or social role, or a body of knowledge' (p. 21), other conceptions of competency range from Randell's (1989) 'nothing more or less than glorious human skills' to 'a dimension of behaviour' (Liam, Healy & Associates 2003). Often equated with skills, competences are also categorized as generic (transferable) and situation specific (van Gelderen 2007), and core and defined (Skills for Health 2007a). By contrast, the Organisation for Economic Co-operation and Development Directorate for Education's (OECD 2005) selection and definition of competences is more holistic, and, in addition to knowledge and skills, 'a competency involves the ability to meet complex demands by drawing on and mobilizing psychosocial resources (including skills and attitudes) in a particular context'. Analogously, Lathi (1999) adopts an inclusive definition of competences – essentially the skills needed to perform specific functions, integrating elements of knowledge, skills and behaviours and/or attitudes.

Competences – typology

Other interpretations of competences are discussed by van Gelderen (2007). He describes three views – the perspective adopted in this chapter. First, competence is an underlying characteristic of an individual (the input approach favoured in the United States of America); next, competence is linked to standards or outcomes (the output model identified in the United Kingdom); and in the final definition, competence is informed by both inputs and outputs and related to behaviour or attitudes.

Competences – applications

In turn, these approaches broadly align with three primary applications of competences – work related skill sets, standards, and 'professionalism'.

The input model of competences – work related skill sets

The input model of competences causally relates competences with successful performance in the workplace (Spencer & Spencer 1993). It also suggests that these work related skill sets are discrete and can be learned; collaborative competencies (Barr 1998) being one example. Much of the revitalized vocational agenda in the United Kindom seems to conform to this assumption, for instance, the 14–19 diplomas (Department for Education and Skills 2005), and advanced and professional apprenticeships (Learning and Skills Council 2005). By accommodating academic and work related learning, these initiatives provide robust alternatives to the traditional A-level educational benchmarks, and in the case of the new diplomas, will replace the current system of around 3,500 separate qualifications. With an overarching goal to improve vocational education, the 14–19 qualifications will be led by employers through the Sector Skills Councils, and create new gateway(s) to higher education and skilled employment (DfES 2005). Similarly, modern apprenticeships are designed to meet employers' present and future skills needs, and offer a progression route into further learning and higher qualifications (Lammy, 2008).

The output model of competences – standards

Standards underline the output conception of competences, and in the United Kingdom, 'National Occupational Standards define the competences which apply to job roles or occupations in the form of statements of performance, knowledge and the evidence required to confirm competence' (Skills for Business 2007). Development of National Occupational Standards and National Workforce Competences for health care is a major commitment of Skills for Health, the Sector Skills Council for the United Kingdom health sector. This National Occupational Standards/National Workforce Competences project also links to key government agendas such as National Service Frameworks, key targets, and the Knowledge and Skills Framework, where appropriate (Skills for Health 2007b). As statements of competence describing good practice and performance criteria, the National Occupational Standards/National Workforce Competences are proactive decision tools related to the demands of employment, the coverage and focus of services, and the structure and content of education and training, and related qualifications. Consequently, they are useful in the management and development of organizations and individuals, job design, recruitment, personal, professional and team development, career planning and appraisal. The interactive competence tool allows cross-referencing and searches according to National Occupational Standard/National Workforce Competences suites and specific functional tasks. Since each National Occupational Standard and National Workforce Competence consists of various elements such as activity scope, the tool also supports competence clustering, team and/or personal and professional profiling, and group and/or self assessment. An additional tool, the Health Functional Map relates competences and functions needed to deliver effective health care services at a strategic level, to the operational National Occupational Standard/National Workforce Competence level (Skills for Health 2007b).

The 'behaviour' model of competences – professionalism

As the third conception of competences addresses both inputs and outputs in terms of behaviour or attitudes, it aligns with many professions. The perception of 'professionalism' and professional competence is strictly regulated and enforced by statutory authorities such as the Health Professions Council in the United Kingdom. Currently registering over 180,000 practitioners from 13 professions, the Health Professions Council only 'accepts' professionals who meet predetermined standards of professional skills, behaviour and health (Health Professions Council 2008).

Most self-regulating professions require evidence of the registrant's competence in the form of mandated continuing education such as attendance at continuing professional development courses and submission of practice hours and/or reflective portfolios.

Competences and education

The symbiotic relationship between competences and education is also reflected in the recent political emphasis on employment and skills in the United Kingdom, primarily via the Leitch Review of Skills (HM Treasury 2006). With an increased emphasis on skills development, the Review aims to maximize economic growth, productivity and social justice, and identify the balance of responsibility for achieving an optimal skills profile. It also recommends investing in a knowledge economy by treating learning as a lifelong activity – one that is responsive to the changing skills demands of a globalized economy, or more pragmatically, a skilling, up-skilling and reskilling agenda. In essence, the Leitch Review of Skills advocates a significant refocusing of the fundamental educational mix of teaching/learning, quality assurance/'fit for purpose', to include employer demand-led provision, thereby leveraging workforce development (competences and skills) with education.

Higher education

A parallel report, the Higher Education Funding Council for England's strategy *Engaging Employers with Higher Education* (2006a) also explores how Higher Education Institutions can be supported to develop dynamic partnerships with employers. For example, Higher Level Skills Pathfinder projects work with employers and their representative bodies to provide specialist skills brokerage to meet regional employment priorities (Higher Education Funding Council for England 2007a). In addition, the Higher Education Funding Council for England's (2007b) Higher Education Business and Community Interaction Survey demonstrates that 88 per cent of Higher Education Institutions offer flexible tailor-made courses for business on campus, and 80 per cent offer similar bespoke education at companies' premises. Furthermore, 78 per cent of Higher Education Institutions also report that employers are actively engaged in the development of content and regular reviewing of curricula. Currently, Higher Education Institutions interact with employers and the 'community' as a supplier and user of 'labour'; in economic development and knowledge transfer initiatives, networks and partnerships; and to support lifelong learning (Hogarth *et al.* 2007).

Further education

Within Further Education, there is a greater emphasis on colleges engaging with employers to ensure provision is demand led and that 'learners and employers are in the driving seat in determining what is funded and how services are delivered. Employers will benefit from training delivered in the workplace, by a provider of their choosing, delivered to suit their operational needs' (DfES 2006). Further Education Colleges are involved in many specialist networks with employers, including Centres of Vocational Excellence, and the 14–19 Diplomas.

Lifelong learning

As noted previously, employer engagement will also be crucial in promoting lifelong learning. By 2020, 70 per cent of the United Kingdom workforce will have completed compulsory education (HM Treasury 2006). To cater for 'non-traditional' workers/learners, such as vocational, mature and part-time learners, increasing flexibility of provision will be important (Universities UK 2007).

Education and employment

Although these burgeoning relationships between education and employers are laudable, challenges remain. Differences in terminology, priorities and outcomes are underscored by Mumford (2007) in his keynote address at the North-West Lifelong Learning Network conference. In his presentation titled 'Employer Higher Education Partnerships. What works well and what needs to improve', Mumford cautions that 'employees are motivated differently to normal students' and 'concepts like "fine grading", "volume of learning" and "level" are counterproductive' (2007). While educational providers often purport to successfully 'engage with employers', confusion over fundamental concepts, such as 'learning' ('academic' and 'vocational'), awards and qualifications ('accreditation' and quality assurance), and competency in the workplace ('fit for practice'), persists.

Competences, education and employment

Exemplars

Nonetheless, some innovative exemplars that link competences, education and employment are evident; specifically work-based learning, accreditation of employer-based training, credit accumulation and transfer schemes, and vocational competence ('fit for practice').

Work-based learning. Recognition of work-based learning opportunities across the United Kingdom, such as Middlesex University Centre of Excellence in Teaching and Learning in Work-based Learning (2007) is increasing. Defined as learning that is derived at, in and from the workplace (Seagraves *et al.* 1996), much work-based learning is integrated into two-year Foundation Degrees (Foundation Degree Forward 2007a). Foundation Degrees are designed with employers to equip learners with the knowledge, understanding and skills relevant to their employment, and are often delivered by innovative teaching/learning methods. A model of work-based learning founded on 'academic' learning in a health care setting is constructed by Irwin (2007).

Accreditation of employer-based training. Accreditation of employer-based training in England is driven by Foundation Degree Forward (2007b). The Employer Based Training Accreditation pilot project enables employers to benefit from the accreditation of existing workplace training by providing a trained Employer Based Training Accreditation facilitator to perform a preliminary analysis of the training and assign notional credits and levels, brokering the accreditation processes between the employer and a Higher Education Institution, and finally, facilitating further progression by employees into and through higher education. To this effect, Foundation Degree Forward engages a range of universities, Further Education Colleges, Chambers of Commerce, UnionLearn and selected employer groups (Phillips 2007).

Credit accumulation and transfer schemes. Various systems of credit accumulation and transfer are being piloted by some Lifelong Learning Networks to 'test' the overarching principles and operational criteria for a 'common approach to credit' developed by the Joint Forum for Higher Levels (Joint

Forum for Higher Levels 2006). For example, the Greater Manchester Strategic Alliance module catalogue/credit accumulation and transfer scheme (GMSA Advance) aims to support institutions in providing employer-led, flexible, work-related higher education provision, centred on small 'bite-sized' units (modules) of learning. Each module offers a clear and coherent 'stand-alone' learning experience. Learners are awarded credit for each module and can also link several modules within the catalogue to form a credit-bearing award or qualification. While 'Advance' is operated by the Greater Manchester Strategic Alliance on behalf of its members, ownership and management of each module is retained by the validating Higher Education Institution and its delivery partners. It is expected that these learning opportunities will suit the needs of part-time learners who may be in employment and seeking personal, professional and/or career development opportunities; and also, employers accessing higher education to help them develop their workforce (Greater Manchester Strategic Alliance 2007a).

Vocational competence/'fit for practice'. In 2004, the University Vocational Awards Council anticipated issues related to competency in the workplace and vocational 'fitness for practice' by advocating the use of National Occupation Standards in higher education to meet the needs of employment. As curriculum 'benchmarks', National Occupational Standards are expected to enhance graduate employability, workplace competence, professional standards and create a gateway to substantial higher education engagement in workforce development (University Vocational Awards Council 2004).

A contrasting model, the Catalyst business interchange scheme (Clark & Craven 2007) permits further education teachers, tutors and trainers in the further education sector to update their business-related skills through a variety of learning experiences in industry. These opportunities extend from one-day industry awareness visits to one academic year industry-based sabbaticals. At present, all sectors of industry are represented and the 'exchange' programme is fully funded.

Employer engagement

Despite these renewed skills, education and employment relationships, a common understanding of 'employer engagement' remains elusive. For instance, the Higher Education Funding Council for England's (2006b, page 4) definition – employer engagement is 'a sub set of the broad range of collaboration between education providers and public and private sector organizations', is vague. Similar reports published in 2007, such as *World Class Skills: Implementing the Leitch review of skills in England* (Department for Innovation, Universities and Skills 2007); *Workforce Development: Employer engagement with higher education* (King 2007); *Higher Education, Skills and Employer Engagement* (Sastry & Bekhradnia 2007); *Response to Higher Education Funding Council for England's Employer Engagement Strategy* (Universities UK 2007); *Employer*

Engagement: Higher education for the workforce: barriers and facilitators (Wedgwood 2007) unpick the higher education/ employer relationship, but circumvent a rigorous analysis of employer engagement. Even the engagement framework, (a five-point classification scale ranging from awareness activity to strategic alliance), produced by The Centre of Education in the Built Environment in 2005, does not elaborate on how education providers can effectively engage with employers (*Accelerating Change in Built Environment Education* 2005).

Competences and employer engagement

To ameliorate this situation and move the employer engagement agenda forward, this chapter proposes that the key to closer education/employer relations rests with competences. By cross matching competences (typology, applications and exemplars) with the simplified outcomes of workforce development (essentially, skilling, up-skilling and reskilling) and education in general (teaching/learning, quality assurance, and fitness for purpose), an interesting resonance with employer engagement emerges. This is reflected in the following table in which three authentic vignettes from Greater Manchester in the United Kingdom briefly illustrate the synergy (employer engagement) between employers and educators at an operational level – enhanced and mediated through competences.

Vignettes

Table 10.1 The relationship between employment and education (employer engagement) mediated through competencies

Context		Operational indicators		
		Vignette 1	*Vignette 2*	*Vignette 3*
Employment (demand)	Workforce development	Skilling	Up-skilling	Reskilling
	Competencies	Input model	Output model	Behaviours (informed by input\ and output models)
Employer engagement	Applications	Work-related skill sets	Standards	Professionalism
	Exemplars	Work-based learning	Accreditation of employer-based training	Fit for practice
Education (supply)	Educational provision	Teaching and learning	Quality assurance	Fit for purpose

Vignette 1 (skilling): Step-In to HE. The 'Step-In to HE' project is a personal development 'taster' that enables Advanced Apprentices who have completed their technical certificate and other framework requirements to study at a higher education level and gain ten transferable higher education credits. Co-sponsored by the Greater Manchester Strategic Alliance and Aimhigher Greater Manchester, the bridging module provides a new, skills-based progression for Advanced Apprentices from work-based learning into higher education (Greater Manchester Strategic Alliance, 2007b). As the module emphasizes research skills, personal development planning and academic writing techniques, it allows learners to access transferable higher level skills, while simultaneously developing their career path in the workplace. Evaluation of the pilot programme (Leech 2008: 11) indicates that 79 per cent of Advanced Apprentices who completed the module intend to progress to higher education within the next two years. This figure compares favourably with an estimated progression rate of 3 per cent for Greater Manchester and 2 to 4 per cent for the United Kingdom nationally (Leech 2008: 1).

Vignette 2 (up-skilling): Digital Pass Programme. The Digital Pass Programme is an innovative public/private collaboration created to develop and deliver inter-institutional continuing professional development modules for freelance workers in the media, digital and creative industries in Greater Manchester. Supported and approved by a Higher Education Institution, the Digital Pass Programme transforms pre-existing employer-based training workshops into four linked modules, leading to a fully accredited qualification – a Certificate of Continuing Professional Development in Digital Pass. As the programme is delivered by industry professionals, and blends academic requirements with learner-specific work-experience placements, it ensures that these freelancers are conversant with the latest technological advances in this rapidly evolving sector. Accordingly, this new programme provides a springboard to up-skill the freelance workforce and grow a world class media economy in the region (University of Bolton, School of Arts, Media and Education 2008).

Vignette 3 (reskilling): Continuing Professional Development awards in Leadership Management. A suite of continuing professional development awards leading to a Certificate, Diploma and Advanced Diploma in Leadership Management will support personal and professional development (reskilling) for selected staff required to undertake team leadership roles within target organizations. The continuing professional development provision is predicated upon stand-alone modules in a targeted aspect of professional leadership, rather than the acquisition of a broader-based management qualification of more significant size. This is a deliberate strategy to enhance 'fitness for purpose' and 'fitness for practice' (Greater Manchester Strategic Alliance 2007c).

Finally, while these vignettes do not claim to be 'best practice', it is hoped that this competence-based approach to employer engagement will stimulate dialogue, and then actively advance education/employment partnerships.

Chapter 11

Developing competence-in-practice

Learning stories of female entrepreneurs in small business

Manuela Perrotta

Introduction

In the last few years, the debate on competence development (CD) has been enriched by new perspectives and has assumed a central role in the field of Workplace Learning. In this chapter, competences will be interpreted as competence-in-practice to stress the performative, relational and situated dimension of the learning process that leads to CD.

There are many reasons for the choice of female small business as the empirical case study. The first is that small businesses, which are quite diffuse and ingrained in Italy, have been little studied in the literature on the development of competences, which has instead concentrated on large organizations. As will be seen in the analysis of the empirical material, small businesses are characterized by an informal management style that could be defined as 'domestic', because for the most part they are family managed. In particular, the research was realized as part of a project that aimed to investigate the quality and make-up of the presence of women in the world of small business. The project expected to collect seventy histories and experiences of female entrepreneurs working in a province in Northern Italy. The objective of the project was to understand how one becomes a female entrepreneur in a social context that is characterized by a traditional division of gender roles.

The international literature on entrepreneurism has overcome a vision entirely masculine in its language and culture (Ahl 2004, 2006; Bruni *et al.* 2004), but often the alternative has been represented by a comparative study of the experiences of men and women in which those of the latter were shown as lacking. The objective of the research was not to understand why the women were not as 'good' as the men, but to pluralize the voices, to give greater visibility to female entrepreneurial experiences without devaluing them. Adopting the adage of Belenky and her colleagues (1986: 5)

> in our study we chose to listen only to women. The male experience has been so powerfully articulated that we believed we would hear the patterns in women's voices more clearly if we held at bay the powerful templates men have etched in the literature and in our minds.

How can one affirm the 'voice' of women within the world of small business if the women themselves do not gain an awareness of their own voices and of their own experiences as female entrepreneurs and women? To give voice to these women we chose to use narrative interviews as the method for the collection of the data, which were then analysed, focusing attention on various aspects (see Gherardi 2008).

In this chapter, I have concentrated on highlighting the way in which CD occurs in female small business, departing from an analysis of the *learning stories* of the interviewees. In the following sections, following a theoretical introduction of the concept of competences-in-practice, I will concentrate on the empirical analysis in order to account for the various nuances of CD.

Studying competences-in-practice from learning stories

In the last few years the concept of competence and the label 'competence development' have been used in various ways to arrive at quite different interpretations and practices. The concept of competence, and its use in literature, is in itself problematic.

According to Ellström and Kock (in this volume) the concept of competence, although often poorly defined in the literature, has a dual meaning: according to one view, competence is considered to be an attribute of the employee, that is, as a kind of human capital or a human resource that can be translated into a certain level of performance; while according to another view, competence is defined in terms of the requirements of the tasks that constitute a certain job. In pointing out this distinction, the authors use the term competence to refer to the capacity of an individual (or a collective) to successfully (according to certain formal or informal criteria, set by oneself or by somebody else) handle certain situations or complete a certain task or job (Ellström 1997). Alternatively, the term qualification is used to refer to the competence that is actually required by the task.

In a way this concept is merely the latest of a number of theories aimed at explaining the competitiveness of a firm (Drejer 2000). In fact, in examining the practitioners' understanding of this notion, it could be said that (generally) CD is something that could and should be planned by the company and in cooperation with the employee. This understanding of CD considers employee needs for further training with regard to their present and future tasks and responsibilities.

According to Sandberg (2000), this understanding of the concept is essentially based on a rationalistic approach and provides theories that regard competence as constituted by a specific set of attributes that workers use to accomplish their work. These attributes are primarily seen as context-independent. An alternative view of the concept of competence is based on an interpretative approach, in which it emerges that attributes used in accomplishing work are not primarily context-free but are situational. Following this second approach, the attributes used in a specific job acquire their context-dependence through the worker's ways of experiencing that work.

However, the interpretative approach, which is the one I will follow in the chapter, does not present an univocal view on competence. A 'generic' approach to competence (Norris 1991), for instance, establishes competences through behavioural event or critical incident interviewing to identify the general abilities associated with expert performers. Furthermore, Keen (1992) states that competence is the ability to cope with a situation, to act and to look forward. According to Keen, competence is the interplay between skills, knowledge, experience, contacts and values.

The problem with these definitions is that the term competence is often used similarly to the way it is used in everyday speech to code a broad range of experiences related to craftsmanship, specialization, intelligence and problem solving. As such, competence remains an experience-near concept (Geertz 1983) which needs further conceptual clarification if it is to serve the purpose of theory building.

In order to respond to this critique, more specific definitions of competence were proposed. According to Sundberg (2001) a pragmatic definition of competence should contain: knowledge, what you learn in education; experience, what you gather in your job, at your workplace and in your social life; abilities, how you use your knowledge and experience. This definition illustrates that competence is the interplay between different characteristics and skills and suggests that competence cannot be seen merely as 'knowledge' – interpreted as what you learn through formal processes – but also in such abilities as the embracing of new knowledge, the ability to learn from each other and the ability to develop personal capabilities. Moreover, CD should deal with many more aspects than just education.

This understanding of competence leads to what has been defined as 'competence in use' (Ellström 1997). Competence-in-use emphasizes that competence is neither primarily an attribute of the individual worker (or the collective of workers), nor primarily an attribute of the job. Rather, the focus is on the interaction between the individual and the job, and on the competence that is actually used by the worker in performing the job. According to a similar perspective, a way of understanding the notion of competence is to consider that it involves 'the ability to think and act appropriately in future situations that are not known and cannot be foreseen at the time when the competences are developed' (Illeris 2008: 2). However, Illeris (2008) argues that competences are not something that can be produced like commodities, but must be developed in and by the person, hence the concept of CD. So competences can be understood as personal (or collective) abilities, capacities and skills developed doing a particular task or job.

The aim of this chapter is to deeply analyse this latter way of understanding CD following a practice-based approach (Gherardi 2000; 2006) that allows for analysing how competences-in-practice are developed by doing. Gherardi argues that

> when a practitioner competently reproduces one of the common practices of his or her occupation, s/he is mobilizing a knowing-how which associates his/her body, social relations in action, artefacts, his/her knowing how to use abstract knowledge, the codes of his/her community, and his/her capacity to see, hear and react to others, and to the situation, as part of a 'seeing', 'doing' and 'saying' deemed appropriate by the co-participants in the situation.
>
> (2006: 228)

Furthermore, there is a need for a better definition of what we mean by knowledge and learning. As we have seen in the definition proposed by some authors, knowledge is something that is static and that you learn in school. In my view, the possible misunderstanding of CD is strictly related to the learning metaphor of acquisition largely diffused in some literature. As Gherardi and colleagues (1998: 273) point out 'when learning is viewed in this way it may be equated to eating: knowledge is food for the mind, and the learner seeks to find the right necessary sort of food and to ingest or consume it'. Moving from the learning metaphor of knowledge acquisition to that of participation invoked by the so-called 'situated learning' theorists (Brown *et al.* 1989; Brown & Duguid 1991; Lave & Wenger 1991; Wenger 1998) means to abandon the idea of knowledge as something that can be owned by individuals. This idea was also introduced by Gergen, who argued that 'knowledge is not something that people possess in their heads, but rather, something that people do together' (1991: 270).

Performing competently means to properly use formal, as well as tacit, knowledge. The term tacit knowledge (Polanyi 1958) refers to those forms of knowledge one cannot account for in terms of rationality, objectivity or detachment, but which are learned through the body, imitation or forms of transmission that do not occur through cognition, but through interpersonal interactions (Bruni & Gherardi 2007: 106). Following a practice-based approach (Gherardi 2000, 2006), to know is to be capable of participating with the requisite competence in the complex web of relationships among people, material artefacts and activities. The concept of knowing-in-practice (Gherardi 2000, 2006; Nicolini *et al.* 2003) assumes that it is an activity and that knowing-in-practice is always a practical accomplishment. Following Gherardi, knowing-in-practice can be defined as 'an accomplishment realized by establishing connections in action' (2006: xxi). In other words, I have interpreted knowledge 'as a social process, human and material, aesthetic as well as emotive and ethical, and that knowledge is embedded in practice, as the domain where doing and knowing are one and the same' (Gherardi 2006: xii). Hence no distinction is drawn between knowing and learning because they are both developed simultaneously through a course of action. Knowledge is not, therefore, in the mind or an 'object' that can be transferred from an existing context to a new one, but is something that is situated in everyday practices and takes place in the flow of experience, with or without our being aware of it (Gherardi 2006: 14). In this way knowing and learning are processes embedded in the performance of a working practice and situated in the body, in a physical context, in the dynamics of interactions, and in language (Gherardi 2006).

In this chapter, the label competences-in-practice is used in a twofold manner: from a theoretical point of view, to suggest a specific interpretation of how competences are developed in the accomplishment of working practices; and from a methodological point of view, referring to the way in which they can be described, studied and analysed.

According to some literature (Drejer 2000; Sundberg 2001), following a rationalistic approach to competence often means trying to operationalize and measure it. On the contrary, my aim in this chapter is to describe and analyse the elements that constitute the entrepreneurial competences-in-practice in female small business. In other words, how do women learn to become entrepreneurs? How do people become competent in their work? How are competences developed?

On the bases of seventy recorded and transcribed interviews with female entrepreneurs I will analyse their 'learning stories' in order to show how competences-in-practice are developed. By learning stories I mean the narratives about how entrepreneurs have learned what they do, including formal and informal learning processes. In particular, in order to collect information on their informal learning process, we used the 'episodic interview' (Flick 1997), which allows for contextualizing experiences and events from the interviewee's point of view. The episodic interview technique is better oriented to obtain narratives of different types of situations than situations which have been defined according to criteria fixed in advance, as in the case of formal learning paths.

The interviews, which lasted between forty-five and 120 minutes, were realized with women that own (or collaborate in the management of) small businesses (from individual enterprises to those with a staff of fifteen people) on the border between handicraft and enterprise in a small city in the North of Italy.

Following a practice-based approach the analysis of the interviews will focus on the situatedness and contingency of the competences-in-practice, paying attention to the description, comprehension, and analysis of the learning stories in which entrepreneurial competences are developed. Particularly, I will analyse three different dimensions of competences-in-practice that emerged from the interviews:

1   *Developing sensible knowledge*: the competences-in-practice more strictly related to manual and craft work;

2   *Learning how to translate materiality*: those that developed performing rela-
    tional practices in order to translate the technical language for those not
    from the trade;
3   *Picking up managing competences by osmosis*: those relating to a more general
    view of the firm's management.

Although the three dimensions are strictly interconnected, this distinction
illustrates some of the features of competence-in-practice that are common to
firms that are otherwise very different in terms of the kind of trade, sector,
management, dimension of the organization and so on.

Developing sensible knowledge

The first dimension that I will analyse is that which corresponds to the development of 'sensible knowledge'. By sensible knowledge I mean 'what is perceived
through the senses, judged through the senses, and produced and reproduced
through the senses. It resides in the visual, the auditory, the olfactory, the gusta-
tory, the touchable and in the sensitive–aesthetic judgement' (Strati 2007: 62).
According to Polanyi (1958), the expression 'personal knowledge' stresses the
individual and subjective commitment to the process of knowing. In a similar
way I have chosen the label 'developing sensible knowledge' to stress those
aspects of competence-in-practice that are embedded, embodied and connected
to the personal knowledge of female entrepreneurs, often tied to knowing how to
work with their hands, to the material and corporeal dimensions of knowledge.

The primary characteristic of developing sensible knowledge is its strong
anchoring in the material dimension of knowledge. The example that appears
most frequently through the various interviews relates to the development of
competence in the materials and products specific to their sector. The capacity to distinguish between one product and another, one material and another,
the recognition of quality and the diverse possibilities for use is one of the key
aspects of the learning stories. For example, a female hairdresser recounts:

> We have always characterized our work, above all, through the careful
> selection of products, because due to many years of work we know what
> to choose. [...] I'd say that in 27 years we have tried all colours, but in
> the true sense of the word. And so, in trying, we are able to choose those
> that work better, and reject the rest, maybe you have a company that you
> like more and so you use that one. For example, shampoo is something
> fundamental to me because I have problems with chapping on my hands.
> When I worked as an employee I destroyed my hands, probably because
> they used shampoo that was particularly alkaline and I thought that I
> would have to leave because of my bleeding hands. [...] I always said: 'if
> I have my own salon I will get the products that I want.' Because I also
> use them, I want them to be quality products, which wash well. The

choice of products is important because there are products that aren't worth anything, and you can tell. Our clients can identify what we use.

The capacity to choose 'the right products' is developed over time, with experience, testing and retesting. The interviewee, however, also draws attention to other elements that are intrinsically linked to the better choice of products: the pleasure of using one product over another, the possibility of distinguishing yourself from your competitors, and the capacity to transmit a particular expression of quality to her clients.

The importance of those aspects tied to materiality in developing competences related to sensible knowledge is not specific to 'manual' work, such as hairdressing, but proves to be fundamental even in companies of a larger scale and belonging to sectors that are less craft-based. For example, the owner of a small family-owned firm that deals with heated flooring describes how she selects their materials.

> It's simple enough: in the case of timber, I join two or three pieces. If they aren't planar, that is, if they are stepped … If I put one beside the other, if there is a slight slope the pieces aren't right because the client won't accept it. For example, in the case that the varnish isn't uniform, that is, when looking at it against the light you see that certain places are missing varnish, or rather in cases where the material on the surface may have peeled off, that is it isn't absolutely perfect, or in the case of laminate, in the case where the staves do this [mimes the disparity of the staves with her hands], that is I look at them, and rather than being straight they are like this, either on the long or the short side. There are many things that can be verified. [...] By sight, many things can be understood by sight, the foundation, the prefinished flooring, we do it with ribs, with a particular foundation rather than another, the thickness of fine timber, the type of choice, the type of veneer.

From the point of view of the interviewee, recognizing the quality of the materials and distinguishing the diverse types 'was simple enough'. The richness of this extract not only draws attention to the competences developed by the interviewee and the embeddedness of her knowledge, but shows a specific competence (which we will speak of in the following section) in transmitting this knowledge through language. In comparison, the extract is less illuminating with respect to how these competences were developed, almost leaving us to understand that they are innate, individual, and scarcely 'transferable' as claimed by a significant body of literature (Nonaka & Takeuchi 1995; Ambrosini & Bowman 2001).

To clarify instead how the development of competences occurs through the everyday execution of work tasks, I will consider the learning story of a female goldsmith who recounts her learning process in these terms:

Obviously in the beginning one looks, comes close to the (goldsmith's) bench and gets to know the basic tools, that is, hammers, saws, files and metal. The metals that one works in the beginning ... I began with copper, with brass, silver. Materials that one uses all the time, everyday, but that aren't precious and so even if there is wastage it doesn't matter. I began to see how they were used, their hardness, their malleability and what these materials could give rise to. Then the blowtorch, the flame, the most beautiful element because it moulds. Let's say that in the same moment it creates and destroys, because when materials are heated, it creates certain effects, oxidization but little is needed to melt it. And this was the most difficult part, you needed experience and materiality to understand when was the moment to decrease the flame, to move it, to increase the heat. All a slow learning process of the uses of the various materials. And then I moved onto yellow and white gold with all of their beautiful effects and the various techniques that one learns over time. And so, to the use of cuttlefish bones for the first smelting, the use of a crucible and slowly, first these things beside him, and then on my own, through trial and error. I then began to produce my first jewellery.

This fascinating story by the interviewee is centred on the material aspects of the particular competences of the goldsmith, of being able to mould and shape the metal. The interviewee underlines the various periods in her development of particular competences, the process of trial and error, and the techniques that one acquires over time. It is the tacit and aesthetic dimensions in particular, that are emphasized by the interviewee in the following passage:

It is difficult to understand the fusion of different materials. To achieve these results means that the research has been appreciated. [...] One does research by keeping informed about the sector, and so you have to follow the exhibitions that occur, obviously taking part as much as possible in classical and contemporary galleries, following all that is the work of the other artists, many of these are also colleagues, and so we meet and we compare our work, what we've seen, we exchange our work. It is of general interest, and one buys a new catalogue on release, and you need to measure yourself against those that are better than you. [...] (There is) an enormous passion for art and so slowly, slowly you learn. Getting to know sculptors and painters has been an enormous help because they taught us how to become acquainted with, above all, the inner workings of the galleries, because it is a difficult world. It is in constant development, one day you're in and another no. It takes a good few years, but once you've arrived or have an important position then the work proceeds on its own.

As can be inferred from this extract, even aesthetic taste, that which is commonly attributed to an individual and innate capacity, is social and is learned through experience and participation, through comparison with more talented colleagues, and in maintaining contact with art galleries. The interviewee describes the development of competences relative to the aesthetic dimension as a long and tortuous process, one that is non-linear, that is accessed by frequenting the 'right' environments and educating one's senses.

From one point of view, their positioning between being a craftsperson and a female entrepreneur, and lastly, the frequent concentration on their sensible knowledge constitutes a way of defining craftsmanship, understood as knowing how to work with their hands, as the core competence of their own activity and relegating management tasks to an ancillary role, as is underlined by this female restorer:

> I don't understand anything about papers. My husband has helped me a lot with the papers, because sincerely they are the things that I detest the most. It is something I can't manage, I work with my hands, but for me papers are a burden.

Learning how to translate materiality

In the previous section the focus was placed on the sensible knowledge developed by the interviewees. In comparison, this section will be focused on how they learn to translate materiality, that is, the capacity to translate their material knowledge so that it becomes comprehensible to those outside the trade, and how this ability is developed in the daily execution of work activities. In the literature, a similar role has been called 'knowledge brokers', defined as 'intermediary actors that facilitate transactions between other actors lacking access to or trust in one another' (Marsden 1982: 202). Even if the question of trust is fundamental in this case, I will not concentrate on this aspect, rather on the ability to connect different and distant worlds.

The first example of the development of this type of competence, that I will call translational competence in order to emphasize its relational dimension, is described in the learning story of an interviewee who is in charge of the administration and management of a carpentry business that produces roofs. The interviewee tells of how in order to 'deal' with her clients she had to learn which aspects were considered to be the 'core' of her business (the real work) and to understand the language to make it comprehensible to her clients:

> Initially I always relied on Franco for everything that I needed to do, and then, as I watched … And so the important thing is to understand the needs of the clients and to also understand the real work, the technical work … Apart from the very technical things, the calculation of forces, you need to be able to understand the system of work and be able to explain to the clients things that before I didn't even know what they were, in the sense that before I only dealt with accounting, and that was

it. They (the clients) come here with a basic design and we try to explain to them how a roof is constructed, the type of materials, the type of insulation, the final cladding, in short, we give them this type of information that I don't ... Before I had to make appointments with Franco at 10 in the evening. Or I had to learn.

From the extract it emerges clearly that learning what the interviewee describes as the 'the real work', that is the technical labour, the practical elements of craftsmanship in the labour in order to 'explain' to her clients the characteristics of the actual product, was necessary to the execution of her work. As the interviewee notes, it wasn't necessary to develop these types of competences 'before', given that she was only occupied with accounting. Understanding the technical aspects in order to explain them to the clients only became necessary when she began to manage the relationship with their clients. In the story told by the interviewee the learning of these types of competences happened through an entirely informal process.

I did it automatically, without doing any courses, just listening. I was here and I listened to what Franco said. Being here you physically see the things and so I learned from living it. Before I was there [referring to the fact that previously the administration office was on a different site] and I didn't even know the difference between bilam and glulam timber ... That is, bilam is two pieces of timber glued together, glulam timber has more laminations glued together. Not seeing the things, you knew the things theoretically, but not ...

As is evidenced in the extract, the learning acquires an everyday – often familiar – dimension of participation, of being present for episodes that produce situations and occasions for learning, of being 'there' even in a corporeal sense. In fact, the interviewee refers to an informal learning that comes through participation similar to that described in the literature on situated learning, but she underlines the corporeal and sensorial aspects by stressing the fact that she learned 'only by listening'.

Translational competences are of fundamental importance to small business where the management of clients determines the success or failure of the enterprise. An interview that dealt with the sales of flooring, for example, described her role and that of her partner as such:

I was employed in sales and he with the laying (of the flooring). The clients come, I show them the materials, and then sell and then the team starts up immediately. It is a chain that turns, if I don't sell the boys don't lay. I am the first link in the chain to start. If I make a mistake everything goes wrong.

Translational competences assume a fundamental role in the interviewee's story that describes in detail how the knowledge of the materials, of the technical labour, of the context in which she works and the competences developed in the management of her clients are central to obtaining good results, in this case the sale of the product and the successive laying of the flooring:

> If a client enters that is looking for a specific product and you don't know how to appeal to them, if you don't know how to show the right characteristics, or you don't know how to please your clients anyway… […] If you find yourself unprepared, you have already lost the clients. Clients think that they know lots about houses because, maybe, they have bought two magazines and they arrive knowing god knows what. In the end it's not true, because there are those environments, those contexts … in the end they can't do what they want to do. Here we live in a place where it is almost always cold, where in winter it is almost always minus 20 degrees, and it's clear that if we do an external area we can't use those materials that they might use in Rome. We have our specific products, or specific things.

So, it is not enough to understand the materials and to have the capacity to translate technical language for those not employed in the sector. Translational competences are developed through the execution of everyday work practices. And they are situated in specific contexts and are based on local knowledge. The following extract of a learning story of the interviewee allows us to understand how these competences may be developed.

> I had a good teacher, because my husband finished middle school and he never enrolled in high school, he has always been a tiler. In the beginning he started by laying tiles for craftsmen, learning, laying as do all young boys, until it became his trade. Now he is 39 years old and he has been laying tiles for more than 20 years. Having started as a boy he better understands any other product, not just his own but even those of the others. And so he gave me an optimum base. Little by little, as I organized the showroom he explained to me: 'this is an external product because … The product is exclusively for internal use because … This can be used internally and externally because …' He explained the reasons, one by one, as we organized the showroom, when he would go I would have all the doubts in the world: why this one? Why that one? Why that one? And what if someone comes in? In short, I lived through moments of panic, also because in here we aren't talking about expenditures of only a few euros. Occasionally there are orders even for large quantities of materials and in spending their money it is only right that the client is as happy with the materials as with the laying of the work. And so in the end, the sales become a huge responsibility.

Even in this case the learning process that brought her to the development of translational competences is an informal, everyday and often domestic process, given that the majority of small businesses are family-run and it is therefore difficult to draw the line between the spaces and times of work and non-work, as will be seen in the following section.

Picking up managing competences by osmosis

The last dimension of entrepreneurial competence-in-practice that I will examine is that which I will refer to as an osmotic development of managing competences. This refers to the acquiring of a more general vision of the management of the business, that which would commonly be defined as an entrepreneurial mentality. In other words, how are these managing competences developed? How does one learn to be a female entrepreneur? An explicit example is one of a female typographer that manages the family business:

> In my case the business belonged to the family, in the sense that in his day my father had launched a typography business, and so when I was studying it so happened that during the summer I would come here to give my father a hand, when I had free time, so half a day I'd be here. My idea was to continue (with my studies), I did architecture, to continue on that path, after which I continued to work while I studied and now I'm still here.

The extract emphasizes well the naturalness, familiarity and everydayness of the learning process. 'Being there', sometimes even against their will, doesn't just determine their path of work, but creates the conditions for the development of managing competences:

> In the beginning, (I learned) working with my collaborators who surely knew more than me and still know more about their specific tasks, they still know more. [...] You learn from the others, working, doing, and also making mistakes. [...] [I learned] from my father and from his associate, because it was always them that managed the sales contracts. Then I even did some course to come closer to a better method of negotiating. I don't know if I am so able now, but in the end I make do.

The interviewee's entrepreneurial path was reconstructed as a path of learning that was situated in a specific familiar dimension and studded with people (collaborators, associates) from whom to learn. The interviewee also refers to 'some course' to imply the interweaving of formal and informal learning. She participated in a course to 'come closer' to a particular mode of negotiating, the best, to acquire knowledge and competences that are useful to her professionalism, but the majority of what she learns is learned through informal and situated processes. For example, another interviewee who manages a small

family-owned business that deals with heated flooring describes her relationship with her working life as follows:

> In reality, in a business like ours the work is part of our lives, that is, it per-
> meates our life entirely, because even when you close the office you are still
> involved, you continue to think about things, you reflect, you are always
> very involved. We don't work like a multinational company with water-
> tight compartments. [...] Evidently you are immersed in the work for
> many hours a day. [In the family] we talk, we certainly talk about work.

In this extract the interviewee establishes a connection between the difficulty
of distinguishing between work and private activity within a small family-
owned business. This same difficulty in defining precise borders is reflected
in the description of her learning process, which is completely inserted within
everyday dynamics and renders difficult the individuation of models that are
valid generally, as the same interviewee underlines:

> I learned it by osmosis, being there and listening and following and
> memorizing things ... [...] It is very difficult to study the process of
> learning within small businesses like ours, where the work is very chaotic
> and very rapid. In my opinion, one needs to understand the secret of the
> trade from the people that are around you because that is the most impor-
> tant thing, going to them, asking them things, picking their brains.

Yet again the attention is focused on an everyday dimension of participation,
in which observing 'the others', those more experienced, and learning from
them seems to represent the model of learning that is most common and
shared. The interviewee defined her learning process as something that happens 'by osmosis', living in a family business where you can develop the
entrepreneurial competences. This account is near to what in the literature is
called 'absorptive capacity' (Cohen & Levinthal 1990; Zhara & George 2002),
that is, the ability of a firm to value, assimilate and apply new knowledge.

In the same extract, though, the interviewee places the attention onto the
difficulty of formalizing the learning processes of small businesses because
these are characterized by activities that are chaotic and rapid, in which the
borders (work/non-work, family/business, formal/informal learning) are often
confused and the process is multiple. The development of managing competences is described as 'understanding the secrets of the trade' rather than as a
linear process, even in the case where one wants to teach others:

> It isn't easy to teach, I think that it is one of the more difficult things to
> do because apart from having procedures which can be standardized and
> so one can go quickly, there is a series of refinements, of things that in my
> opinion are difficult to teach. In the sense that you would say to them:

look at me, stay here with me. Look at what I do and try to memorize it and to take home that which might be useful to you. [...] For example, how to manage the clients in a certain manner, because to one person you can say one thing, to another you need to say another. For example, it is difficult to codify the relationship that we have with our suppliers, there is one that is less relevant, one that is more relevant, one that has a monopoly, someone that you need to keep, someone that you can let go, and so the relationships are therefore very personal. Then the problem is this: obviously a person that has a 360 degree view [this is an idiomatic Italian expression that implies an overall vision, a 'holistic understanding' of a situation] of the whole business can manage it in a certain manner, any other person that comes into my business and sees only a small piece has greater difficultly in managing a whole series of things.

The selected extract tells of a learning process that is delineated through occasions, actively participating in daily work practices to finally develop that which has been described as a 'situated curriculum' (Gherardi *et al.* 1998), that is a specific form of social order that instructs the socialization of novices within the context of ongoing work activities, which permits a '360 degree view of the whole business'.

The importance of developing an overall view of their business that includes elements and competences that are connected to the specific trade or to administrative and management questions of greater breadth is highlighted by the learning story of an interviewee that takes care of the administrative and management part of a business that is occupied in building management:

I have an excellent capacity to organize people, to have people follow me, and I exploit this capacity of mine. These are skills that one learns (through) work experience, working, always gaining greater familiarity with the instruments that are needed, financial instruments, of relationships, of competences in the management of resources. [...] If you don't know your product, or the market in which you could sell it, or the people you should deal with, offering services becomes difficult, and so there needs to be greatest knowledge. For example, knowing all of the opportunities an association of craftsmen can offer you, with all of the offices that exist. We have difficulty accessing a line of credit, there aren't banks that will finance us, and there are instruments that the associations can get access to, extra-regional, extra-national finance. However small businesses don't know this, and so they have an idea and the bank doesn't approve their loan, the idea is put away. This occurs because there isn't the knowledge of the alternative resources, by now you need to work as part of a network, I really believe in working as a team because it allows you to manage better the things that one can't do on your own because there isn't the time. The problem of the craftsman is that he has a very small organization and sometimes he misses some knowledge.

The competences that the interviewee speaks of in her extract are in themselves of a diverse nature: organizing people, having familiarity of the various tools, materials, knowledge of the services and the opportunities offered by the territory, the market, learning how to work in a group. Learning to recognize all of these elements signifies developing entrepreneurial competences that allow one to manage a small business tied to a familiar and craft dimension.

The relationship between the craft and entrepreneurial aspects of small businesses is often lived contradictorily, as if one must position oneself exclusively in one of the two categories. If in the accounts of developing competences related to sensible knowledge the interviewees stress the manual and craft aspects of the work, in the accounts of developing managing competences they emphasize the aspects which represent them as entrepreneurs. The extract from an interview with a female restorer highlights the lived antithesis between craftsmanship and entrepreneurialism:

This is a critical moment for me, in fact, I am actually quite vulnerable, because this site is a real burden to me, because it is really difficult to manage. [...] It is the first time that I am inside the logic of the site, there is a whole dynamic there, due to which I am seen badly with respect to the others, in the sense that it never happens that an employer would go there to work. I go to work and naturally I check that everything is done as I want it. It has created a strange situation within the site and within my team. Getting to the end of this thing is really weighing on me and I need to be able to create some emotional distance, therefore I'm promising myself that when I've finished I will re-examine my own entrepreneurial capacity. I won't ever take on something so massive, because everything in this experience creates baggage. It is from the point of view of everything that is implied by managing many people, organizing, of having these negative sensations just because you go on-site, listening to the jokes of the officials: 'the only female restorer, the only business woman that works.' Just because I went on-site to work. You can laugh, but it's only because I went on-site. [...] It is the first time that I've experienced something like this, because I know how to do many things ... I restored the small church. You arrive, you have already made contact with the parish, with the municipal government. You arrive and they already know who you are, it is a different dynamic.

As is evidenced in this extract, the interviewee has developed competences that allow her to execute the technical part of her work without difficulty, but that does not equate to having developed that which I have called managing competences. Being able to manage complex situations, broad networks, and controlling the dynamics of the site are competences that differ with respect to being able to restore a fresco, but are as important. That which the diverse dimensions have in common is the path of informal learning that is primarily tied to the situated work experience that allows one to develop them.

Conclusions: developing entrepreneurial competence in female small business

In the preceding sections I have considered three diverse dimensions of entrepreneurial competences-in-practice that female entrepreneurs develop in the daily accomplishment of their work practices.

The three dimensions are not intended to be representative of the various professional figures within the companies. These have emerged from the analysis of the interviews and I have described them, using ample extracts of the learning stories to highlight the diverse elements that characterize these competences. At this point I would like to specify that the relationship between these elements also assumes diverse nuances due to the way in which the female entrepreneurs see their own role. In small businesses, which are often on the border between handicraft and entrepreneurial activity, attributing themselves with one role over another does not just have a 'labour' value, but is part of the construction of a larger, personal history. For example, in one of the previous sections a restorer distanced herself from all of the management, administrative and bureaucratic activities of the job expressing a 'hatred for papers' and underlining that hers was one of 'working with her hands'. A similar description also characterizes the last extract analysed in the preceding section in which the interviewee declares that she has to revisit her own managerial capacity after a negative experience on the building site.

Positioning themselves as manual labourers and craftswomen almost seems to have a defensive aim in a social environment that is characterized by a traditional division of labour on the basis of gender. The sociocultural context of small business in Northern Italy seems to discourage one from pursuing some lines of entrepreneurial work on the grounds that it was 'unfeminine' or incompatible with female capabilities.

This interpretation is also sustained by the examples presented in the section on translational dimension of competences. The learning to recognize materials through an informal process (often listening to their business partner), gaining a technical language and the knowledge to translate it to non-professionals are described as competences that were developed naturally, almost in a banal and obvious way. The two interviewees underline the difficulty that they met in the development of competences as subjective issues that were tied to their incapacity to do the 'real work'. Even though they allow the business to survive, these translational competences are not valued but experienced as responsibilities.

A greater assurance and consciousness was expressed in the narratives regarding managing competences, as if the experience that is accumulated in addition to the development of competences also allows one to position oneself as a figure that is closer to that of the entrepreneur than to the craftswoman.

At this point, I would like to underline the dual understanding of the three dimensions of CD that I analysed in the chapter: on the one hand, I focused attention on 'developing sensible knowledge', 'learning how to translate materiality', and 'picking up managing competences' as situated knowledges; on the other hand, I paid attention to how female entrepreneurs learn. I would like to stress the informality and the domesticity of the learning process. In small businesses CD occurs daily through the participation in work practices, which are distinguished from private practices with difficulty. The borders between work and non-work, between family and business, and formal and informal learning are ephemeral and are constantly renegotiated. For these reasons the 'single' female entrepreneurs, those that are not part of a family business and do not manage to insert themselves into a network that substitutes for the function of the family, have greater difficulty in developing competences, given that they have reduced access to occasions and situations for learning as described in the preceding pages. Given the characteristics of situatedness and contingency in developing competences-in-practice and their context-based essence, a policy proposal that could contribute to future competitiveness seems to be one that invests in the construction and maintenance of the network of small businesses and in exchange programmes in which the female entrepreneurs could gain direct experience in other environments.

Finally, I would like to highlight the specificity of female entrepreneurship. As we have seen in the extracts, female ways of doing business are based on what has been called 'knotworking' (Engeström 1999), which includes various forms of tying and untying of otherwise separate threads of activities. What emerges from the analysis of the interviews is the continuous relational work that is at the base of the entrepreneurial competences. Female entrepreneurship seems to be more oriented to 'taking care' of the business than to dominating it. As a New Penelope the female entrepreneur weaves a web more than discovers a new land or builds an empire. But exactly as a New Penelope she seems to destroy her work during the night, failing to recognize all the efforts invested in doing it and all the competences she develops in the accomplishment of her never-ending task.

Acknowledgements

This study sets out preliminary reflections on a more wide-ranging project entitled 'Family enterprise and the development of entrepreneurial skills' supported by the Provincia di Trento. I want to to thank the coordinator of the project, Silvia Gherardi, for our fruitful discussions and for the invaluable advice she gave me on a previous draft of this chapter. The assistance of Katie Hepworth in translating the chapter into English is greatly appreciated.

Part IV

Competence development as a national strategy

Chapter 12

Enhancing competences and skills in China

Xianjin Dou

Nearly a decade into the twenty-first century, a broad consensus is emerging from research and development about the critical need for students to have twenty-first-century competences such as problem solving and technological savvy. Competences are critical for today's workforce and will be essential for the workforce of tomorrow. On an individual level, these competences affect educational and professional opportunities and, on a large scale, they impact the quality of the labour force and, ultimately, the strength of national economy competition.

Murnane and Levy (2004) have documented that with the advent of new information communication technologies, there is less demand for lower order job skills and a much greater demand for new twenty-first-century competences and skills. Concerning China, we have many more workers with lower level skills and there is a need to reform the education system to ensure basic competences and skills for all. This affects all types of workers, from office secretaries to company presidents, from car mechanics to car manufacturers.

In order to respond to the new challenges, Chinese education has generated a new focus in pedagogical processes where there is a balance between teaching students the core content knowledge *and* the ability of students to apply that knowledge to the competences that support student learning. In other words, these competences differ from traditional educational outcomes because they value not only mastering a discrete concept or memorizing a particular formula but also practically applying what is learned across subject matters and in a variety of settings. Under a competence approach, students need to master new knowledge, skills and attitudes relevant for functioning in a twenty-first-century global economy. Therefore, Chinese education should be reformed and public resources reallocated to support students in achieving the identified twenty-first-century competences and core content knowledge in the twenty-first-century priority areas (mathematics and science; career and technical education; learning other languages and ICT and systemic reform).

With the fast growth of the knowledge-based economy in China, twenty-first-century Chinese employees need relevant competences to respond to the demands of the workplace. The recent rising unemployment among highly

educated people, notably college graduates, and the severe shortage of technical workers signal the structured shortage and serious mismatch between
skills supply and demand in China. To address this, the Chinese government
is taking a series of measures to reform education and enhance youth and
labourer competences and skills through career and technical education.

This chapter analyses the trends of socio-economic development and summarizes the development of career and technical education in recent years in
China and how to respond to a competence-based society.

China is entering the competence-based society

The recent rising unemployment among highly educated people, notably college graduates, and the severe shortage of technical workers in the labour
markets not only signal the structured shortage and serious mismatch between
skills supply and demand, but also indicate China is entering the competence-
based society. In the competence-based society, it will be not enough to know
about something – the competence to solve a practical problem is a decisive factor in personal success. This new development has very important implications
for advancing the world of education in China to think about trends of work
and how to help students entering a rapidly changing workplace.

The rise in the number of unemployed graduates of tertiary institutions in
recent years is the natural result of the very rapid increase in the number of
entrants to higher education institutions of 50 per cent a year since 1997. In
2002 among 1.45 million college graduates, 440,000 (30 per cent) were not
able to find a job; in 2003, of 2.1 million graduates, 630,000 (30 per cent)
were still unemployed in September (Bengali 2004); and in 2004, of 2.8 million graduates, a 32 per cent increase from the previous year, as many as
600,000 (around 21 per cent) were jobless. According to the Ministry of
Education statistics, by September 2005, of 3.4 million graduates, about
913,000 (27 per cent) had not found jobs (Wu 2006). In 2006, it is expected
that 4.1 million college students will graduate and that the job situation will
worsen. Why? It is mainly because of poor course design, out-of-date training
methods, maladjusted curricula, poor information services and incomplete
job markets. There is also a mismatch between what students specialize in
and the needs of the market, due to vestiges of the old system, where the type
of students produced was centrally decided, as was the allocation of students
to jobs. Today, highly educated Chinese students can no longer be assured of
a job just through holding a graduate certificate. What competences and
skills they have grasped are directly related to their career development.
Therefore the student has more freedom to decide what to study.

What competences and skills do employers want? How are these competences and skills being developed through the education system? All these
new problems are very important for education institutions because they are
directly related to their development. With the development of the market

economy, all education institutions must respond to the demands of the labour market. In terms of studies, the International Labour Office, with the Centre of Labour Market Studies, University of Leicester, responded to a request from the China Enterprise Confederation to determine employer views on the quality of the education and training system and its relevance to enterprises. A survey was conducted July to September 2000 of 465 organizations located mainly in eastern, southern and coastal areas of China, with a broad cross-section of enterprise sizes and ownership types.

The study found that employers require not only higher level skills but also a much broader range of skills for managers and, to a lesser extent, for technicians, than for other types of workers. These broader skills include the ability to organize, solve problems, communicate with others and work in teams. While the Chinese-owned firms (particularly state-owned enterprises) tend to place a higher value on the more tangible, measurable skills and certification, the foreign-funded firms tend to place more value on imagination and the softer skills, such as adaptability, and skills for contributing through ideas and flexibility. Organizations operating in international markets, whether foreign or Chinese-owned, have the highest skill demands, both hard (advanced information technology, numeracy and formal qualifications) and soft (communication, innovation and organization). While foreign-owned enterprises can minimize the impact of the shortage of managerial workers through their attractive salary packages, smaller Chinese firms, especially the private ones, experience considerable difficulties in attracting managers and technicians because they have few benefits to offer prospective recruits.

Employers also felt that the training system is geared to meet the needs of state-owned enterprises and the public sector, not those of the new economy and enterprises operating in international product markets. The survey also found that there has been a rapid growth of IT use in enterprises over the last five years. Most of these skills have been delivered through private training providers. The use of IT is highest among those firms competing in international markets. Those firms use training not just to deliver task skills but also to inculcate a high level of commitment from their employees.

An assessment of likely skill deficiencies in four key sectors – state-owned enterprises, the private sector, foreign-owned and joint venture firms, and the emerging high-tech sector – suggests that the most deficient skills (occurring twice or more in different sectors) are effective human resources management, intellectual property management, marketing and strategic planning. According to a senior executive from ABB China, the most desirable skills for its salespersons include the following:

- Integrity
- Drive for results
- Interpersonal skills

- Technical and industrial knowledge
- Communications and persuasive skills
- Teamwork
- Control capability.

It is hoped that Chinese higher education graduates can improve in attitude, flexibility, commitment and moving from knowing to doing. International experience shows that programmes with flexibility and a strong market orientation can serve the changing market needs for just-in-time learning better than long-term academic degree programmes.

To address this, the Chinese government is taking a series of measures to reform education and enhance youth and labourer competences and skills through career and technical education.

The emerging competences and skills of the labour market in China

In China, we live in an era of innovation characterized by urbanization, marketization and globalization. The emerging knowledge-based economy integrated with rapid technological development is changing the nature of work and the skills required in almost every occupation. With the rapid development of science and technology and social progress, the total amount of knowledge being created is growing at a great pace. The knowledge and skills acquired in schools or universities have not caught up with those demanded for work and personal fulfilment. The rapid changes in the structure of employment and in the organization of work have drastically altered the form and content of jobs. People have to continue learning and upgrading their skills to keep pace with development.

China has a population of about 1.3 billion, with a large working-age population. With the development and establishment of a market-oriented employment mechanism, the Chinese government is clearly aware that the country will face severe employment pressure due to various factors, such as the huge population base, population migration from rural regions to towns or cities, age structure of the population and employment structure change. In the five years between 2001 and 2005, the population of working age increased by 13.6 million annually on average. By the year 2020, the total population of working age will reach 940 million. There are now 150 million surplus rural labourers who need to be transferred, and over 11 million unemployed and laid-off persons who need to be employed or re-employed. The contradiction between overall supply of and demand for labour is thus severe.

China has a complex labour market system with many different groups seeking employment and many different providers of education and training. There has been a rapid growth in higher education enrolment at the same time as working adults are being forced to make a transition in employment, either from rural farming work or from secure jobs in state-owned enterprises to market-based employment in the cities. Different government institutions have a shared responsibility for the welfare of youth and adults in this transition including, but not limited to, the Ministry of Education, the Ministry of Human Resource and Social Security, the Ministry of Agriculture, etc.

As the economy shifts, new demands are being placed on education institutions. Students and parents are beginning to demand more freedom of choice in their studies. The education and training delivery systems were traditionally highly structured and rigid, and responded to an equally structured job system. The system was developed to serve the needs of the organization of production, which featured rule-driven, routine production processes controlled by management with little requirement for creativity on the part of workers. But the new market-led economy requires a different type of organization of production that calls for changes in the relationship of worker to work, worker to worker, and worker to consumer, and seeks to stimulate continuous improvements made by workers which are as significant as those resulting from design changes by engineers and scientists.

To maintain relevance in this knowledge-based economy and market-based economy, new demands of competences and skills, such as team-working skills and transferable skills, are emerging along the way. The rising skill demands of the labour market have made qualifications at the upper secondary level of education the minimum credential for the youth and sustainable labour market entry. Occupations are changing dramatically. It is estimated that over half the jobs done by Chinese today didn't exist in the 1980s and dozens of new occupations are emerging annually. We live in a world in which 80 per cent of the fastest-growing jobs will require upper-secondary education. Therefore, the Chinese government is taking various measures to make a breakthrough in the bottleneck for upper secondary education. By 2020, it is planning to universalize upper secondary education. The central government has adopted a special state grant of 800 million yuan (US$ 99 million) for upper secondary students, to cover tuition from 2006. This new action will increase the attractiveness for the young and promote more rural students to enter the competitive labour market.

The strong workforce supply has made the labour market more competitive and delayed wages growth. It will move the Chinese economy forward maintaining growth in a relatively long period. The economy grew at a fast rate, with an astounding 9.6 per cent per annum from 1978 to 2005. China's share of world exports increased from 1 per cent to almost 6 per cent between 1980 and 2003. The export or import/GDP ratio increased from 5 per cent to 25 per cent during the same period. It is reported that China ranks among the top growth performers in world economic history.

We are aware that such amazing successes do not guarantee that the future will be devoid of major difficulties. Some of the challenges that lie ahead are quite formidable. This is because the quality of economic growth is too low. We need to confront natural resource depletion and the environmental effects. This has resulted in discussions on socio-economic development strategy. In China, we have relatively inadequate resources per capita. Human resources are China's main asset and advantage. Human resources are central to the creation and transmission of knowledge and a determining factor in socio-economic development. Investing in education and training is a prerequisite for achieving the economic, social and environmental goals set by the nation. With the development of economic restructuring and urbanization in China, more and more youths and labourers will be educated and trained to meet the needs of occupations.

In the future, employees will work in more decentralized, specialized firms and employer–employee relationships will become less standardized and more individualized. The labour market not only needs the traditional competences of reading, writing, language, mathematics, but also demands team-working skills and transferable skills to adapt to the continuous job changes. In terms of a survey related to 154 enterprises, 555 managers and 8176 workers in China, carried out by the National Centre of Education Development Research in 2005, managers think team working-skills, operating skills or problem solving skills and lifelong learning competences are the basic skills for holding a job.

At the moment, there has also been an increasing focus on competences and skills and how they can best be developed around China. But there are no exact definitions of competences and skills, and the terms 'competences' and 'skills' are often used interchangeably. Many efforts to define such competences and skills are under way, and a broad consensus seems to be emerging. The OECD recently completed its four-year study, the Definition and Selection of Competencies (DeSeCo) Project, defining key competences for a successful life and a well-functioning society (Rychen & Salganik 2003). Twelve country reports were produced with some key competences frequently mentioned. Based on the research on theory and practice, the DeSeCo identified key competences in three broad categories – interacting in socially heterogeneous groups, acting autonomously, and using tools interactively. It helps us understand the meaning of competences and what they comprise, but they are also theoretical and abstract.

In the world of education in China, we are concerned with creativity and critical thinking skills, feeling the need to generate more creative thinkers as essential for innovation. This is why we have changed the curricula in recent years to address concerns that the education systems are too structured and disciplined. In big developed cities such as Beijing and Shanghai, the local education administration is actively engaged in lifelong learning. The education administration assures that not only traditional competences – numeracy and literacy (foundation skills), basic competences in mathematics, science and technology – but also foreign languages, ICT skills and use of technology, learning to learn, social skills, entrepreneurship and general culture are necessary for the competence and skill of all students. They ask schools not only to pay much attention to the updated knowledge but also to be concerned with students' attitudes (curiosity, motivation, creativity, scepticism, honesty, enthusiasm, self-esteem, reliability, responsibility, initiative and perseverance) and ICT, foreign languages, basic science and technology.

As a whole, China's education achievements have been very impressive in recent years. The school entrance rates at different levels have risen steadily. China has basically realized the nine-year compulsory education and eliminated illiteracy among the young and middle-aged population. The school entrance rate to upper secondary school has been maintained at the level of 47.5 per cent. The gross rate of enrolment in schools of higher learning reached 23 per cent in 2007 which indicates that China has entered the stage of popular education. However, one of the most important problems facing China's education is that too much attention has been paid to school-based education and the school certificate in the past. This has resulted in an extremely negative impact on youth education. The emerging competences and skills in the labour market are now igniting the reforming curriculum and pedagogy of education.

Developing career and technical education to meet demands of the labour market in China

In today's world, our constantly changing society requires the sustainable renewal of knowledge and competences, especially the professional expertise of all working people. This continuous updating of professional knowledge or the so-called competences and skills is not satisfied only by the conventional formal education system. To be able to learn any subject at any time independently or in a group is indispensable in the twenty-first century to cope with an uncertain future. Nobody can prepare their career paths at school age, but career and technical education will play a very important role for people's career development in the twenty-first-century. We need to strengthen career and technological education to respond to the continuous challenges of the twenty-first century from the viewpoint of a lifelong learning society.

The rapid change of production systems demands greater flexibility of the labour force. Knowledge and skills have to become both broader and deeper. Broad qualifications help workers to orientate themselves in an entire production process and within a larger occupational field. For those who are disposed to broad knowledge, it will be easier to change working tasks or working place and participate in integrative or even innovative work. At the same time, enterprises need a specialized labour force, able to understand the very specific production processes. The world of education is trying to integrate flexibility and standardization for redesigning career and technical education. The following policies and measures are being carried out.

Strengthening career education and guidance from primary school to university

Nearly all schools have adopted the course on career guidance that helps youth and adults make informed career choices. The major components of a career counselling and guidance system include clients, information, delivery strategy, staffing, and governance and administration. The major actors for a career counselling and guidance system are education and labour institutions, schools (compulsory education), tertiary education institutions, public employment services, employer-based services, and private and non-government agencies. The aims are to help students understand the situation of supply and demand in the labour market and to plan their future career development. Finally, the system is beneficial for the students' choices of what kinds of schools and specialized curriculum.

Embedding the core competences and skills into the curriculum

The growing attention on enhancing students' employability responds to their motivation to be available for the job. In order to move employability forward into the curriculum, the Ministry of Education initiated the National Action Programme of Curriculum Reform to ensure the education and training programmes were directly linked to the needs of the workplace in 2003. The programme included all the courses from secondary vocational education to tertiary professional and technical colleges. They invited many teachers from the schools and experts from the world of work. Employer participation is critical to ensure that the process is demand and output driven. Up to today, the programme has completed thousands of new curricula and updated the contents of teaching.

Developing technical education

All the new competences and skills are available through non-academic education. To address this need, new providers such as technical and community colleges, and polytechnics are being advanced by the central government. These institutions usually offer courses in professional or vocational subjects in a more practical way. They also provide custom education and training services on contract to enterprises – they are often more efficient and useful than regular training, and at lower cost.

In recent years, the rapid development of Chinese industries and the expansion of its international trade and high domestic consumption of daily goods have stimulated a variety of industries to explore new business, with enlarged employment opportunity. Along with the gradual improvement in living standards, parents have raised their aspirations in education, encouraging their children to receive a better education. At the secondary education

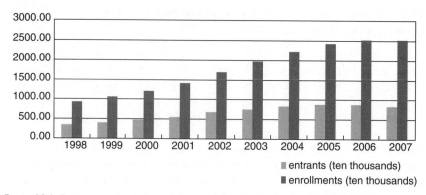

Figure 12.1 Entrants and enrolments in secondary general schools, 1998–2007.

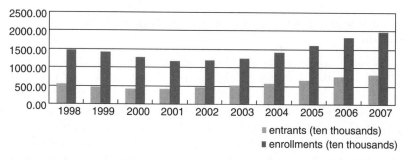

Figure 12.2 Entrants and enrolments in secondary vocational schools, 1998–2007.

level, both in general schools and vocational schools entrants have increased in the past ten years (see Figures12.1 and 12.2).

In the higher education level, not only those students registered in professional and technical colleges but also those registered in universities increased fast than ever before (see Figures 12.3 and 12.4).

China is facing a transitional period in the history of education to meet the demands of twenty-first century competences and skills. The rapid expansion of entrants in secondary education indicates China is on the way to the compulsory twelve years education.The growth of entrants in science and engineering to university indicates that higher education is responding to the demands of labour markets. Educational administrators are energetically responding to these demands and moving forward to the real needs of students, to prepare them to adapt to the great diversity of abilities, aptitudes, interests, concerns and career paths.

The notion that dependence on academic achievement to plan one's future career and educational institution ranking or schools ranking are related to one's living conditions is fast disappearing. The young generation have to give

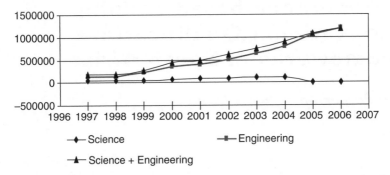

Figure 12.3 The science and engineering entrants to professional and technical colleges, 1997–2006.

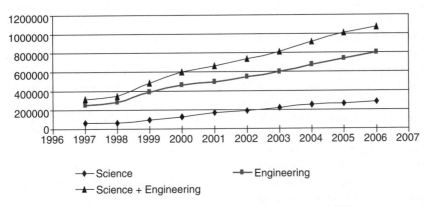

Figure 12.4 The science and engineering entrants to university, 1997–2006.

up the traditional values whereby success in school guarantees their future promotion in any occupation, whether in public services or industries. More students are planning their future career in terms of ability, economic conditions and supply and demand of the labour markets. In technologically advanced production systems, workers have to solve increasingly complex problems. Pre-defined solutions do not work anymore. To deal with unstructured situations like this, students need a solid base of new competence and skills. Specialized knowledge restricted to only one workplace is not sufficient any more. The youths are supposed to understand not only their own job, but also the whole production process, to be competitive in the labour markets.

In conclusion, the China of today is very different from that of the past. In that world, a single occupation could last for a lifetime and ensure a comfortable life for a family. Today, careers are decided by the competences and skills that have been grasped and not by university certificates. Therefore, it is not only the structure but also the contents of education that are changing.

Competence-based training and National Qualifications Frameworks in South Africa

Ben Parker and Shirley Walters

Introduction

From the early years of the twentieth century, the relations between education, training and work have become increasingly complex and contested. One example of such contestation is apparent in discourses around competence-based training (CBT) and the relationship between this form of training and more classical forms of education that have dominated schooling and higher education as found, for example, in the Trivium and Quadrivium that dominated the curriculum of schooling in Europe for hundreds of years and traces of which still remain (Bernstein 1996: 82–90). During the last thirty years, competence-based National Qualification Frameworks (NQFs) have emerged as an attempt to 'manage' the relations between education, training and work and, unsurprisingly, have been highly contested.

The number of NQFs, which emerged in the late 1980s in some anglophone developed countries, has grown rapidly with more than sixty countries and at least three regions at various stages of qualifications framework development by 2007. Their initial emergence was informed by perceptions of fundamental changes in the global economy, which had implications for the traditional divide between education and training and for the formal recognition of workplace and life 'experience' (Illeris 2003: 167). These views complemented the views of business and government, which saw qualification frameworks as a means to make education more 'relevant' to the work place and as a 'steering mechanism' by which the state could achieve 'social objectives' such as educational reform and equity. South Africa provides an intriguing example of how a confluence of global influences were indigenized and adapted to meet national objectives and how, after ten years of development, the architecture and practices are being reshaped.

South Africa's NQF, which was conceived and established in the transition to a post-apartheid democracy, embodied many of the aspirations of the time, above all, transformation of the apartheid education system through an NQF that addressed access, redress, portability and progression and enabled people to become lifelong learners (Allais 2007: 225). Given the idealism of the times, hindsight understands the impractical idealism of the model and of the qualifications and standards setting processes, which emerged as policy was implemented. This chapter traces how, in the South African case, in the 1990s, an indigenized version of CBT became the dominant political discourse guiding educational reform and was 'implanted' in the education and training system through the creation of an NQF managed by the South African Qualifications Authority (SAQA) in concert with government, Sectoral Education and Training Authorities (SETAs) and other stakeholders.

Drawing on South African experiences of ten years of NQF development, this chapter highlights the areas of greatest contestation and achievement. We argue for a view of NQFs as a work-in-progress and as contestable artefacts of modern society, which can contribute to the way in which a society manages the relations between education, training and work by finding 'common ground' between distinct forms of learning. There is no doubt that NQFs can become divisive and make little, if any contribution, to lifelong learning or educational reform. This is not preordained, however, as NQFs can provide an opportunity to address, in a modest manner, aspects of lifelong learning in ways which contribute to economic development, social justice and personal empowerment.

The indigenization of competence-based training and the development of South Africa's NQF

Thirteen years after the election of South Africa's first democratic government, South Africans have become all too aware of the difficulties of education change posed by the challenges of transforming the legacies of apartheid: the persistence of inequalities, learners lack of access and success, weak management practices and poor teaching practices. Our collective failure to produce significant successful change is all the more depressing because of the dazzling array of our transformative policy interventions. South Africa has a strong and progressive constitution and comprehensive policy and regulations focused on achieving freedom, equality and human dignity. One of the major education policy initiatives of the newly elected government was signalled by the promulgation, in October 1995, of the South African Qualifications Act, which formally established the NQF. At the time, the NQF was seen as a key instrument for transformation. In 2001, however, the Minister of Education set up a process to review the NQF. Six years later, in September 2007, the Ministers of Education and Labour issued a Joint Policy Statement (MoE and MoL 2007), which concludes the NQF Review process. This early and lengthy review process indicates ongoing intense political contestation surrounding the NQF and SAQA and their role in the transformation of South African education and the ways in which we can best understand different forms of learning and the relations between them (Allais 2007: 34; Lugg 2007: 182).

The overarching objectives and vision of the NQF were forged over a period of ten years starting in the late 1980s and were shaped by a confluence of external and internal dynamics (Allais 2007: 72; Lugg 2007: 46). The key external influences came from Western developed countries where changing modes of economic production were placing increasing emphasis on the importance of a skilled flexible labour force, which was thought to require an integration of education and training and which led to the emergence of NQFs (of particular importance were the New Zealand, English and Scottish models) (Mukora 2006: 26). Internally, there were economic and political imperatives prioritizing a need to move away from the racial segregation of apartheid education, which excluded the majority of the population from access to education and training opportunities, towards an integrated education and training system promoting equity and development (Allais 2007: 221; Parker and Harley 2007: 18).

As part of an overall strategy to foster a culture of lifelong learning, SAQA focuses on ensuring the development of an NQF that is underpinned by systemic coordination, coherence and resource alignment in support of South Africa's Human Resource Development Strategy and the National Skills Development Strategy. The objectives of the NQF are stated in the SAQA Act: create an integrated national framework for learning achievements; facilitate access to and mobility and progression within education, training and career paths; enhance the quality of education and training; accelerate the redress of past unfair discrimination in education, training and employment opportunities; and, contribute to the full personal development of each learner and the social and economic development of the nation at large.

South Africa's NQF was conceived as a comprehensive and unified ladder of learning with multiple pathways enabling learners to move from one field of education to another and to progress up the ladder. Those excluded from educational opportunities in the past would be given access onto a rung of the ladder through recognition of their prior learning and experience (RPL). In addition, to its focus on setting standards through pegging qualifications onto rungs of the ladder, SAQA has responsibility for the overarching coordination and evaluation of the quality assurance, undertaken by Education and Training Quality Assurance bodies, of the programmes that lead to qualifications and of the providers of those programmes.

All South African qualifications are included on the NQF, both those that were developed prior to the NQF (historical qualifications), and those developed through SAQA's standards setting structures (new qualifications). Education and training providers submitted their historical qualifications for registration on the NQF between 1998 and 2003 and had to align with NQF requirements, which included an outcomes-based format intended to provide a basis for comparability of learning achievements that would create a platform for mobility, portability, progression and RPL.

The use of an outcomes-based education (OBE) approach to standards setting has its origins in the CBT movement. In the early 1990s, South African educators and policy makers drew strongly on developments in CBT in England, America and Australia. Broadly, CBT is an approach to vocational and occupational training that places emphasis on what a person can do in the workplace as a result of completing a programme of training where competence refers to knowledge, skills and values required to perform a specific occupation. Drawing on this approach, the idea emerged and took hold in what has become an international movement among governments, that competence could be expressed in the outcome statements of a qualification without '... prescribing any specific learning pathway or programme' (Young 2005: 5).

In the South African debates, there was a concern that CBT could be too 'behaviourist' and 'atomistic' and narrowly focused on specific 'items' of skills performance. The fear was that knowledge and skills would be understood as referring only to performances that can be observed and measured thereby excluding the 'interiority' of the learner and reducing assessment to a checklist approach of 'correct behaviours'. A policy decision was made in the mid-1990s, to use the term 'Outcomes Based Education' to ensure a more holistic and 'constructivist' view of learning that would not reduce competence to only the observable but would include the consciousness and conscience of the learner (Moll 2002: 7; Moll *et al.* 2005: 78–115). With respect to psychological theories of learning this marked a shift from the behaviourism associated with the work of Skinner, to the constructivist theories of learning associated with Piaget and Vygotsky (Moll 2007).

Currently, SAQA's operational structure is configured around three key strategic areas, namely standards setting, quality assurance and the electronic management of learner achievements through the National Learners' Records Database (NLRD). The key instrument in standards setting is the design of qualifications standards, which are expressed through outcome statements. Qualifications can be based on 'unit standards' which are 'units of learning' with specific learning outcomes but smaller than a full qualification. These units range in time demand from 20 hours of learning up to 160 hours of learning. Both qualifications and unit standards are registered on the NQF. The achievements of SAQA in its implementation of the NQF from 1997 to 2007 in relation to standards setting include:

- By May 2001, 180 Standards Generating Bodies (SGBs) had been formed and 137 new qualifications and 2207 new unit standards had been registered on the NQF. In addition, over 7000 historical provider-generated qualifications had been recorded on the NQF.
- By December 2004, over 250 SGBs had been formed and 631 new qualifications and 8797 new unit standards had been registered. In addition, 7695 historical provider-generated qualifications were recorded on the NQF.

- By July 2007, 74 SGBs were operating, and 787 new qualifications and 10,988 unit standards had been registered. In addition, there were 7092 provider-generated qualifications recorded on the NQF (of which 492 were new qualifications, and 6600 were historical qualifications).
- By July 2007, 7.5 million learners' achievements were registered on the NLRD and there were 23,990 providers accredited for 6683 qualifications. There were thirty-one accredited Education and Training Quality Assurance bodies (of which 25 are Sectoral Education and Training Authorities).

A comparison between 'historical' qualifications developed by providers and 'new' qualifications developed by SGBs after the NQF was established shows a significant increase in qualifications available at NQF levels 3, 4 and 5. The highest level of activity has been in manufacturing, engineering and technology. Provider-generated qualifications are registered, in the main, at levels 5 and above. By contrast, unit standards have been registered primarily from levels 2 to 5.

Joint implementation plans have been entered into enabling Sector Education and Training Authorities, professional bodies, government departments and other bodies such as the Independent Electoral Commission to establish SGBs to generate qualifications and standards that meet their particular needs. By July 2007, over thirty-five joint implementation plans had been established. These included a broad range of partners and cover a variety of standards and qualifications including: Local Government and Water Services SETA, Mpumalanga Government, Services SETA, Financial and Accounting Services SETA, Health and Welfare SETA, National Department of Arts and Culture, Independent Electoral Commission, Mining Qualifications Authority and the National Treasury.

The impact of an outcomes led qualifications framework on qualifications and quality assurance in higher education and in schooling has been mixed. In the case of higher education, institutions have become more aware of quality assurance issues and most have instituted quality assurance management systems and have done some standardizing of their programmes and qualifications. The light-touch approach adopted by the Council on Higher Education and the Higher Education Quality Committee to outcomes and the developmental approach to quality assurance reviews and audits has encouraged academics to scrutinize their own curriculum, pedagogic and assessment practices without impinging overly on their academic autonomy, although some would express concern at the increased administrative loads now required as part of curriculum development and programme management.

The recent history of the schooling system is more complex. The specific interpretation of outcomes-based education, which took hold in SA in the mid-1990s, informed the development of the NQF and of the school curriculum.

However, the dominance of OBE was soon challenged within schooling and, in the last five years, there has been an increasing emphasis placed on providing detailed curriculum guidance, professional development of teachers and national external assessments. In higher education and schooling there are causes for serious concern about quality – especially the vast divergences in quality of provision, which suggest that our nascent quality managements systems are proving ineffective in addressing the weaknesses of the system.

In the field of occupational learning, weaknesses are most apparent in the persistence of both high levels of unemployment and high levels of skills shortages in key areas of the labour market, which led to the establishment, in 2006, of the Accelerated and Shared Growth Initiative for South Africa (ASGISA) and the Joint Initiative on Priority Skills Acquisition (JIPSA). Part of the explanation for this ineffectiveness lies in a lack of systemic coherence and collaboration between the role players and of clear differentiation of their roles and responsibilities. For example, the uptake of unit standards-based qualifications is low. There are, however, myriad potential explanations for this failure, which attribute responsibility to different role players. Could it be that the Sectoral Education and Training Authority system, which should be the main channel for the flow of learners into unit standards-based occupational qualifications has not functioned efficiently? Or is it the conceptual design model used by SAQA? Or perhaps, it just takes time for new kinds of qualifications to become established.

Implementation of the NQF has clearly been affected by the climate of uncertainty created by the lengthy review process, and the differences between standards setting and quality assurance practices across the three knowledge fields have impeded progress towards the NQF objectives. The release of the Joint Policy Statement (JPS), in September 2007, by the Ministers of Education and Labour attempts to address the challenges described above and is intended to mark the beginning of a new phase in the development of South Africa's NQF (MoE and MoL 2007).

The two major changes to South Africa's NQF are moves away from 'standardization' to 'differentiation' and away from an up-front, design-down and prescriptive approach to standards setting to a practice-based, design-up and descriptive approach. There will be a shift from an 8-level to a 10-level NQF to accommodate greater differentiation in higher education. The standards setting and quality assurance functions carried out by SAQA will shift to three Quality Councils: the Quality Council on Higher Education (NQF Levels 5 to 10); the Quality Council for General and Further Education (Umalusi) (NQF Levels 1 to 4 – the schooling system and technical colleges); and, the Quality Council for Trades and Occupations (occupational qualifications: NQF Levels 1 to 10). This will allow for the emergence of different sub-frameworks shaped to the needs of each distinct knowledge field and its associated forms of learning.

The major changes to standards setting and the design and delivery of programmes and qualifications are likely to occur in the field of occupational qualifications. Currently, occupational qualifications are integrated with no formal distinction between different forms of learning, in future, they will contain three components: General *knowledge and theory*; General and occupationally relevant *practical skills*; and, requisite *work experience*. These components can be learnt and assessed separately in different sites; their achievement will be recorded formally and will count towards certification of a unit standard or qualification made up of specific sets of components (DoL 2007: 3).

The development of occupational qualifications and unit standards will be informed by the development of a curriculum, which will structure knowledge, skills and values into a meaningful process of developing occupational competence through selecting, sequencing, pacing and assessment and includes classroom activities, practical activities and workplace experience and a strong emphasis will be placed on the role of external national assessments in quality assurance (DoL 2007: 5). The key shift here is that the process of curriculum development begins with work place practices rather than with outcome statements.

The government expects these changes to make the system simpler and more efficient by recognizing different forms of learning in the different parts of the education and training system. Broadly, this is a move away from a top-down model that tried to use OBE as a prescribed 'common ground' applicable to all education and training towards a bottom-up model that allows for differentiation and sees the NQF as a 'common ground' that will be constructed slowly and incrementally.

Underneath the surface: a brief overview of key debates that have informed the development of South Africa's NQF

In South Africa, the early ambitious dreams of what could be achieved through national qualifications frameworks have been replaced by more modest views of NQFs as frameworks of communication that grow incrementally. Parker and Harley (2007: 18) draw a distinction between two archetypes of NQFs that distinguish between frameworks that describe and coordinate *'what is'* and frameworks that try and prescribe *'what ought to be'*, with the former being favoured by developed countries and the latter by developing countries. The descriptive frameworks of developed countries develop incrementally towards 'common standards'. By contrast, the normative frameworks of developing countries tend towards a radical rupturing with the past and are intended to transform education and training systems. The review of South Africa's NQF marks a shift from a normative approach to a descriptive approach to standards setting.

The initial impetus for the development of NQFs was focused strongly on articulating academic schooling with vocational or occupationally oriented education, and education and training more generally with the economy. This has been supplemented, in the last decade, by an increasing need for a free flow of intellectual capital and skilled labour and a growing economic need to commodify and massify education and training. This tramples on traditional autonomies and vested interests leading to contestation over the meaning and purposes of qualifications and the curriculum, pedagogic and assessment practices associated with them. Developing communicative articulating frameworks, which enable a free flow of intellectual capital and skilled labour, perhaps most evident in the Bologna process, is an exercise in harmonization and standardization – creating rules of recognition and evaluation by which diverse qualifications can be compared and categorized as having x, y and z in 'common'. Whether one approaches this with a 'transformative' and prescriptive approach to reform (by diktat) or an incremental and generative approach (by recognition of 'good' practices), the target remains harmonization and/or standardization.

Access, redress, mobility, portability and progression all depend in some or other way on the assumption that it is possible to recognize and evaluate 'something' that is comparable between different qualifications or different forms of learning. The original design of South Africa's NQF located this function in the learning outcomes of a qualification. Whether a qualification was discipline-based and achieved through an institution or craft-based and achieved through workplace experience, the learning outcomes embedded in the qualification were supposed to be 'learning-mode' neutral and could therefore be used as a 'proxy-function' to map one set of knowledge, skills, and values onto another.

It is this aspect of South Africa's NQF that has been most contested. At the heart of these debates lie two very distinct understandings of learning processes and their outcomes, which are grounded in the debates between behaviourist and constructivist views of learning. The latter extol the esoteric nature of learning: knowledge, skills and values can only be acquired through initiation into 'worthwhile practices and grammars' of a specific knowledge discourse (Ensor 2003: 330). This takes time and a conducive environment, motivated and intelligent learners and appropriate curriculum, pedagogic and assessment practices. From this perspective, outcome statements are 'formal' rather than substantive standards and provide little specification of the selection, pacing, sequencing, progression and evaluation criteria that will characterize the curriculum and there is no indication of appropriate depths of content knowledge and levels of cognitive demand (Allais 2003: 308). While this allows for a significant degree of autonomy over the curriculum, it presupposes that educators can read the criteria in a way that is meaningful and 'aligned with' the meaning intended by the designers.

From a behaviourist perspective, outcome statements are descriptions of observable and measurable behaviours. However, because this learning can't be captured by simple descriptions of behaviour, outcome statements become increasingly specified (Allais 2007: 272). The risk is that what is supposed to be a platform for public communication and participation instead becomes a domain of esoteric jargon understood only by experts – leaving learners, providers and employers struggling to make sense of basic matters such as curriculum and assessment. Trying to prescribe quality up front through ever increasing levels of specification and complexity is a doomed enterprise, which assumes that outcome statements are transparent descriptions of 'competence'. A design-down approach, which begins with outcome statements, is oriented away from actual curriculum, pedagogic and assessment practices towards policy and design criteria. Approval of qualifications becomes a matter of compliance with technical regulations rather than a fit-for purpose practice-oriented approach.

In recent South African debates, emphasis has been placed on a distinction between 'competence standards' and 'academic standards'. Competence standards are linked to job descriptions and their associated skills sets, which are expressed through outcome statements. A person who has a qualification and designation as a 'plumber' must be able 'to do the job' and can have their performance evaluated against a set of 'performance/outcome statements'. Although these descriptions of practices can never be 'thick' enough to capture everything we expect of a person who has certified occupational or professional competence, they do provide a 'rule of thumb' sufficient for the purposes of a rather crude performance management tool.

While competence standards speak to skill sets and job description/performance measurement indicators, 'academic standards' relate to domains of knowledge and the curriculum and assessment practices by which they are achieved. The thinness of outcome statements in relation to these institution-based educational practices prevents them from playing a similar measurement and grading role. Confusion abounds when an NQF attempts to construct overarching 'qualification standards' to bridge the divide and describe knowledge domains, curriculum and assessment practices, skills sets and job descriptions in a common language. There is a necessary impossibility about these endeavours; however elaborate our languages of description we cannot create a 'perfect picture'. Outcome statements are not the same as outcomes or competences. Ironically, within current debates in South Africa, academics are defending idealism (the intrinsic worth of knowledge) by grounding their standards in real educational practices, while their counterparts in the occupational learning system are defending realism (skills outcomes) by grounding their standards in the ideal world of design policy and tools. This suggests the importance of a strong distinction between mastery of a body of knowledge certified by a qualification and the achievement of a set of competences certified by a professional or occupational designation.

Building opportunities for lifelong learning requires a clear understanding of 'comparability' and 'transferability' and reiterates the importance of initiatives such as credit accumulation and transfer and recognition of prior learning, which are understood to have the potential to improve access, progression, mobility and portability – nationally and internationally. What instruments, tools and practices can be used for comparability? Moving away from outcomes implies moving towards different approaches to recognizing and evaluating different 'units of comparability'. By themselves, specifications of curriculum content and of assessments do not avoid the conundrums of interpretation.

If we can no longer pre-specify the 'unit of comparability', how do we begin to establish a framework for developing communicative models that articulate different forms of learning? We believe that the best way to address these challenges is through research-driven policy, which informs the political and organizational shape of the NQF. In the South African case, there is already a considerable body of research on learning and on the NQF that can provide a foundation for future research. Two theoretical approaches that have become prominent within this research draw on Bernstein's (1996: 169–180) account of different knowledge fields and the power and control relations between and within these fields, and on Lave and Wenger's (1991: 53) notion of communities of practice as learning communities which emerge in workplaces.

For Bernstein, pedagogic discourse is constructed by a recontextualizing principle, which selectively appropriates, relocates, refocuses and relates other discourses to constitute its own order (Bernstein 1996: 47). This recontextualization delocates discourses from their substantive practice and context and relocates them in an arbitrary space according to principles of selective reordering and refocusing that remove the discourses from the social basis of their practice (Bernstein 1990: 184). Understanding the inside of a pedagogic practice, recognizing its intrinsic worth and purpose, is inextricably interwoven with recognizing what is outside of the practice – the social order within which the practice is embedded.

The concept of communities of practice is primarily a means of categorizing a particular set or web of relations between people as having a particular identity, value orientation and purpose (Lave and Wenger 1991: 98). Within a strong community of practice there is a strong sense of shared values and beliefs; a consciousness of, and commitment to, an overall holistic purpose that shapes the activities of the community; and, agreement on the set of practices that constitute 'competent practice' (Wenger 1998: 95). At some level, learning is always induction into a community whose boundaries are marked by commitment to a set of beliefs about what counts as knowledge and skills and what are 'good' values and attitudes to underpin and infuse learning as a process of enlightenment, enhancement and attunement. This approach emphasizes the social and constructive nature of learning. Learning is simultaneously a path to knowledge, initiation into a community of practitioners and a shaping of one's identity. These reflections suggest that when talking about qualifications frameworks it is useful to distinguish between distinct knowledge fields and the ways in which they are cognitively structured and socially organized.

Although we are not advocating the use of these two particular theorists, we are suggesting that their already existing productive use in South African research indicates that it is possible to conceptualize a vantage point from which to develop languages of description to explore the development of quality management systems and the role of qualification frameworks within these systems. Recognizing differences between the fields, understanding the nature of their boundaries and hence the possibility of boundary crossings will inform how we develop an integrated approach to a national qualifications framework with articulations that enable comparability between different forms of learning and the different knowledge fields within which learning takes place and between these fields and the world of work.

There have been some suggestions, within South African debates, that the boundaries between the academic field and the 'everyday' field, between school and street knowledge, are very strong and that institutions, curriculum and assessment should be the primary foci of qualifications design and quality assurance. There is a particular emphasis on the importance of institutions as bedrock of quality education and training. This is obviously correct when applied to schooling and higher education. However, many occupational qualifications are delivered by non-institutional providers or in the workplace, thus raising questions about approaches to quality assurance and development in non-institutional settings. Although the knowledge field of occupationally oriented education is far more context specific and delivery is less institutionalized, this does not mean that this non-academic knowledge field is content-less, nor that curriculum, pedagogy and assessment are less important. Rather than dichotomizing and demonizing the everyday knowledge field, we should be researching curriculum, pedagogic and assessment practices in these fields to better understand how we can improve quality. Although, the existence of different knowledge fields and communities of practice does make agreement and articulation difficult to achieve, it does perhaps make it all the more worthwhile.

Some insights on competence-based training and National Qualifications Frameworks from South Africa's experience

South Africa's experience illuminates the importance of coherent and systemic implementation and the slow nature of educational transformation. Qualifications frameworks can play an important role in the transformation of education and training systems, provided that they are seen as a platform for communication and coordination rather than an arena of contestation and confusion. South Africa's NQF has already made some progress towards achieving its objectives and the changes proposed by the Joint Policy Statement should further enhance the efficacy and efficiency of the NQF. Among other benefits, NQFs should enable: the development of relevant and appropriate qualifications, which address national and personal needs; improvements in quality assurance systems; and, monitoring and evaluation of progress towards national education and training objectives.

The NQF introduced new language, procedures and processes, which some found opaque and complex. Systems have continued to be simplified and streamlined in response to this and the NQF is now 'coming of age' with citizens more familiar with its workings. After ten years of development, the South African NQF is seen as an important reference point for new national and regional qualifications frameworks that are developing in many parts of the world. South African experience indicates that qualifications frameworks should be built cautiously, modestly and incrementally. Development should have a strong experimental scientific approach in which failures or falsifications are seen as evidence.

South Africa's initial move to privilege CBT or OBE as the template for the whole education and training system through the use of outcomes statements as an up-front, prescriptive and design-down approach, which was intended to create a 'communication's platform' for portability of learning between different knowledge and occupational fields, has not succeeded. The schooling and higher education systems did not 'buy-in' to the approach, nor has South Africa's skills development system prospered. South Africa's deepening skills crisis, which is 'blamed' by many politicians and business leaders on disjunctures between schooling and higher education on the one side and the economy and labour market on the other side, has been exacerbated by the massive decline in apprenticeships and other types of work-based learning. The number of apprenticeships has declined from a high of 80,000 per annum in the mid-1980s to 5000 in the mid-2000s. South Africa's NQF has not met the expectations of business with respect to improving the supply of appropriately trained skilled labour or intellectual capital, nor the expectations of labour with respect to increasing access to educational and occupational opportunities. Far from contributing to the development of a lifelong learning system, the NQF appears to have impeded South Africa's progress towards these objectives.

The reasons for this failure lie in factors internal and external to an outcomes based NQF. Key among the external factors was an underestimation of the weaknesses of institutions and the lack of competent educators and trainers inherited from apartheid. Key among the internal factors was conceptual confusions and contestations over what was meant by competences and outcomes (and forms of learning underpinning their achievement) and how they might best be described in qualification statements and used for quality assurance. Central to both sets of factors was a lack of clarity about the purposes of the NQF with stakeholders having very different perspectives and objectives ranging from the state's perspective of an administratively driven quality management system that could steer the education and training system towards its economic and political objectives to organized labour's view of the NQF as a portal to lifelong learning with strong emancipatory and empowering objectives.

NQFs are best understood as a work-in-progress and as contestable artefacts of modern society, which can contribute in a modest way to how a society manages the relations between education, training and work by finding 'common ground' between distinct forms of learning and their articulation with workplace practices. This can best be done through a strong research-driven collaborative approach to NQF development that seeks 'means of portability', ways of enabling boundary crossings, of improving quality and relevance and of understanding better different forms and sites of learning. There is no doubt that NQFs can become divisive and make little, if any contribution, to lifelong learning or educational reform. This is not preordained, however, as NQFs can provide an opportunity to address, in a modest manner, aspects of lifelong learning in ways which contribute to economic development, social justice and personal empowerment.

Chapter 14

Towards enhanced competence of the Thai workforce

Patcharawalai Wongboonsin and Kua Wongboonsin

Introduction

Thailand has recently envisioned repositioning itself from a lower-middle income economy to an upper-income one and beyond. It looks forward to more skilled-intensive activities and higher technology to secure its competitive edge in the world market. Such an effort is launched against the backdrop of the pressure from newly emerging, low-wage countries, such as China and India. This chapter argues that the challenges for Thailand not only derive from such external sources, but also from within the country itself.

Despite a series of education reforms and the performance of a certain proportion of Thai students being identified as comparable with that in the developed world, a shortage of skilled workforce remains a key shortcoming in Thailand. Limited skills acquisition in both the stock and flow of the workforce are pronounced in the majority of the Thai population, particularly those in rural areas and with relatively low socio-economic status.

A competitive world market and changing comparative advantage are major trends in the era of globalization. Countries throughout Asia are restructuring their economies and upgrading the capacities of their national economies so as to compete effectively in the world market. Located at the heart of Southeast Asia, Thailand is a developing country of 65.7 million people under a structural shift from a factor-driven to an investment-driven, and even further towards an innovation-driven, economy (NSO 2008). Enhancing productivity through innovation, buttressed by higher rates of private investment, is an objective for the Thai economy and is reflected in the country's Tenth Economic and Social Development Plan. This is to move away from a 'middle income trap' into a knowledge-based economy on a par with other leading East Asian economies while sustaining the momentum of growth in the longer term.

Improvement of skills to move Thailand towards a knowledge-based economy is the key for enhancing productivity and competitiveness. This is to be emphasized before Thailand moves into a demographic structural change towards an ageing society in the next 10–15 years.

The second demographic dividend, or else the onus

Thailand's economic development during recent decades was contributed to by the demographic dividend, which refers to a feature of an age structure with the tendency for the working-age population to grow more rapidly than the overall population once fertility has begun to decline. It normally takes place only once in the middle phase of a demographic transition, and lasts for just a few decades. The rising proportion of the population of working age relative to that of dependent age is considered a window of opportunity to accrue economic benefits to both the society and each individual person in the society (Bloom *et al.* 2003). An increase in the dependency ratio signals the fading away of the opportunity to capitalize on the demographic conditions for a demographic dividend. During that time, there is an increasing proportion of the population who are elderly, due to low fertility and stable mortality (K. Wongboonsin & Guest 2005). This may lead to a situation, called a 'demographic onus', which constitutes burdens to the society, the family, and the individual population (Ogawa *et al.* 2004).

In Thailand, changes in population growth, driven by changing fertility over the last four decades, are expected with profound impacts on population compositions. The proportion of the population below 15 years of age is projected to decline from 24.65 per cent in 2000 to 17.95 per cent in 2025. After the projected peak in the proportion of the population in the labour force age range (15–59) at 67.08 per cent in 2009 the proportion will decline and reach 62.05 per cent in 2025 (see Figure 14.1).

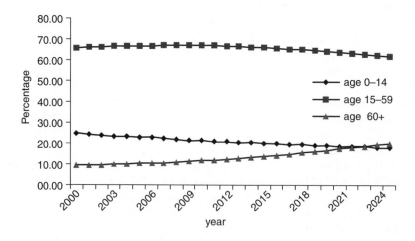

Figure 14.1 Per cent of population below 15, 15–59 and 60 and above (medium fertility assumption).

Source: Based on data from NESDB (2005).

Against the dwindling curve of the proportion of the population below 15 and between 15 and 59 years of age, the proportion curve of the ageing population (60+ years) is having a surge with a double increase from 10 to 20 percentage points. It is like a Tsunami wave that carries negative impacts on the society. This study calls such a situation as a 'Tsunami ageing population phenomenon'. This phenomenon is expected to have negative impacts on Thai society in the near future. In other words, Thailand will have a chance to enjoy the optimum conditions of the demographic dividend for no more than two years from 2009. Thereafter, Thailand will be in transition to a demographic onus, unless an appropriate policy intervention is adopted.

This study maintains that Thailand will still have a chance for a second demographic dividend, if a demand-driven competence approach is adopted in enhancing the productivity of the workforce. This is based on the notion raised by Becker (1991) in terms of the possibility of an increase in human capital in an ageing society should there be a trade-off between the number of children and investment in human capital in children. Mason and Lee (2006) suggest further that the second dividend would be possible if changes in the age structure influence the accumulation of wealth and capital. Should that be the case, ageing can lead to a sustained increase in standards of living that persist after the first demographic dividend has long disappeared.

Productivity, competence development, and lifelong education for all

One may note that the economic dividend is not solely a function of demographic change. To realize the economic benefits, there must also be higher productivity of the workforce, which is contributed by appropriate competency in both technical and social terms. The nexus between competence and productivity of the workforce is also reflected in a notion of fundamental human competence, in terms of the ability to do what needs to be done, to deal productively with other people and their environments. Used and usable knowledge, skills and attitudes are often considered as essential parts of competence, while skills may also refer to practical knowledge. The latter can be categorized into two kinds: explicit and tacit. One may find skills resembling tacit knowledge once the latter is defined in terms of an individual's familiarity with his work and his ability to make judgements about performances (Freden & Nilsson 2003; Nonaka & Takeuchi 1995).

Knowledge and skills are transferable. Learning theories maintain that explicit knowledge, or that which an individual can declare, can be converted into a more complex set. Leaning by doing can internalize explicit into tacit knowledge. Socialization, such as when a learner watches and interacts with an expert, contributes to a whole body of experience. Once the tacit knowledge is

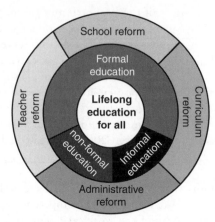

Figure 14.2 Lifelong education for all in Thailand.

Source: P. Wongboonsin (2006).

translated and expressed into forms that are comprehensible to the conscious mind of an individual and to others, the tacit knowledge is externalized into explicit knowledge (Delahaye & Becker 2006).

Such a process of knowledge generation is further supported by a concept of the transposition of competency and learning. The latter spells out the possibility for a learner's level of competency and professionalism to be elevated to a higher plane along expanding circles in the competency theory. According to the trans-positioning notion, learning can turn into competency itself (Azemikhah 2006).

The above notions imply that lifelong learning should be the basis for competence development, particularly in the knowledge-based society of the twenty-first century. This is supported by a common notion in the current debates of skills development on the ever-shifting requirements for competence development due to the changing needs of growing economies, the changing nature of work as well as the opportunities globalization presents.

'Lifelong Education for All' serves as a major principle of education reform to upgrade the skills of people at all ages towards a knowledge-based society in Thailand. According to section 4 of the National Education Act, the term incorporates formal, non-formal and informal education for continuous lifelong development in both quantity and quality dimensions (see Figure 14.2).

Projected workforce from 2003 to 2025

Of the total Thai population of 65.7 million people in 2007, approximately 36.7 million make up the total labour force. Out of the 35.7 million employed persons, approximately 20.7 million had no more than a primary school education (NSO 2008). Despite universal primary enrolment rates, Thailand still has a low rate of enrolment at secondary and tertiary levels.

Against the general notion of an increase in educated workforce above primary education reflected in a projection of the Thai workforce from 2003 to 2025 (see Figure 14.3), a closer look into the proportion of educational attainment from the secondary level onwards does not exactly suggest a very bright future for the Thai economy.

First, the Thai workforce is moving more towards basic education at the secondary level than the vocational education. This reflects an ongoing trend of the common preferences towards general upper secondary schools as a prestige route for further education at university level (P. Wongboonsin 2006).

Second, the proportion of those with vocational education remains low. This implies an on-going trend for vocational education to be an unpopular educational choice for the young population, albeit the general notion that vocational education is a key factor for attaining international competitiveness in the new and technologically dynamic world economy, and that the practical skills and corresponding theories taught to vocational students in certain vocational schools are sufficient for a clean transition to the workplace (P. Wongboonsin *et al.* 2004).

Third, there will only be a slight increase in the proportion of the workforce with tertiary education to 22.97 per cent in 2025.

Such a future trend of the workforce reflects that Thailand will not be in an appropriate position to secure their competitive edge in the world market in years to come.

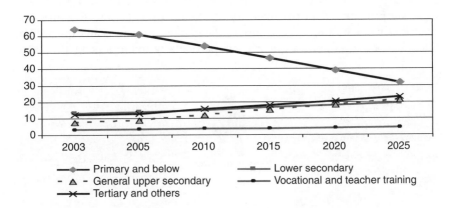

Figure 14.3 Proportion of projected workforce by educational attainment.

Source: K. Wongboonsin (2003).

Looming shortage of skilled workforce

While Thailand has recognized the need to move up the value-added chain, the factor conditions in terms of the shortage of skilled workforce and a mismatch between the demand and supply of skills represent key constraints that need to be addressed, as compared to inadequacy of infrastructure and regulatory environment. Skill deficiency of the available workforce was the topmost concern of the private sector in Thailand while skills shortage was 'costing firms 15% of their sales on average' (World Bank 2006). This is despite the following indicators for the Thai workforce to be competitive in the face of intensified challenges from existing players and newcomers in Asia such as China, India and Vietnam: low costs, low unemployment, relatively productive labour relations with low industrial disputes and high average working hours, high level of overall and female labour force participation, as well as high level of labour force growth – all have contributed to its strength (Ahuja *et al.* 2006).

The above notions are supportive of the findings of another study, shown in Figure 14.4, based on perceptions of companies in niche industries, such as automotive, textile, and electronics and information technology, that the shortcomings in the Thai labour market include a shortage of high-skilled workers, lack of motivation, work ethic, and responsibility of the workforce. The latter was reflected in terms of lack of concern with deadlines and punctuality. Figure 14.4 also reflects that adult training is encouraged, since the strengths of the Thai workforce are that they are easy to train, they learn quickly and they are respectful. Accordingly, such an encouragement should not be subject to any confrontational reactions from the workforce side.

Despite a series of education reforms and the performance of a proportion of Thai students being identified as comparable with that of developed economies, limited skill acquisition in both the stock and flow of the workforce are pronounced in the majority of the Thai population. Rigidity and inadequacy of education in response to the market demand is an explanation. Such a problem of skill acquisition is particularly found among people in

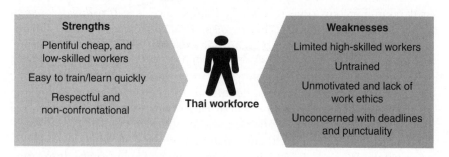

Figure 14.4 Strengths and weaknesses of Thai workforce.

Source: Authors, based on Biron *et al.* (2004).

rural areas and those with relatively low socio-economic status. According to Ahuja *et al.* (2006), a big gap in educational attainment is noticeable between the more developed parts of the country, particularly Bangkok Metropolitan Area as well as its vicinities, and the rural areas, which contribute to 50 per cent of the workforce in Thailand.

Case study: Textile industry

The Thai textile industry has played a critical role in Thailand's economy. It is comprised of a wide spectrum of factories and human resources. Both outdated and new facilities exist, with a mix of both skilled and unskilled labour. Due to changing needs in technological innovation, globalization and new competitors in the international market, the textile industry is in the process of restructuring. Thailand currently attempts to gain the status of a world leader in the manufacture of quality textiles. Technologies in factories are in the process of being improved to allow for the production of high quality, modern fabrics with minimal labour. Upgrading technology requires not only changes in machinery, but also changes in the skills and competencies of the human capital in the labour market. An effective means of facilitating these changes is to begin with educating, training and preparing the future workforce before they enter the industry. Workers entering the textile industry are usually educated and trained in vocational schools. Industry reforms are likely to progress more rapidly if supplemented by curricular reforms that develop a broader range of skills for students. Such areas are deemed crucial for the future success of the Thai textile industry (P. Wongboonsin *et al.* 2004).

It is clear that the advantages of the information age, such as specialized computer software, internet access, and many kinds of visual aids are used extensively to enhance different areas of the relevant curriculum. A pilot study carried out in 2004 suggested that the competence of students can be improved, if they attain education that is equipped with curricula relevant to the market demand (P. Wongboonsin *et al.* 2004).

Needed strategies towards future Thai workforce

Against the background of skill competency and educational attainment of the workforce that is below the level needed in the competitive world economy, a highly skilled and productive workforce is necessary for Thailand to advance in economic terms while ensuring investment prospects from abroad. The role of education and training in upgrading the competency of the workforce and the reduction of skill mismatching remains further encouraged.

Educational reform and skills training should, at most, be levelled up to enhance competencies and productivity of both the stock and flow of the Thai workforce with basic, general and specific skills to sustain the quality of work life in the twenty-first century, as shown in Figure 14.5.

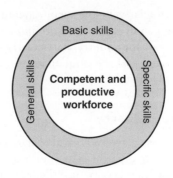

Figure 14.5 Skills needed for competent and productive workforce.

Source: P. Wongboonsin (2006).

Competence development for flow of the Thai workforce

A study of human resource trends suggests that the demand in quantity will rise for only ten more years, and decline to reach a steady level thereafter (K. Wongboonsin *et al.* 2003). This is in comparison to a rising demand for quality human resources. The study also suggests that Thailand is in urgent need of a human resource development (HRD) reform, which should be comprehensive and adjustable at all times with visions and database information. Education and skill development should be integrated with an emphasis on learning by doing while enabling students to think effectively (K. Wongboonsin *et al.* 2007).

Figure 14.6 lists skills and attitudes identified by HR experts as essential for students to possess, so as to be a competitive workforce in the next 10 to 15 years.

Students should be provided with a sound foundation of basic knowledge and self-adjustment capability in developing skills to learn and be further trained in the workforce market. The role of workplace learning is to be further strengthened along with strong collaboration among the ministries of education, labour and industry. Given rapid change of science and technology and rapid knowledge obsolescence, a strong technological and scientific orientation of vocational education and training systems is encouraged with increasing national investment and greater involvement of the private sector to boost indigenous R&D in response to the market economy.

Considering the future trend towards a knowledge-based and dynamically changing society, a previous study suggests the following (K. Wongboonsin *et al.* 2003, 2007).

- Vocational students should be equipped with upgraded vocational knowledge and the following skills to meet the demand in the labour market:

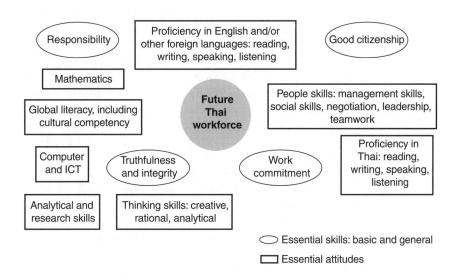

Figure 14.6 Essential attributes of future Thai workforce.

Source: Authors, based on K. Wongboonsin *et al.* (2003, 2007).

thinking; operating; technical; management; human relations; and communication skills. Vocational education should also emphasize upgrading proficiency in languages – Thai, English and other languages used in business – as well as competency in mathematics, science and technology. Learning and training systems at vocational schools are subject to a highlight on competencies that meet the demand of the labour market.

- Secondary education should add the following dimensions into the educational system: mentality, activities in support of job creation, and consciousness. It is important for secondary-education managerial teams to have a broad vision aiming at international competitiveness. The final year students in secondary schools should be provided with thinking, operational, and problem-solving skills as well as a responsibility attribute. In addition, they must have the skills to learn by themselves.
- Tertiary education should emphasize the improvement of basic education and basic competence with curriculums that meet the future trends. Students in a higher learning institution should have appropriate attitudes towards the knowledge-based and dynamically changing society with appropriate knowledge in general terms and basic skills in specific areas for their careers.
- The quality of vocational and tertiary education should be upgraded so that graduates at both levels of education are equipped with the following: 1) multidisciplinary knowledge that gives a balance between

sciences and social sciences; 2) capability to learn by themselves; 3) good skills in listening, reading, writing and verbal communication; 4) competence in English language and computers.

- The workforce should be well prepared for the information technology society. This can be done by reorientating educational curricula in vocational and tertiary education towards a multidisciplinary dimension with a focus on the development of analytical ability and critical thinking. The students should have opportunities to practice with entrepreneurs and to develop their knowledge in science and technology in order to keep apace with the world in the age of information.

- In all, competencies to be commonly possessed by students at all levels of education in Thailand include: English, information technology, teamwork; knowledge application; knowledge development; and problem solving. They should also be of good character, diligent and have good attitudes towards a working life in the knowledge-based economy.

Evaluation of HRD management should be an integral part of the development process at all levels of education. For secondary education, the evaluation should be focused on educational quality assurance, teacher-development plans, appropriate ages of students, training courses, and provision of career standards at the national level. For vocational education, the international standards and criteria should be used to analyse the cost and benefit as well as economic returns in the short and long term. For first-year university education, the evaluation process should include both internal and external auditing. First-year university students should be evaluated in terms of knowledge, skills, knowledge application, attitudes and potentialities for further development. For university graduates, issuing a practitioner licence should be part of the process besides an emphasis on quality control within an institution. Institutional evaluation mechanisms may be the government or specialized agencies. As a matter of fact, all are subject to evaluation by the market at the end of the process (K. Wongboonsin *et al.* 2003, 2007).

Competence development for the stock of the Thai workforce

Thailand is in need of upgrading low-skilled workers to desired standards of technical proficiency responding to market signals. Teaching and learning in schools should be able to help students make connections between their school activities and the basic skills, competencies required in the labour market with appropriate qualifications to adjust themselves either to a new environment, further education as well as training prior to and during employment. Appropriate training after schools is also to be prioritized to help the workforce adjust with the necessary skills to the new environment in workplaces.

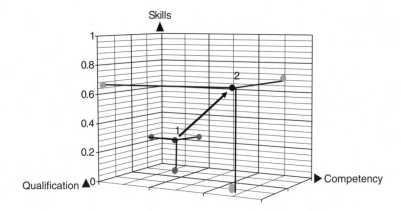

Figure 14.7 Improvement of skills, competency, and qualifications, from level 1 to level 2.

Source: K. Wongboonsin (2003).

Figure 14.7 reflects the notion that new graduates of good vocational or higher education are able to attain a basic level (Level 1) of skills, competency and qualifications. Normally, only the new employees that enter the workforce are affected. It may not influence the cumulative human capital for ten or more years, which is the approximate turnover period for the current labour pool population to exit the workforce. Appropriate training after schooling helps augment the gradual improvement of skills, competency and qualifications (Level 2).

An explanation is an unequal strength of schools in Thailand that contribute to the literacy skills of students despite years of schooling (Ahuja *et al.* 2006). Even with appropriate schooling, literacy skills can deteriorate if they are not maintained through on-the-job training, informal learning or regular practice (Somers 2005).

Workplace learning has become a trend in Thailand. A previous study finds two factors affecting the drive for training and enhanced learning within firms. One is governmental factors, including governmental policy initiatives and supporting mechanisms. The other is non-governmental, including: the challenge of globalization; regionalization; market pressures in the knowledge economy, which have affected prospects for profit making and/or business survival, while leading to redefinition of firm performance; international trends and growing use of international standards as well as quality accreditation systems; technological, product and organizational change within firms; vision, leadership and commitment at the top-management level within firms (P. Wongboonsin & Rojvithee 2007).

It is clear that production-based industries in Thailand are very much (60%) in need of a skill-based workforce with quality vocational training and schooling compared to those with tertiary education. Large, medium and small-scaled enterprises share the notion that a knowledgeable and competent workforce is one of the most essential resources for a business to survive. This is particularly so when a firm recognizes the combining forces of the market pressure, the concept of intellectual capital and the growing use of international standards as well as quality accreditation systems. Workplace learning is part of business strategies to meet the challenges of globalization. The case is clear once an enterprise sees that the knowledge-based economy is forging ahead (P. Wongboonsin and Rojvithee 2007).

Yet, workplace learning as competence development is still limited in scope. Certain businesses in manufacturing put little effort into increasing the basic skill level of their employees. They tend to provide training programmes to help their employees learn job-specific skills rather than basic competencies. Only some of the businesses offer their skilled workers the opportunity for additional training and job advancement (Biron *et al.* 2004; P. Wongboonsin & Rojvithee 2007).

Despite incentives and attempts in workplaces to provide training for their staff, workplace learning in Thailand is, accordingly, to be further strengthened. The government should be assured that employees are receiving high-quality training according to the national and international standards. The concept of social investment should be encouraged among the private sectors in preference to the common notion among a number of entrepreneurs that the training and retraining of their workers is costly (Biron *et al.* 2004; P. Wongboonsin & Rojvithee 2007).

Conclusion

Thailand is currently under a structural shift from a factor-driven to an investment-driven, and even further towards an innovation-driven economy, so as to move away from a 'middle income trap' into a knowledge-based economy on a par with other leading East Asian economies, while sustaining the momentum of growth in the long term. Yet, despite a series of education reforms and the performance of a certain proportion of Thai students being identified as comparable with that in the developed world, Thailand is short of skilled workforce. A projection on the future trend of the workforce also warns that Thailand's competitive edge in the world market is insecure in years to come, unless their workforce is repositioned towards higher skills and productivity along the approach of competence development and lifelong education for all. This is to allow a second demographic dividend to help materialize the vision.

Educational reform and skills training should be leveled up to enhance competences and productivity of both the stocks and flows of the Thai workforce with basic, general and specific skills to sustain a quality of work life and the quality of life in the twenty-first century. Against the background of a declining labour-intensive demand, a list of essential skills for the workforce within the next 10–15 years is identified. Students at all levels of education in Thailand should be provided with these basic skills: English, information technology, team-work, knowledge application, knowledge development and problem solving. They should also be of good character, diligent and have good attitudes towards a working life in the knowledge-based economy. Students in vocational and higher education are particularly encouraged to equip themselves with the following: 1) multidisciplinary knowledge that gives a balance between sciences and social sciences; 2) capability to learn by themselves; 3) good skills in listening, reading, writing and verbal communication; 4) competence in English language and computer skills. Educational curricula should be reorientated towards a multidisciplinary dimension with a focus on the development of analytical ability and critical thinking. Evaluation of HRD management should be an integral part of the development process at all levels of education.

Even with appropriate schooling, literacy skills can deteriorate if they are not maintained through on-the-job training, informal learning, or regular practice. Appropriate training after schools is accordingly to be prioritized to help the workforce adjust with needed skills to the new environment in workplaces. This is based on the notion of trans-positioning knowledge, which spells out the possibility for a learner's level of competency and professionalism to be elevated to a higher plane along expanding circles in the competency theory. The concept of social investment in workplace learning is, accordingly, encouraged.

References

Introduction

APER (*Asian Pacific Education Review*) (2008) *Special Issue: Competence Development.* Guest Editor: Knud Illeris. Volume 9, Number 1.

OECD (2005) *The Definition and Selection of Key Competencies: Executive Summary.* Online at: www.oecd.org/dataoecd/47/61/35070367.pdf

Chapter 1

ASTD Policy Brief by American Association of Training and Development (2007, Spring) Retrieved on September 2, 2008 from: http://www.astd.org/NR/rdonlyres/8C6FDB15-3861-4C27-86DF-7F35917E4A57/12976/Spring07APBFinal.pdf

Baldwin, C. and Clark, K. (2005) *Designs and design architecture: The missing link between "knowledge" and the "economy."* Paper presented at the Advancing Knowledge and the Knowledge Economy Conference, National Academies, Washington, DC.

Beechler, S. and Javidan, M. (2007) Leading with a Global Mindset. In M. Javidan, R. M. Steers and M. A. Hitt (eds), *The Global Mindset.* New York: Elsevier, pp. 131–169.

Bloom, B. S. (1956) *Taxonomy of Education Objectives, Handbook 1: The cognitive domain.* New York: David McKay.

Boyatzis, R. E. (1982) *The Competent Manager: A model for effective performance.* New York: Wiley.

Burgelman, R. A. and Siegel, R. E. (2008) Cutting the strategy diamond in high-technology ventures. *California Management Review*, 50(3): 140–167.

Collis, D. J. and Montgomery, C. A. (2008) Competing on resources. *Harvard Business Review*, 86(7/8): 140–150.

Committee on Prospering in the Global Economy of the 21st Century: An agenda for American Science and Technology: The National Academy of Sciences, National Academy of Engineering, Institute of Medicine.

Competency Development (2008) Retrieved on July 14, 2008 from http://www.danskebank.com/en-uk/csr/employees/Pages/competency-development.aspx

Cross, T., Bazron, B., Dennis, K. and Isaacs, M. (1989) *Towards a Culturally Competent System of Care: A monograph on effective services for minority children who are severely emotionally disturbed: Volume I.* Washington, DC: Georgetown University Child Development Center.

Cseh, M. (2002) Management learning and development in Central and Eastern Europe: The case of Romanian small business owner-managers. *Journal of Transnational Management Development*, 7(4): 55–71.

Cseh, M. and Coningham, B. (2007) Learning experiences of organization development and change consultants working across cultures. In M. Xiao, A. M. Osman-Gani, B. Yang and J. Gong (eds), *Proceedings of the Sixth Asian Conference of the Academy of Human Resource Development: Developing Talents for Organizations and Nations* (CD-E-051). Beijing.

Deloitte Research (2007) Managing the talent crisis in global manufacturing: Strategies to attract and engage Generation Y. Retrieved July 8, 2008, from http://www.deloitte.com/dtt/research/0,1015,cid%253D161887,00.html

Elkin, G. (1990) Competency-based human resource development. *Industrial & Commercial Training*, 22(4): 20–25.

Garavan, T. N. and McGuire, D. (2001) Competencies and workplace learning: Some reflections on the rhetoric and the reality. *Journal of Workplace Learning*, 13(3/4): 144–163.

Grantham, C. and Ware, J. (2005) Closing the talent gap. The work design collaborative. Retrieved July 8, 2008, from http://www.thefutureofwork.net/resources_whitepapers.html

Gurchiek, K. (2007) Leadership gap poses biggest talent crisis, executives say. *HRNews*. Retrieved July 8, 2008, from http://www.shrm.org/hrnews_published/archives/CMS_021090.asp

Henderson, F., Anderson, E. and Rick, S. (1995) Future competency profiling: Validating and redesigning the ICL graduate assessment center. *Personnel Review*, 24(3): 19–31.

Klemp, G. L. (1981) *Job Competence Assessment: Defining the attributes of the top performer.* Alexandria, VA: American Society for Training and Development, Vol. 8.

Kochanski, J. T., & Ruse, D. H. (1996) Designing a competency-based human resources organization. *Human Resource Management*, 35(1): 19-33.

Kottolli, A. (2007) Developing a global mindset. Retrieved February 7, 2008, from http://www.geocities.com/akottolli/developing_a_global_mindset.htm

Levy, O., Beechler, S., Taylor, S. and Boyacigiller, N. A. (2007) What we talk about when we talk about 'global mindset': Managerial cognition in multinational corporations. *Journal of International Business Studies*, 38: 231–258.

McLagan, P. A. (1982) The ASTD training & development competency study: A model building challenge. *Training & Development Journal*, 36(5): 18–24.

National Academy of Sciences (2005) *Rising above the Gathering Storm: Energizing and employing America for a brighter economic future.* Committee on Prospering in the Global Economy of the 21st Century: An agenda for American Science and Technology. The National Academy of Sciences, National Academy of Engineering, Institute of Medicine. Retrieved September 29, 2008, from: http://books.nap.edu/openbook.php?isbn=0309100399&page=212

Peterson, B. (2004) *Cultural Intelligence: A guide to working with people from other cultures.* Yarmouth, ME: Intercultural Press.

Prahalad, C. K. and Hamel, G. (1990) The core competence of the corporation. *Harvard Business Review*, 68(3): 79–91.

Rhinesmith, S. H. (1996) *A Manager's Guide to Globalizations: Six skills for success in a changing world.* New York: McGraw-Hill.

Rodriguez, D., Patel, R., Bright, A., Gregory, D. and Gowing, M. K. (2002) Developing competency models to promote integrated human resource practices. *Human Resource Management*, 41(3): 309–324.

Sandberg, J. (2000) Understanding human competence at work: An interpretative approach. *Academy of Management Journal*, 43(1): 9–25.

Swanson, R. and Holton, E. (2001) *Foundations of Human Resource Development.* San Francisco, CA: Berrett-Koehler.

The Economist (2006) Survey: Masters of the universe (2006, October) *The Economist*, 381(8498), 15. Retrieved September 29, 2008, from ABI/INFORM Global database (Document ID:1142599051).

Thomas, D. C. and Inkson, K. (2003) *Cultural Intelligence: People skills for global business*. San Francisco: Berrett-Koehler.

Thorn, M. (2007) Leadership in international organizations: Global leadership competencies. Retrieved January 15, 2008, from www.academy.umd.edu/pubilcations/global_leadership/marlene_thorn.htm

Thunderbird School of Global Management (2008) Retrieved September 15, 2008 from http://newsandopinions.thunderbird.edu/blog/2008/09/10/eight-minutes-well-spent-before-going-global/#more-374

Walker, D., Walker, T. and Schmitz, J. (2003) *Doing Business Internationally: The guide to cross-cultural success* (2nd edn), New York: McGraw-Hill.

Watkins, K. E. and Marsick, V. J. (1993) *Sculpting the Learning Organization*. San Francisco: Jossey-Bass.

Watkins, K. E. and Marsick, V. J. (1997) Dimensions of the Learning Organization Questionnaire (survey). Warwick, R.I.: Partners for the Learning and Leadership (www.partnersforlearning.com).

Watkins, K. E. and Marsick, V. J. (2003) Summing up: Demonstrating the value of an organization's learning culture. *Advances in Developing Human Resources*, 5(2): 129–131.

Werhane, P. H., Posig, M., Gundry, L. Powell, E., Carlson, J. and Ofstein, L. (2006) Women leaders in corporate America: A study of leadership values and methods. In M. F. Karsten (ed.), *Gender, Race, and Ethnicity in the Workplace: Issues and challenges for today's organizations* pp. 1–29. Westport, Conn: Praeger Publishers.

White, R. W. (1959) Motivation reconsidered: The concept of competence. *Psychological Review*, 66(5): 297–333.

Wright, P. M., Dunford, B. B. and Snell, S. A. (2001) Human resources and the resource based view of the firm. *Journal of Management*, 27(6): 701–721.

Chapter 2

Delors, Jacques (ed.) (1998) *Education: A treasure to be discovered*. São Paulo: Cortez/Unesco.

Freire, Paulo (1997) *Pedagogy from Autonomy: The knowledge necessary for educational practice*. São Paulo, Cortez.

Furter, Pierre (1983) *Training Gaps*. Lausanne: Presses Polytechniques Romandes.

Gadotti, Moacir (2006) *To Educate for Another Possible World*. São Paulo: Publisher Brasil.

Haan, Gerhard de (2007a) Education for sustainable development: a new field of learning and action. *Unesco Today*, Journal of the German Commission for UNESCO, Bonn, 2007, pp. 6–10.

Haan, Gerhard de (2007b) *ESD Guide, Secondary Level: Justifications, Competences, Learning, Opportunities*. Berlin: Frie Universität.

Illeris, Knud (2004) *Adult Education and Adult Learning*. Malabar, FL: Krieger Publishing.

Kane, Liam (2001) *Popular Education and Social Change in Latin America*. London: LAB.

La Belle, Thomas J. (1986) *Informal Education in Latin America and the Caribbean: Stability, Reform or Revolution?* New York: Praeger.

Leicht, Alexander (2005) Learning Sustainability – the UN Decade of Education for Sustainable Development (2005–2014) in Germany: an International Education Initiative. *Unesco Today*, Journal of the German Commission for UNESCO, Bonn, 2005, pp. 26–31.

Lima, Licínio (2006) Europe is looking for a new higher level of education. In: *The DNA of Education: Legislators play the lead role in the most profound and current reflections on public policies*. São Paulo: Instituto DNA Brasil, pp. 63–77.

Lima, Licínio C. (2007) *Lifelong Learning: Between Miró's left and right hands*. São Paulo: Cortez.

Mészáros, István (2004) *The Power of Ideology*. São Paulo: UNESP.

Minvielle, Yvon (1991) *The year of education: outcome 89-90*. Paris: Païdeia.

Monereo, Carlos and David Duran Gisbert (2005) *Plots: Cooperative Learning Procedures*. Porto Alegre: Armed.

OECD (2001) *Investing in Competencies for Everyone*. Paris: OECD.

O'Sullivan, Edmund (2004) *Transformative Learning: An educational vision for the 21st Century*. São Paulo: Cortez/Paulo Freire Institute.

Paulo Freire Institute (2006–2008) *Sectorial Plan of Social and Professional Qualification in Solidarity Economy*. São Paulo: Paulo Freire Institute.

Perrenoud, Philippe (2002) *Constructing Competencies from School*, Porto Alegre: Artmed.

Piaget, Jean (1974) *Learning and Knowledge*. São Paulo: Freitas Bastos.

Ramos, Marise Nogueira (2001) *Competence Pedagogy: autonomy or adaptation?* São Paulo: Cortez.

Rivero, José H. (1993) *Adult Education in Latin America: Challenges of equality and modernisation*. Lima: Tarea.

Ropé, Françoise and Luicie Tanguy (1997) *Knowledge and Competence: The use of such notions in school and the company*. Campinas: Papirus.

Silva, Monica Ribeiro (2008) *The Curriculum and Competencies: Management training*. São Paulo: Cortez.

Torres, Carlos Alberto (1990) *The Politics of Informal Education in Latin America*. New York: Praeger.

Torres, Rosa Maria (ed.) (1987) *Popular Education: An encounter with Paulo Freire*. São Paulo: Loyola.

Wals, Arjen E. J. (ed.) (2007) *Social Learning: Towards a sustainable world*. Wageningen: Wageningen Academic.

Chapter 3

Adler, P. S. (2004) Skill trends under capitalism and the socialisation of production. In C. Warhurst, I. Grugulis and E. Keep (eds), *The Skills That Matter*. Houndmills: Palgrave Macmillan.

Alvarez, K., Salas, E. and Garofano, C. M. (2004) An integrated model of training evaluation and effectiveness. *Human Resource Development Review*, 5(4): 385–416.

Becker, G. S. (1975) *Human Capital: A theoretical and empirical analysis*. New York: Columbia University Press.

Bell, E., Taylor, S. and Thorpe, R. (2002) Organizational differentiation through badging: Investors in people and the value of sign. *Journal of Management Studies*, 39: 1071–1086.

Billett, S. (2001) Learning through work: Workplace affordances and individual engagement. *Journal of Workplace Learning*, 13(5): 209–214.

Brown, P., Green, A. and Lauder, H. (2001) *High Skills: Globalization, competitiveness and skill formation*. Oxford: Oxford University Press.

Burke, L. A. and Hutchins, H. M. (2007) Training transfer: An integrative literature review. *Human Resource Development Review*, 6(3): 263–296.

Collins, R. (1979) *The Credential Society: A historical sociology of education and stratification*. New York: Academic Press.

Colquitt, J. A. and LePine, J. A. (2000) Towards an integrative theory of training motivation: A meta-analytic path analysis of 20 years of research. *Journal of Applied Psychology*, 85(5): 678–707.

Edwards, R. (1979) *Contested Terrain*. London: Heineman.

Ellström, P-E. (1997) The many meanings of occupational competence and qualification. *Journal of European Industrial Training*, 21(6/7): 266–274.

Ellström, P-E. (2006) Two logics of learning. In E. Antonacopoulou, P. Jarvis, V. Andersen, B. Elkjær and S. Høyrup (eds), *Learning, Working and Living: Mapping the terrain of working life learning*. London: Palgrave Macmillan.

Ellström, P-E. and Nilsson, B. (1997) *Kompetensutveckling i små- och medelstora företag: En studie av förutsättningar, strategier och effekter* [Competence development in SMEs: A study of conditions, strategies, and effects]. Linköping: CMTO och Institutionen för pedagogik och psykologi, Universitetet i Linköping, LiU-PEK-R-199.

Gooderham, P. N., Nordhaug, O. and Ringdal, K. (1999) Institutional and rational determinants of organizational practices: Human resource management in European firms. *Administrative Science Quarterly*, 44: 507–531.

Hendry, C., Jones, A., Arthur, M. and Pettigrew, A. M. (1991) *Human Resource Development in the Small to Medium Size Enterprise: Final report to the employment department*. Sheffield: Employment Department.

Hendry, C., Pettigrew, A. and Sparrow, P. (1988) *Linking Strategic Change, Competitive Performance and Human Resource Management: Results of a UK empirical study*. University of Warwick, Coventry, England: Centre for Corporate Strategy and Change.

Holton, E. F. (1996) The flawed four-level evaluation model. *Human Resource Development Quarterly*, 7(1): 5–21.

Høyrup, S. and Ellström, P-E. (2007) *Arbejdspladslæring: forudsætninger, strategi/metoder, resultater* [Workplace learning: Strategy/methods, results]. Copenhagen: Nordisk Ministerråd, TemaNord.

Illeris, K. (2004) *Adult Education and Adult Learning*. Malabar, FL: Krieger.

Illeris, K. (2005) Lifelong learning and the low-skilled. *International Journal of Lifelong Education*, 25(1): 15–28.

Illeris, K. (2007) *How We Learn: Learning and non-learning in school and beyond*. London: Routledge.

Karasek, R. and Theorell, T. (1990) *Healthy Work: Stress, productivity and the reconstruction of working life*. New York: Basic Books.

Kirkpatrick. D. L. (1959) Techniques for evaluating training programmes. *Training and Development Journal*, 13: 3–9.

Kirkpatrick, D.L. (1996) Invited reaction: Reaction to Holton article. *Human Resource Development Quarterly*, 7(1): 23–26.

Kock, H., Gill, A. and Ellström, P-E. (2007) *Practices of competence development in the workplace: Relations between learning environments, strategies and learning outcomes in SMEs*. Paper presented at The Second Nordic Conference on Adult Learning, Linköping.

Kock, H., Gill, A. and Ellström, P-E. (2008) Why do small firms participate in a programme for competence development? *Journal of Workplace Learning*, 20(3): 181–194.

Kraiger, K. (2002) Decision-based evaluation. In K. Kraiger (ed.), *Creating, Implementing, and Managing Effective Training and Development*. San Fransisco: Jossey-Bass pp. 331–375.

Larsson, S., Alexandersson, C., Helmstad, G. and Thång, P-O. (1986) *Arbetsupplevelse och utbildningssyn hos icke facklärda*. [Work experience and educational points of view of the low-skilled]. Göteborg, Sweden: Göteborg Studies in Educational Sciences 57.

Lorenz, E. and Lundvall. B-Å. (eds) (2006) *How Europe's Economies Learn: Coordinating competing models*. Oxford: Oxford University Press.

Meyer, J. H. (1977) The effects of education as an institution. *American Journal of Sociology*, 83(1): 55–77.

Mintzberg, H. (1983) *Power in and around Organizations*. Englewood Cliffs, NJ: Prentice-Hall, Inc.

Mulder, M. (1998) *What makes training programs effective? Evaluation of effectiveness of projects in the field of corporate education*. Paper presented at the AERA Conference, San Diego, April, 1998.

Nordhaug, O. (1991) *The Shadow Educational System: Adult resource development*. Oslo: Norwegian University Press.

Offe, C. (1976) *Industry and Inequality: The achievement principle in work and social status*. London: Edward Arnold Publication.

Pfeffer, J. (1981) *Power in Organizations*. Marchfield, MA: Pitman.

Pettigrew, A. M., Hendry, C. and Sparrow, P. R. (1988) *Training in Britain: A study of funding, activity and attitudes: Employers' perspectives on human resources*. London: Training Agency, HMSO.

Powell, W. W. and DiMaggio, P. J. (eds.) (1991) *The New Institutionalism in Organizational Analysis*. Chicago: The University of Chicago Press.

Ram, M. (2000) Investors in people in small firms: Case study evidence from the business services sector. *Personnel Review*, 29(1): 69–91.

Rubenson, K. (2006) The Nordic model of lifelong learning. *Compare: A Journal of Comparative Education*, 36(3): 327–341.

Rubenson, K. and Willms, D. (1993) *Human Resources Development in British Columbia*. Vancouver: Centre for Policy Studies in Education, UBC.

Salas, E. and Cannon-Bowers, J. A. (2001) The science of training: A decade of progress. *Annual Review of Psychology*, 52: 471–499.

Scott, W. R. (1995) *Institutions and Organizations*. Thousand Oaks: Sage.

Scott, W. R. and Meyer. J. W. (1991) The rise of training programs in firms and agencies: An institutional perspective. *Research in Organizational Behavior*, 13: 297–326.

Skule, S. and Reichborn, A. N. (2002) *Learning-conducive Work: A survey of learning conditions in Norwegian workplaces. CEDEFOP Panorama series; 30*. Luxembourg: Office for Official Publications of the European Communities.

Spicer, D. P. and Sadler-Smith, E. (2003) *Organizational Learning in Smaller Firms* (Working paper No. 0329). University of Bradford, England: School of Management.

Tannenbaum, S. I. and Yukl, G. (1992) Training and development in work organizations. *Annual Review of Psychology*, 43: 399–441.

Tichy, N. M. (1983) Managing organizational transformations. *Human Resource Management*, 22(1/2): 45–62.

Tuomisto, J. (1986) The ideological and sociohistorical bases of industrial training. *Adult Education in Finland*, 23: 3–24.

Warhurst, C. and Thompson. P. (2006) Mapping knowledge in work: proxies or practices? *Work, Employment and Society*, 20(4): 787–800.

Chapter 4

Apple, M. W. (1993) *Official Knowledge: Democratic education in a conservative age*. New York and London: Routledge.

Allee, V. (1997) *The Knowledge Evolution: Building organizational intelligence*. Boston: Butterworth-Heinemann.

Brewer, A. (1984) *A Guide to Marx's Capital*. Cambridge: Cambridge University Press.

Brien, K. M. (2006) Humanistic Marxism and the transformation of reason. *Dialogue and Universalism* (5–6): 39–58.

Burton-Jones, A. (1999) *Knowledge Capitalism: Business, work, and learning in the new economy*. Oxford: Oxford University Press.

Drucker, P. (1998) From capitalism to knowledge society. In D. Neef (ed.), *The Knowledge Economy*. Boston: Butterworth-Heinemann.

Field, J. (2002) *Lifelong Learning and the New Educational Order*. Sterling: Trentham Books.

Foucault, M. (1977) *Discipline and Punishment: The birth of prison*. New York: Random House.

Giroux, H. (1993) *Border Crossings: Cultural workers and the politics of education*. New York and London: Routledge.

Goodson, I. and Dowbiggin, I. (1990) Docile bodies: Commonalities in the history of psychiatry and schooling. In S. J. Ball (ed.), *Foucault and Education: Discipline and knowledge*. London and New York: Routledge pp. 105–129.

Hall, B. (1979) Knowledge as a commodity and participatory research. *Prospects*, 9(4): 393–408.

Han, S. (2008) The lifelong learning ecosystem in Korea: Evolution of learning capitalism? *International Journal of Lifelong Education*, 27(5): 517–524.

Jarvis, P. (2007) *Globalization, Lifelong Learning and the Learning Society: Sociological perspectives*. New York: Routledge.

Liston D.P. (1988) *Capitalist Schools: Explanation and ethics in radical studies of schooling*. New York and London: Routledge.

Marcuse, H. (1972) The foundation of historical materialism. In *Studies in Critical Philosophy*. New York: Beacon Press.

McClelland, D. C. (1973) Testing for competency rather than for intelligence, *American Psychologist*, 28(1): 1–14.

OECD (2002) *Understanding the Brain: Towards a new learning science*. Paris: OECD.

OECD (2004) International schooling for tomorrow forum: Background OECD papers, The schooling senarios. *International Schooling For Tomorrow Forum*, June 6–8, 2004, Toronto, Canada.

Olssen, M. (2006) Understanding the mechanisms of neoliberal control: lifelong learning, flexibility and knowledge capitalism. *International Journal of Lifelong Education*, 25(3): 213–230.

Raven, J. (2001) The conceptualization of competence. In J. Raven (ed.) *Competence in the Learning Society*. New York: Peter Lang.

Rychen, D. S. and Salganik, L. H. (eds) (2003) *Key Competencies: For a successful life and a wellfunctioning society*. Cambridge, MA: Hogrefe & Huber.

Schuetze, H. G. (2006) International concepts and agendas of lifelong learning. *Compare*, 36(3): 289–306.

Senge, P., Kleiner, A., Roberts, C., Ross, R. and Smith, B. (1994) *The Fifth Discipline Fieldbook: Strategies and tools for building a learning organization*. New York: Doubleday.

Stevenson, M. A. (1999) Flexible education and the discipline of the market. *Qualitative Studies in Education*, 12(3): 311–323.

Swanson, R. A. (2001) *Foundations of Human Resource Development*. San Francisco: Berrett-Koehler Publishers.

Wills, G. (1998) *The Knowledge Game: The revolution in learning and communication in the workplace*. London: Cassell.

Young, M. F. D. (1998) *The Curriculum of the Future: From the 'New Sociology of Education' to a critical theory of learning*. London: Palmer Press.

Chapter 5

Beckett, D. (2001) Hot Action at Work: A Different Understanding of 'Understanding', In T. Fenwick (ed.) *Sociocultural Perspectives on Learning Through Work*, New Directions for Adult and Continuing Education Series. San Francisco: Jossey-Bass.

Beckett, D. (2004) Embodied competence and generic skill: The emergence of inferential understanding. *Educational Philosophy and Theory*, 36(5): 497–508.

Beckett, D. and Hager, P. (2000) Making judgements as the basis for workplace learning: Towards an epistemology of practice. *International Journal of Lifelong Education*, 19(4): 300–311.

Beckett, D. and Hager, P. (2002) *Life, Work and Learning: Practice in postmodernity*, Routledge International Studies in the Philosophy of Education. London: Routledge.

Brandom, R. (2000) *Articulating Reasons: An introduction to inferentialism*. Cambridge Ma: Harvard University Press.

DeVries, W. and Triplett, T. (2000) *Knowledge, Mind, and the Given: Reading Wilfred Sellars's 'Empiricism and the Philosophy of Mind'*. Indianapolis, IN: Hackett Publishing Company Inc.

Flyvbjerg, B. (2001) *Making Social Science Matter: Why social inquiry fails and how it can succeed again*. Cambridge: CUP.

Gigerenzer, G. (2007) *Gut Feelings: The intelligence of the unconscious*. London: Penguin Books.

Gonczi, A., Hager, P. and Oliver, L. (1990) *Establishing Competency Standards in the Professions: NOOSR Research Paper No. 1*. Canberra: Australian Government Publishing Service.

Groopman, J. (2007) *How Doctors Think*. New York: Houghton Mifflin Company.

Hager, P. and Beckett, D. (1995) Philosophical underpinnings of the integrated conception of competence. *Educational Philosophy and Theory*, 27(1): 1–24.

Hager, P., Holland, S. and Beckett, D. (2002) *Enhancing the Learning and Employability of Graduates: The role of generic skills*, Business/Higher Education Round Table Position Paper No. 9, BHERT, Melbourne.

Hyland, T. (1997) Reconsidering competence. *Journal of Philosophy of Education*, 31(3): 491–501.

Montgomery, Kathryn (2006) *How Doctors Think: Clinical judgment and the practice of medicine*. New York: OUP.

Mulcahy, Dianne (2000) Body matters in vocational education: The case of the competently-trained. *International Journal of Lifelong Education*, 19(6): 506–524.

Chapter 6

Alheit, Peter (1994) The biographical question as a challenge to adult education. *International Review of Education*, 40 (3/4): 305–319.

Argyris, Chris (1992) *On Organizational Learning*. Cambridge, MA: Blackwell.

Argyris, Chris and Schön, Donald (1996) *Organizational Learning II: Theory, method, practice*. Reading, MA: Addison-Wesley.

Beckett, David and Hager, Paul (2002) *Life, Work and Learning: Practice in postmodernity*. London: Routledge.

Braverman, Harry (1974) *Labor and Monopoly Capital*. New York: Monthly Review Press.

Ellström, Per-Erik (2001) Integrating learning and work: conceptual issues and critical conditions. *Human Resource Development Quarterly*, 12(4): 421–436.

Engeström, Yrjö (1987) *Learning by Expanding: An activity theoretical approach to development research*. Helsinki: Orienta Kunsultit.

Flavell, John H. (1963) *The Developmental Psychology of Jean Piaget*. New York: Van Nostrand.

Freud, Anna (1942 [1936]) *The Ego and the Mechanisms of Defence*. London: Hogarth Press.

Illeris, Knud (1991) Project Education in Denmark. *International Journal of Project Management* 1: 45–48.

Illeris, Knud (1998) Adult learning and responsibility. In Knud Illeris (ed.) *Adult Education in a Transforming Society*. Copenhagen: Roskilde University Press.

Illeris, Knud (1999) Project work in university studies: Background and current issues. In Henning Salling Olesen and Jens Højgaard Jensen (eds) *Project Studies*. Copenhagen: Roskilde University Press.

Illeris, Knud (2004) *Adult Education and Adult Learning*. Copenhagen: Roskilde University Press/Malabar, FL: Krieger Publishing.

Illeris, Knud (2007) *How We Learn: Learning and non-learning in school and beyond*. London: Routledge.

Illeris, Knud (2009) Transfer of Learning in the Learning Society. *International Journal of Lifelong Education* (in press).

Illeris, Knud *et al.* (2004) *Learning in Working Life*. Copenhagen: Roskilde University Press.

Jørgensen, Per Schultz (1999) Hvad er kompetence? *Uddannelse*, 9: 4–13. [What is competence?].

Lave, Jean and Wenger, Etienne (1991) *Situated Learning: Legitimate, peripheral participation*. New York: Cambridge University Press.

Leithäuser, Thomas (1976) *Formen des Alltagsbewusstseins*. Frankfurt a.M.: Campus [The forms of everyday consciousness].

Mager, Robert F. (1961) On the sequencing of instructional content. *Psychological Reports*, 9: 405–413.

Mezirow, Jack (1991) *Transformative Dimensions of Adult Learning*. San Francisco, CA: Jossey-Bass.

Olesen, Henning Salling and Jensen, Jens Højgaard (eds) (1999) *Project Studies*. Copenhagen: Roskilde University Press.

Piaget, Jean (1952 [1936]) *The Origin of Intelligence in Children*. New York: International Universities Press.

Rogers, Carl R. (1951) *Client-Centered Therapy*. Boston, MA: Houghton-Mifflin.

Rogers, Carl R. (1969) *Freedom to Learn*. Columbus, OH: Charles E. Merrill.

Vygotsky, Lev S. (1978) *Mind in Society: The development of higher psychological processes*. Cambridge, MA: Harvard University press.

Weil, Susan Warner, Jansen, Theo and Wildemeersch, Danny (2004) *Unemployed Youth and Social Exclusion in Europe: Learning for inclusion?* Aldershot: Ashgate.

Wenger, Etienne (1998) *Communities of Practice: Learning, meaning and identity*. Cambridge, MA: Cambridge University Press.

Chapter 7

Bell, D. (1973) *The Coming of Post-Industrial Society*. New York: Basic Books.

Benner, P. (1984) *From Novice to Expert*. Menlo Park, CA: Addison Wesley.

Collins English Dictionary (1979).

Daloz, L., Keen, C., Keen, J. and Parks, S. (1996) *Common Fire*. Boston, MA: Beacon.

Delors, J. (1996) *Learning: The treasure within*. Paris: UNESCO.

Dreyfus, S. and Dreyfus, H.L. (1980) A five stage model of the mental activities involved in directed skill acquisition. Unpublished Report: University of California at Berkeley.

Feigenbaum, E.A. and McCorduck, P. (1984) *The Fifth Generation*. New York: Signet.

Jarvis, P. (1977) Protestant ministers: job satisfaction and role strain in the bureaucratic organisation of the Church. Birmingham: University of Aston. Unpublished PhD thesis.

Jarvis, P. (1987) *Adult Learning in the Social Context*. London: Croom Helm.

Jarvis, P. (1999) *The Practioner-Researcher*. San Francisco: Jossey-Bass.

Jarvis, P. (2006) *Towards a Comprehensive Theory of Human Learning*. London: Routledge.

Jarvis, P. (2008) *Learning to be a Person in Society*. London: Routledge.

Livingstone, D. (2002) Lifelong learning in the knowledge society: a North American perspective. Reprinted in R. Edwards, N. Miller, N. Small and A. Tait (eds) *Making Knowledge Work: Supporting lifelong learning (Vol 3)*. London: RoutledgeFalmer.

Lyotard, J-F. (1984) *The Post-Modern Condition: A report on knowledge*. Manchester: Manchester University Press.

Nyiri, J. C. (1988) Tradition and Practical Knowledge. In J. C. Nyiri and B. Smith (eds) *Practical Knowledge: Outlines of a theory of traditions and skills*. London: Croom Helm.

Reich, R. (1991) *The Work of Nations*. London: Simon Schuster.

Schutz, A. and Luckmann, T. (1974) *The Structure of the Life World*. London: Heinemann.

Stikkers, K. (1980) (ed.) Scheler, M. ([1926]1980) *Problems of a Sociology of Knowledge*. London: Routledge and Kegan Paul.

Stehr, N. (1994) *Knowledge Societies*. London: Sage.

Swanson, R. A. (2001) *Foundations of Human Resource Development*. San Francisco, CA: Barrett-Koehler Publishers.

Tuomi, I. (1999) *Corporate Knowledge: Theory and practice of intelligent organizations*. Helsinki: Metaxis.

Vaillant, G. E. (1993) *The Wisdom of the Ego*. Cambridge, MA: Harvard University Press.

Chapter 8

Abott, A. (1988) *The System of Professions: An essay on the division of expert labour*. Chicago: The University of Chicago Press.

Andersen, A. S., Gleerup, J., Hjort, K. E., Sommer, F. M. (2003) Office work and competence development in work and lifelong learning in different contexts: Proceedings book IV: Theme 6: Learning processes and work processes. 3rd International Conference of Researching Work and Learning, Tampere, Finland, 25-27 juli 2003 (pp. 1–11). University of Tampere: Department of Education.

Argyris, C. and Schön, D. A. (1996) *Organizational Learning*. Reading, MA: Addison-Wesley.

Bregn, K. (ed.) (1998) *Omstilling i den offentlige sektor i et finansielt perspektiv*. Copenhagen: DJØF. [Transforming the Public Sector in a financial perspective].

Dale, E. L. (1989) *Pædagogisk Professionalisme*. Oslo: Norsk Gyldendal [Educational professionalism].

Dich, J. (1973): *Den herskende klasse. En kritisk analyse af social udbytning og midlerne imod den*. København: Borgen [The ruling class: A critical analysis of social exploitation and the means against it].

Drevsholt, E., Friis, K., Hjort, K., Olesen, A., and Petersen-Testrup, S. (2001) *Helhedsforståelse og delforandring*. Roskilde University: EVU [Holistic understandings and transformation of the small elements].

Dreyfus, H. L. and Dreyfus, S. E. (1986) *Mind over Machine: The power of human intuition and expertise in the era of the computer*. Oxford: Blackwell.

European Commission (1995) *Teaching and Learning. Towards the learning society.* Luxembourg: European Commission.

European Commission (2000) *Memorandum on Lifelong Learning.* Luxembourg: European Commission.

Evetts, J. (2004) The sociological analysis of professionalism: occupational change in the modern world. *International Sociology.* 18(2): 395–415

Finansministeriet (2000) *Vejledning om kompetenceudvikling i statens institutioner.* Copenhagen: Finansministeriet [The Danish Ministry of Finance: Guidance to Competence Development in the Institutions of the State].

Freidson, E. (2001) *Professionalism, the Third Logic.* Oxford: Polity Press.

Foucault, M. (1997) Truth and Power. In Gordon, C. (ed.) *Power/Knowledge.* New York: Prentice Hall.

Goodson, I. F. and Hargreaves, A. (1996) Teachers' professional lives: aspirations and actuality. In I. F. Goodson and A. Hargreaves (eds) *Teachers' Professional Lives.* London: Palmer.

Greenwood, I. and Stuart, M. (2002) *Employability or Lifelong Flexibility?* Roskilde University: ESREA.

Hargreaves, D. H. (2000) The production, mediation and use of professional knowledge among teachers and doctors. In OECD/CERI: *Knowledge Management in the Learning society.* Paris: OECD.

Hjort, K. (2001) *Moderniseringen af den offentlige sektor.* Copenhagen: Roskilde University Press [Modernisation of the Public Sector].

Hjort, K. (ed.) (2004) *De professionelle.* Copenhagen: Roskilde University Press. [The Professionals].

Hjort, K. (2005) *Professionaliseringen i den offentlige sektor.* Copenhagen: Roskilde University Press [Professionalising in the Public Sector].

Hjort, K. (2008) *Demokratiseringen af den offentlige sektor.* Copenhagen: Roskilde University Press [Democratisation in the Public sector].

Illeris, K. (2004) *Adult Education and Adult Learning.* Malabar, FL: Krieger Publishing.

Illeris, K. (2007) *How We Learn: Learning and non-learning in school and beyond.* Abingdon: Routledge.

Jarvis, P. (1999) *The Practitioner-Researcher: Developing theory from practice.* San Francisco: Jossey-Bass.

Klausen, K. K. and Ståhlberg, K. (eds) (1998) *New Public Management i Norden.* Odense: Odense Universitets Forlag [New Public Management in the Nordic Countries].

Kompetencerådet (1999) *Kompetencerådets Rapport 1998.* Copenhagen: Ugebrevet Mandag Morgen [Report from the Danish Competence Council 1998].

Krag, Ejler (1997) *Debatoplæg – kompetenceudvikling i sundhedsvæsenet.* Copenhagen: Sundhedsstyrelsen [Debate: Competence Development in the Health System].

Laclau, E. and Mouffe, C. (1985) *Hegemony and Socialist Strategy.* London: Verso.

Lave, J. and Wenger, E. (1991) *Situated Learning: Legitimate peripheral participation.* Cambridge, MA: Cambridge University.

Ministeriet for Finans, Industri m.fl. (2003) *Det nationale kompetenceregnskab.* Copenhagen [The Danish Ministry of Finance: National competence account].

Nielsen, S. B. (2003) Mænd søges. In K. Hjort and S. B. Nielsen (eds) *Mænd og omsorg.* Copenhagen: Reitzel. [Men and Care].

Parsons, T. 1968, 'Professions,' in *International Encyclopedia of the Social Sciences*, D. L. Sills, ed., pp. 536-546. New York: Imprenta.

Pedersen, D. (1998) Mod forhandlet ledelse – resultatet af en dansk moderniseringsstrategi. In: *Arbejdspladser og medarbejdere i amter og kommuner*. Copenhagen: Personalepolitisk Forum [Workplaces and employees in regions and municipalities].

Petersen-Testrup, S. (2004) *Kompetence Udvikling – Et casestudium fra et offentligt hospital i København*. Copenhagen: Danish University of Education [Competence development – a case study from a public hospital in Copenhagen].

Polanyi, M. (1966) *The Tacit Dimension*. New York: Doubleday.

Rolf, B. (1991) *Profession, Tradition og Tavs Viden*. Lund: Nye Doxa [Profession, Tradition and Tacit Knowledge].

Rose, N. (1999) *Governing the Soul: The shaping of the private self*. London: Free Association Book.

Wackerhausen S. and Wackerhausen, B. (1993) Tavs viden og læringsteori. Dansk Pædagogisk Tidsskrift, 4 [Tacit Knowledge and Learning Theory].

Weber, K. (ed.) (2002) *Lifelong Learning*. Copenhagen: Roskilde University Press.

Weber, M. (1905) *The Protestant Ethic and the Spirit of Capitalism*. London and Boston: Unwin Hyman.

Chapter 9

Anonymous (2004) $37M boost to sector councils. *Canadian HR Reporter*, 17(7): 3.

Atkins, M. J. (1999) Oven-ready and self-basting: Taking stock of employability skills. *Teaching in Higher Education*, 4(2), 267–278.

Baldry, C., Bain, P. and Taylor, P. (1998) Bright satanic offices: Intensification, control and team taylorism. In P. Thompson and C. Warhurst (eds) *Workplaces of the Future*. London: Macmillan pp. 163–183.

Boreham, N. (2004) A theory of collective competence: Challenging the neo-liberal individualisation of performance at work. *British Journal of Educational Studies*, 52(1): 5–17.

Braverman, H. (1974) *Labor and Monopoly Capital: The degradation of work in the 20th century*. New York: Monthly Review Press.

Brown, P., Green, A. and Lauder, H. (2001) *High Skills: Globalisation, competitiveness and skill formation*. Oxford: Oxford University Press.

Burawoy, M. (1979) *Manufacturing Consent: Changes in the labour process under monopoly capitalism*. Chicago: University of Chicago Press.

Canadian Labour Congress (2005, August) *Essential Skills and the Labour Movement*. Ottawa: Canadian Labour Congress.

Canadian Labour Congress (2006) To the house of commons standing committee on human resources, social development and the status of persons with disabilities. Retrieved November, 2007, from http://canadianlabour.ca/updir/HUMA-Brief-FINAL-E.pdf

Coffield, F. (2000) Introduction: A critical analysis of the concept of a learning society. In F. Coffield (ed.) *Different Visions of a Learning Society*. Bristol: Policy Press, pp. 1–38.

Cooney, R. and Stuart, M. (eds) (2004) *Trade Unions and Training: Issues and international perspectives*. Caulfield: National Key Centre in Industrial Relations, Monash University, pp. 1–18.

Courtney, S. (1992) *Why Adults Learn: Towards a theory of participation in adult education*. New York: Routledge.

Fenwick, T., Guo, S., Sawchuk, P., Valentin, C. and Wheelahan, L. (2005, December) *Essential Skills, Globalization and Neo-liberal Policy: Challenging skills-based agendas for workplace learning*. Paper presented at the Fourth International Conference on Researching Work and Learning. Sydney.

Forrester, K. (2005) Learning for revival: British trade unions and workplace learning. *Continuing Education*, 27(3): 257–270.

Frenkel, S., Korczynski, M., Shire, K. and Tam, M. (1999) *On the Front Live: Organization of work in the information economy*. Ithaca, NY: Cornell University Press.

Green, A. (2002) The many faces of lifelong learning: Recent education policy trends in Europe. *Journal of Education Policy*, 17(6): 611–626.

Hayes, B. (2005) Canadian organizations move to develop workplace literacy and numerical skills. *Canadian HR Reporter*, 18(13): 7–10.

Heyes, J. and Stuart M. (1994) Placing symbols before reality: re-evaluating the low skills equilibrium, *Personnel Review*, 23(5): 35–49.

HRSDC (2005a) *Essential Skills*. Ottawa, ON: Human Resources and Skills Development of Canada. Retrieved May, 2007, from http://www.hrsdc.gc.ca/en/hip/hrp/essential_skills/essential_skills_index.shtml

HRSDC (2005b) *Essential skills: Tools and applications*. Retrieved May, 2007, from http://www15.hrdc-drhc.gc.ca/English/general/Tools_Apps_e.asp

Hurd, R. (2001) Contesting the dinosaur image: The US labour movement's search for a future. *Transfer*, 7(3): 451–465.

Jackson, N. (1991) *Skills Formation and Gender Relations: The politics of who knows what*. Geelong: Deakin University Press.

Kelly, J. (1999) Social partnership in Britain: Good for profits, bad for jobs and unions. *Communist Review*, 30: 3–10.

Lafer, G. (2004) What is 'skill'? Training for discipline in the low-wage labour market. In C. Warhurst, I. Grugulis and E. Keep (eds) *The Skills that Matter*. London: Palgrave Macmillan, pp. 109–127.

Littler, C. (1982) *The Development of the Labour Process in Capitalist Societies: A comparative analysis of work organization in Britain, the USA and Japan*. London: Heinemann.

Livingstone, D. W. (2004) *Education–Jobs Gap* (2nd edn) Toronto: Broadview.

Martin, A. and Ross, G. (eds) (1999) *The Brave New World of European Labour*. New York: Berghahn.

Martinez Lucio, M., Skule, S., Kruse, W. and Trappmann, V. (2007) Regulating skill formation in Europe: German, Norwegian and Spanish policies on transferable skills. *European Journal of Industrial Relations*, 13(3): 323–340.

Mojab, S. (1999) Deskilling immigrant women. *Canadian Woman Studies*, 19(3): 123–128.

Nonaka, I. and Takeuchi, H. (1995) *The Knowledge-Creating Company: How Japanese companies create the dynamics of innovation*. New York: Oxford University Press.

OECD (2002) *Review of National Policies for Education: Lifelong learning in Norway*. Paris: OECD publications.

OECD (2004) *Developing Highly Skilled Workers: Review of Norway*. Paris: OECD publications.

Olsen, M., Codd, J. and O'Neill, A. M. (2004) *Education Policy: Globalisation, citizenship and democracy*. London, Thousand Oaks and New Delhi: Sage publications.

Payne, J. (2000) The unbearable lightness of skill: The changing meaning of skill in UK policy discourses and some implications for education and training. *Journal of Educational Policy*, 15(3): 353–369.

Payne, J. (2006) The Norwegian competence reform and the limits of lifelong learning. *International Journal of Lifelong Education*, 25(5): 477–505.

Peetz, D. (1998) *Unions in a Contrary World: The future of the Australian trade union movement*. Cambridge: Cambridge University Press.

Pencavel, J. (2005) Unionism viewed internationally. *Journal of Labor Research*, 26(1): 65–97.

Rainbird, H. (ed.) (2000) *Training in the Workplace*. London: Macmillan.

Rikowski, G. (2001) Education for industry: A complex technicism. *Journal of Education and Work*, 14(1): 29–49.

Sawchuk, P. H. (2003a) *Adult Learning and Technology in Working-Class Life*. New York: Cambridge University Press.

Sawchuk, P. H. (2003b) The 'unionization effect' amongst adult computer learners. British *Journal of Sociology of Education*, 24(5): 639–648.

Sawchuk, P. H. (2006) 'Use-value' and the re-thinking of skills, learning and the labour process. *Journal of Industrial Relations* 48(5): 593–617.

Sawchuk, P. H. (2007) *Understanding the work/learning implications of 'community unionism' in Canada: The case of hotel workers organizing in Toronto*. Paper presented at the Fifth International Conference on Researching Work and Learning, Capetown, South Africa.

Shah, C. and Burke, G. (2005) Skills shortages: Concepts, measurement and policy responses. *Australian Bulletin of Labour*, 31(1): 44–71.

Skule, S. and Reichborn, A. (2002) *Learning-Conducive Work: A survey of learning conditions in Norwegian workplaces*. Luxembourg: CEDEFOP (Luxembourg Office for Official Publications of the European Communities).

Skule, S., Stuart, M. and Nyen, T. (2002) International briefing: Training and development in Norway. *International Journal of Training and Development*, 6(4): 263–276.

Spenner, K. (1979) Temporal changes in work content. *American Sociological Review*, 44(6): 968–975.

Teige, B. (2004) Trade union involvement in lifelong learning in Norway. In R. Cooney and M. Stuart (eds), *Trade Unions and Training: Issues and international perspectives*. Caulfield: National Key Centre in Industrial Relations, Monash University, pp. 162–174.

Thompson, P. (2003) Disconnected capitalism: Or why employers can't keep their side of the bargain. *Work, Employment and Society*, 17(2): 359–378.

Vince, R. (2005) Ideas for critical practitioners. In C. Elliot and S. Turnbull (eds), *Critical Thinking in Human Resource Development*. New York: Routledge.

Waddington, J. (2000) Towards a reform agenda? European trade unions in transition. *Industrial Relations Journal*, 31(4): 317–330.

Waddington, J. (2001) Articulating trade union organisation for the new Europe? *Industrial Relations Journal*, 32(5): 449–463.

Waddington, J. and Kerr, A. (1999) Trying to stem the flow: Union membership turnover in the public sector. *Industrial Relations Journal*, 30: 184–196.

Warhurst, C., Grugulis, I. and Keep, E. (2004) *The Skills that Matter*. London: Palgrave Macmillan.

Wood, S. (1982) *The Degradation of Work? Skill, deskilling and the labour process*. London: Hutchinson.

Zimbalist, A. (1979) *Case Studies on the Labor Process*. London: Monthly Review Press.

Chaper 10

Accelerating Change in Built Environment Education (2005) Salford: Annual Report, Centre of Education in the Built Environment.

Barr, H. (1998) Competent to collaborate: Towards a competency-based model for interprofessional education. *Journal of Interprofessional Care*, 12(2): 181–187.

Boyatzis, R. E. (1982) *The Competent Manager*. New York: Wiley.

Clark, A. and Craven, A. (2007) *Catalyst: Taking further education forward*. Retrieved December 2007, from http://www.lifelonglearninguk.org/documents/docs/lluk

Department for Education and Skills (2005) 14–19 *Education and Skills* (White paper). Norwich: Her Majesty's Stationary Office (HMSO).

Department for Education and Skills (2006) *Further Education: Raising skills, improving life chances*. Nottingham: DfES.

Department for Innovation, Universities and Skills (2007) *World Class Skills: Implementing the Leitch review of skills in England*. Norwich: DIUS.

Foundation Degree Forward (2007a) *Foundation Degrees*. Retrieved December 2007, from www.fdf.ac.uk

Foundation Degree Forward (2007b) *Employer Based Training Accreditation*. Retrieved December 2007, from http://www.fdf.ac.uk/home/information_for_employers

Greater Manchester Strategic Alliance (GMSA) (2007a) *Module Catalogue*. Retrieved December 2007, from http://www.gmsa.ac.uk/projects/view/?id=679

Greater Manchester Strategic Alliance (2007b) *Step up to HE*. Retrieved January 2008, from http://www.gmsa.ac.uk/casestudies/view/?id=756

Greater Manchester Strategic Alliance (2007c) *Continuing Professional Development (CPD) awards in leadership management*. Retrieved January 2008, from http://www.gmsa.ac.uk/casestudies/view/?id=731

Health Professions Council (2008) *Fitness to Practice*. Retrieved January 2008, from http://www.hpc-uk.org/complaints/ftp/

Higher Education Funding Council for England (2006a) *Engaging Employers with Higher Education*. Retrieved December 2007, from http://www.hefce.ac.uk/News/ HEFCE/2006/employer.htm

Higher Education Funding Council for England (2006b) What is the scope of our strategy? In *Engaging Employers with Higher Education*. Retrieved December 2007, from http://www.hefce.ac.uk/learning/employer/ strat/Board_strategy

Higher Education Funding Council for England (2007a) *Higher Level Skills Pathfinders* (Train to gain) Retrieved January 2008, from http://www. hefce.ac.uk/learning/employer/path/

Higher Education Funding Council for England (2007b) *Higher Education – Business and community interaction survey*. Retrieved July 2007, from http://www.hefce.ac.uk/pubs/hefce/2007/07_17/

HM Treasury (2006) *Leitch Review of Skills*. Retrieved October 2007, from http://www.hm-treasury. gov.uk/independent_reviews/leitch_review/review_leitch_index.cfm

Hogarth, T., Winterbotham, M., Hasluck, C., Carter, K., Daniel, W. W., Green, A. E., *et al.* (2007) *Employer and University Engagement in Use and Development of Graduate Level Skills*. Warwick: Institute for Employment Research.

Irwin, P. (2007) Towards a shared understanding of work-based learning. *Journal of Advanced Perioperative Care*, 3(2): 73–79.

Joint Forum for Higher Levels (2006) *Overarching Principles and Operational Criteria for a 'Common Approach to Credit'* (Briefing paper) Retrieved January 2008, from http://www.qca.org.uk/libraryAssets/media/020207joint_forum_for__higher_levels_brief.pdf

King, M. (2007) *Workforce Development: Employer engagement with higher education*. London: The Council for Industry and Higher Education.

Lammy, D. (2008) Exanding and delivering apprenticeships. Retrieved Januray 2008, from http://dius.gov.uk/speeches/lammy_Apprenticeships_030408.html

Lathi, R. K. (1999) Identifying and integrating individual level and organizational level core competencies. *Journal of Business and Psychology*, 14(1): 59–75.

Learning and Skills Council (2005) Advanced Apprenticeship Frameworks. Retrieved January 2008, from http:// www.apprenticeships.org.uk/partners/frameworks/apprenticeships/

Leech, S. (2008) *The Step-In to HE Project*. Manchester: Aimhigher Greater Manchester Coordination Unit.

Liam, Healy and Associates (2003) Defining competencies. In Selection System Design and Validation. Retrieved January 2008, from http://www.psychometrics.co.uk/ selection.htm

Middlesex University (2007) *Centre of excellence in teaching and learning (CETL) in work based learning (CEWBL)* Retrieved January 2008, from http:// www.mdx.ac.uk/wbl/cfe/ index.asp

Mumford, J. (2007) *Employer-HE Partnerships in Work Based Learning*. What works well and what needs to improve (Keynote address) Greater Merseyside and West Lancashire Lifelong Learning Network Regional Conference. Retrieved January 2008, from http:// www.merseyandwestlancslln.ac.uk/shared/documents/JMumfordPresentation.ppt

Organisation for Economic Co-Operation and Development Directorate for Education (2005) Overview. In *The Definition and Selection of Key Competencies*. Retrieved January 2008, from http://www.oecd.org/dataoecd/ 47/61/35070367.pdf

Phillips, K. (2007) *Employer Based Training Accreditation (EBTA)*. Retrieved January 2008, from http://www. cumbriahigherlearning.ac.uk/files/EBTA%20Presentation%20130907. pdf

Randell, G. (1989) Employee appraisal. In K. Sisson (ed.), *Personnel Management in Britain*. Oxford: Blackwell, pp. 149–174.

Sastry, T. and Bekhradnia, B. (2007) *Higher Education, Skills and Employer Engagement*. Retrieved January 2008, from http://www.hepi.ac.uk/downloads/30HEskillsandemployerengage mentfull.pdf

Seagraves, L., Osborne, M., Neal, P., Dockrell, R., Hartshorn, C. and Boyd, A. (1996) *Learning in Smaller Companies* (Final report) University of Stirling: Educational Policy and Development.

Skills for Business (2007) *National Occupational Standards*. Retrieved January 2008, from http://www.ukstandards.org/About_occupational_standards/default.aspx

Skills for Health (2007a) *Multidisciplinary/Multi-agency /Multi-professional Public Health Skills and Career Framework – Consultation version 22 June 2007*. Bristol: Public Health Resource Unit

Skills for Health (2007b) *Competences*. Retrieved December 2007, from www.skillsforhealth. org.uk/ page/competences.

Spencer, L.M. and Spencer, S.M. (1993) *Competence at Work. Models for superior performance*. Wiley: New York.

University of Bolton, School of Arts, Media and Education (2008) *Digital Pass Programme*. Bolton: University of Bolton.

University Vocational Awards Council (2004) *Fit for Purpose. The use of national occupational standards in higher education to meet the needs of employment*. Bolton: UVAC.

Universities UK (2007) *Response to HEFCE's Employer Engagement Strategy*. Retrieved July 2007, from http://www.universitiesuk.ac.uk/skills/

van Gelderen, M. (2007) *Research Based Yet Action Oriented: Developing individual level enterprising competencies* (Research working paper series 4) Massey University: Department of Management and International Business.

Wedgwood, M. (2007) *Employer Engagement: Higher education for the workforce: barriers and facilitators* (preliminary report). DfES.

Chapter 11

Ahl, H. (2004) *The Scientific Reproduction of Gender Inequality: A discourse analysis of research texts on women's entrepreneurship*. Copenhagen: Copenhagen Business School Press.

Ahl, H. (2006) Why research on women entrepreneurs needs new directions. *Entrepreneurship Theory and Practice*, 30(5): 595–621.

Ambrosini, V. and Bowman, C. (2001) Tacit knowledge: Some suggestions for operationalization, *Journal of Management Studies*, 38: 811–829.

Belenky, M. F., Clinchy, B. M., Goldberger, N. R., and Tarule, J. M. (1986) *Women's Ways of Knowing: The development of self, voice, and mind*. New York: Basic Books.

Brown, J.S., Collins, A., and Duguid, P. (1989) Situated cognition and the culture of learning, *Educational Researcher*, 18(1): 32–42.

Brown, J. S. and Duguid, P. (1991) Organizational learning and communities-of-practice: Toward a unified view of working, learning, and innovation. *Organization Science*, 2(1): 40–57.

Bruni, A., Gherardi, S. and Poggio, B. (2004) *Gender and Entrepreneurship: An ethnographic approach*. London: Routledge.

Bruni, A. and Gherardi, S. (2007) *Studiare le pratiche lavorative*, Bologna, Il Mulino [Studying Working Practices].

Cohen, W. M. and Levinthal, D. A. (1990) Absortive capacity: A new perspective on learning and innovation. *Administrative Science Quarterly*, 35: 128–152.

Drejer, A. (2000) Organisational learning and competence development. *The Learning Organization*, 7(4): 206–220.

Ellström, P.-E. (1997) The many meanings of occupational competence and qualification. *Journal of European Industrial Training*, 21(6/7): 266–274.

Engeström, Y. (1999) Innovative learning in work teams: analysing cycles of knowledge creation in practice, in Engeström, Y., Miettinen, R., Punam ki, R.L. (eds) *Perspectives on Activity Theory*, Cambridge: Cambridge University Press, pp. 377–406.

Flick, U. (1997) The Episodic Interview. Small scale narratives as approach to relevant experiences. Online at http://www.lse.ac.uk/collections/methodologyInstitute/pdf/QualPapers/Flick-episodic.pdf

Geertz, C. (1983) *Local Knowledge*. New York, NY: Basic Books.

Gergen, K. J. (1991) *The Satured Self: Dilemmas of identity in contemporary life*. New York: Basic Books.

Gherardi S. (2000) Practice-based theorizing on learning and knowing in organizations. *Organization*, 7(2): 211–223.

Gherardi, S. (2006) *Organizational Knowledge: The texture of workplace learning*. Oxford: Blackwell.

Gherardi, S. (ed.) (2008) *Storie di imprenditrici e di imprese artigiane*, Franco Angeli, Milano [Female entrepreneurs and craft enterprises stories].

Gherardi, S., Nicolini, D. and Odella, F. (1998) Toward a social understanding of how people learn in organizations: The notion of situated curriculum, *Management Learning*, 29(3): 273–298.

Illeris, K. (2008) Competence Development – the key to modern education, or just another buzzword? *Asia Pacific Education Review*, 9(1): 1–4.

Keen, K. (1992) Competence: What is it and how can it be developed? In J. Lowyck, P. de Potter and J. Elen (eds) *Instructional Design: Implementation issues*: Brussels, IBM Education Center, pp. 111–122.

Lave, J. and Wenger, E. (1991) *Situated Learning: Legitimate peripheral participation*, Cambridge: Cambridge University Press.

Marsden, P. V. (1982) Brokerage Behavior in Restricted Exchange Networks. In P. V. Marsden and N. Lin (eds) *Social Structure and Network Analysis*. Beverly Hills, Sage, pp. 201–218.

Nicolini, D., Gherardi, S. and Yanow, D. (2003) *Knowing in Organizations: A practice-based approach*: London: Sharpe.

Nonaka, I. and Takeuchi, H. (1995) *The Knowledge-Creating Company*. New York, Oxford University Press.

Norris, N (1991). The trouble with competence. *Cambridge Journal of Education*, 21(3): 331–341.

Polanyi, M. (1958) *Personal Knowledge. Towards a post-critical philosophy*. Chicago: University of Chicago Press.

Sandberg, J. (2000) Understanding human competence at work: An interpretative approach. *The Academy of Management Journal*, 43(1): 9–25.

Sundberg, L. (2001) A holistic approach to competence development. *Systems Research and Behavioral Science*, 18: 103–114.

Strati, A. (2007) Sensible knowledge and practice-based learning, *Management Learning*, 38(1): 61–77.

Wenger, E. (1998) *Communities of Practice: Learning, meaning, and identity*, Cambridge: Cambridge University Press.

Zhara, S. A. and George, G. (2002) Absortive capacity: a review, reconceptualization, and extention. *Academy of Management Review*, 27(2): 185–203.

Chapter 12

Autor, D. H., Levy, F. and Murnane, R. J. (2003) The skill content of recent technological change: an empirical exploration. *Quarterly Journal of Economics*, 118(4): (November)

Bengali, A. (2004) *Economic Trends: Degree No Guarantee for Grades*. Detroit Free Press, July 1.

Dahlman, C. (2007) *Enhancing China's Competitiveness through Lifelong Learning*. Washington: World Bank Institute.

Dou, X. (2007) Lifelong learning in the national strategy reform in China. *Lifelong Learning in Europe*, 1.

Levy, F. and Murnane, R.J. (2004) *The New Division of Labor: How Computors are Creating the Next Job Market*. Princeton, NJ: Princeton University Press.

Rychen, D. S. and Salganik, L. H. (eds) (2003) *Key Competencies for a Successful Life and a Well-Functioning Society*. Cambridge, MA: Hogrefe & Huber.

Wu, Y. (2006) *The Thriving and the Threat of Higher Education*. Chinese Financial News, January 26.

Chapter 13

Allais, S. (2003) The National Qualifications Framework in South Africa: A democratic project trapped in a neo-liberal paradigm. *Journal of Education and Work*, 16(3): 305–324.

Allais, S. (2007) The Rise and Fall of the NQF: A critical analysis of the South African National Qualifications Framework. Thesis type. University of the Witwatersrand.

Bernstein, B. (1990) *The Structuring of Pedagogic Discourse: Volume IV, class codes and control*. London: Routledge.

Bernstein, B. (1996) *Pedagogy, Symbolic Control and Identity: Theory, research, critique*. London: Taylor and Francis.

Department of Labour (2007) *Draft Occupational Qualifications Framework: Discussion document*. Pretoria: Department of Labour.

Ensor, P. (2003) The National Qualifications Framework and higher education in South Africa: some epistemological issues. *Journal of Education and Work*, 16(3): 325–346.

Illeris, K. (2003) Workplace learning and learning theory. *Journal of Workplace Learning*, 15(4): 167–178.

Lave, J. and Wenger, E. (1991) *Situated Learning: Legitimate peripheral participation*. New York: Cambridge University Press.

Lugg, R. (2007) Making different equal? Social practices of policy-making and the National Qualifications Framework in South Africa between 1985 and 2003. Thesis type. University of London.

Minister of Education and Minister of Labour (2007) *Enhancing the Efficacy and Efficiency of the National Qualifications Framework*. Pretoria: Department of Education and Department of Labour.

Moll, I. (2002) Clarifying constructivism in a context of curriculum change. *Journal of Education*, 27: 5–32.

Moll, I. (2007) *Understanding Learning, Assessment and the Quality of Judgements*. Presentation at SAQA Seminar, 16 November 2007. Pretoria: SAQA.

Moll, I., Steinberg, C. and Broekmann, I. (2005) *Being a Vocational Educator: A guide for lecturers in FET colleges*. Braamfontein: South African Institute for Distance Education.

Mukora, J. (2006) Social justice goals or economic rationality? The South African Qualifications Framework considered in the light of local and global experiences. Thesis type. University of Edinburgh.

Parker, B. and Harley, K. (2007) The NQF as a socially inclusive and cohesive system: communities of practice and trust. *SAQA Bulletin*, 10(2): 17–37. Pretoria: SAQA.

Wenger, E. (1998) *Communities of Practice: Learning, meaning, and identity*. New York: Cambridge University Press.

Young, M. (2005) *National Qualifications Frameworks: Their feasibility for effective implementation in developing countries*. InFocus Programme on Skills, Knowledge and Employability, Skills Working Paper No. 22. Geneva: International Labour Office.

Chapter 14

Ahuja, Ashvin, Chucherd, Thitima and Pootrakool, Kobsak (2006) *Human Capital Policy: Building a competitive workforce for 21st century Thailand*. Monetary Policy Group, Bank of Thailand.

Azemikhah, Homi (2006) *The 21st Century, the Competency Era and Competency Theory*. Open Learning Institute of TAFE. Paper presented at the AVETRA 9th Annual Conference, University of Wollongong, Australia, 19-21 April. Available from http://www.avetra.org.au/ABSTRACT2006/PA%200068.pdf

Becker, Gary S. (1991) *A Treatise on the Family*. Cambridge, MA: Harvard University Press. Cited in Andrew Mason (2008) Sustainable Economic Policies in an Aging World. Presented at the Shanghai Forum 2008: Economic Globalization and the Choice of Asia, Fudan University, Shanghai, May 25–27.

Biron, Mathew, Comkowycz, Lisa, Holberger, Laura, and Holemo, Cody (2004) *The Private Sector and Improving Human Capital in Southeast Asia*. Bangkok: College of Population Studies and Institute of Asian Studies, Chulalongkorn University.

Bloom, David E., Canning, David and Sevilla, Jaypee (2003) *The Demographic Dividend: A new perspective on the economic consequence of population change*. Santa Monica: Rand.

Delahaye, Brian L. and Becker, Karen L. (2006) Unlearning: A revised view of contemporary learning theories. Available from http://eprints.qut.edu.au

Freden, Karolina and Nilsson, Fredrik (2003) *The Individual's Expectations on Competence Development in A Transition Organization*. Linköping, Ekonomiska Institutionen.

Mason, Andrew and Lee, Ronald (2006) *Reform and Support Systems for the Elderly in Developing Countries: Capturing the second demographic dividend*. Cited in Andrew Mason (2008) Sustainable Economic Policies in an Aging World. Presented at the Shanghai Forum 2008: Economic Globalization and the Choice of Asia, Fudan University, Shanghai, May 25–27.

NESDB (2005) *Population Projections for Thailand, 2005–2025*. Bangkok: Office of the National Economic and Social Development Board.

Nonako, Ikujiro and Takenchi, Hirotaka (1995) The Knowledge Creating Company: How Japanese companies create the dynamics of innovation. New York: Oxford University Press.

NSO (2008) *Report of the Labor Force Survey*. Bangkok: National Statistical Office.

Ogawa, Naohiro, Kondo, Makoto and Matsukura, Rikiya (2004) *Japan's Transition from the Demographic Bonus to the Demographic Onus*. Presented at the International Conference on the Demographic Window and Healthy Aging, Beijing, 10–11 May.

Somers, Marie-Andrée (2005) Disentangling Schooling Attainment from Literacy Skills and Competencies. Background paper prepared for the Education for All Global Monitoring Report, 2006, *Literacy for Life*. UNESCO 2006/ED/EFA/MRT/PI91.

Wongboonsin, Kua (2003) *Population and Human Resource Development*. Bangkok: Chulalongkorn University Printing House.

Wongboonsin, Kua and Guest, Philip (eds) (2005) *The Demographic Dividend: Policy options for Asia*. College of Population Studies; Asian Development Research Forum and Thailand Research Fund. Bangkok: Chulalongkorn University Printing House.

Wongboonsin, Kua, Kunwat, Malika, Prabpal, Kanjana, Surasiangsang, Suwanee, Hongladarom, Soraj, Opanonamata, Prakaikaew, Bunjoedpongchai, David and Potisiri, Tanyawat (2003) *Desirable Skills of Future Thai Workforce*. Bangkok: Chulalongkorn University Printing House.

Wongboonsin, Kua, Surasiangsung, Suwanee, Wongboonsin, Patcharawalai and Iamkanjanalai, Somkiat. (2007) *Workforce Development for Population in the Studying and Labor-Force Age Groups to Prepare for an Ageing Society in Thailand*. Bangkok: College of Population Studies, Chulalongkorn University.

Wongboonsin, Patcharawalai (2006) *Education and Training for the Thai Workforce: Needed strategies in the 21st century*. Paper presented at the APEC Conference on Strategies for Workforce Development, Hanoi, 18–20 September.

Wongboonsin, Patcharawalai, Pinrat, Kmol, Kuanniyom, Monchai, Jubkolsuk, Krisda, Junpen, Vullapa and Rodmebun, Supanan (2004) *An Investigation into the Working Skills and Competencies of Thai Labor in the Textile Industry: Measures, trends, and differentials*. Bangkok: Institute of Asian Studies, Chulalongkorn University.

Wongboonsin, Patcharawalai and Rojvithee, Areeya (2007) Competence Development as Workplace Learning in Thailand. In Lynne Chisholm, Helmut Fennes, Reingard Spannring (eds): *Competence Development as Workplace Learning*. Innsbruck: Innsbruck University Book, pp. 43–61.

World Bank (2006) *Thailand Investment Climate, Firm Competitiveness and Growth*. Bangkok: World Bank Thai Office.

Index